FROM THE LIBRARY OF

....

Weddings

THE BEST OF
MARTHA STEWART LIVING

Weddings

CLARKSON POTTER/PUBLISHERS

NEW YORK

TO *Alexis Stewart* AND *John Cuti* FOR A LIFE OF HAPPINESS TOGETHER

Originally published in book form by
Martha Stewart Living Omnimedia LLC
in 1999. Published simultaneously
by Clarkson Potter Publishers, Inc.,
Oxmoor House, Inc., and Leisure Arts.

A portion of this work was previously
published in MARTHA STEWART LIVING.

Published by Clarkson Potter Publishers,
201 East 50th Street, New York, NY 10022.

Member of the Crown Publishing Group.
Random House, Inc.
New York, Toronto, London,
Sydney, Auckland
www.randomhouse.com
Clarkson N. Potter, Potter, and colophon
are trademarks of Random House, Inc.

Manufactured in the
United States of America.

Library of Congress Cataloging in
Publication Data is available upon request.
ISBN 0-609-60426-0

10 9 8 7 6 5 4 3 2 1 First Edition

ACKNOWLEDGMENTS
from Martha

CREATING A BOOK AS EXQUISITE AS THIS ONE REQUIRES the collaborative effort of a great many people. Special thanks to Eric A. Pike, my design director, whose talent and vision have shaped the visual personality of Martha Stewart Living Magazine and Martha Stewart Weddings for the last seven years. His dedication to the subject of weddings–and to this book—is unsurpassed. Thank you to editor Kathleen Hackett, for her tireless, heroic efforts to ensure that this book is as informative, well-organized and useful as it can be. Esther Bridavsky assisted in creating a design that, like a good marriage, will stand the test of time. Patricia Beard wrote text as engaging and inspiring as the images. Thank you to Molly Tully, who never wavered in her pursuit of perfect copy.

This book would not have been possible without the talented team of editors from Martha Stewart Weddings, where the photographs in this book originally appeared. Special thanks to weddings editor Darcy Miller for consistently producing a magazine that is as instructive as it is beautiful.

A wedding would not be a wedding without a delicious cake. The beautiful, well-crafted cakes on these pages are the result of a collaborative creative effort between food editor Susan Spungen and contributing food editor Wendy Kromer.

A beautiful bouquet of flowers is essential, too, and none are more romantic than those created by crafts editor Hannah Milman and her very talented, hardworking team of stylists.

Thank you to the editors, art directors, and stylists who contributed to the creation of this volume, notably Gia Russo Adams, Celia Barbour, Lynn Butler Beling, Claudia Bruno, Stephana Bottom, Ellen Burnie, Anthony Cochran, Jeanine Colgan, Amy Conway, Stephen Drucker, James Dunlinson, Stephen Earle, Kimberly Gieske, Agnethe Glatved, Claudia Grimaldi, Jill Groeber, Joelle Hoverson, Jodi Levine, Bobbi Lin, Helen Lund, Whitney Jewett, Fritz Karch, Hope Meyers, Melissa Morgan, Amy Nebens, Sara Neumeier, Page Marchese Norman, Ayesha Patel, Heidi Posner, Nikki Rooker, Scot Schy, Kevin Sharkey, Gabrielle Simon, Curtis Smith, Eva Spring, Duane Stapp, Susan Sugarman, Lindsey Taylor, Rebecca Thuss, and Gael Towey.

Many thanks to all my longtime friends at Clarkson Potter and to everyone at Oxmoor House, Applied Graphics, and R.R. Donnelley & Sons Company.

Finally, heartfelt thanks to the many real brides and grooms, and their families and friends, who inspire us to create and document the special ideas that make a wedding day extraordinary.

CONTENTS

THE BEST OF MARTHA STEWART LIVING Weddings

SEPTEMBER 7, 1937 Jersey City, New Jersey

My mother and father fell madly in love, eloped, and then married formally in church in December, 1937. Mother looked radiant, dressed stylishly in rust silk velvet with her gorgeous hair gathered into a golden bronze kerchief. In all her portraits, she smiles as beautifully as Leonardo's Mona Lisa.

JULY 1, 1961 New York, New York

My wedding took place on the tiniest budget imaginable. With the help of my mother, I designed and made a very full-skirted dress with long full sleeves, a scooped neckline, and a back closure featuring a row of cloth-covered buttons. When I look at the dress in the attic, I'm amazed at how well it has withstood the march of time.

JULY 5, 1970 Nutley, New Jersey

Thinking back to the day she was married, I remember how lovely Kathy, our most beautiful sister, the middle of three, was. Her perfect oval face, unblemished skin, slightly elongated eyes, and finely arched brows always reminded me of our maternal grandmother.

JULY 28, 1990 Cutchogue, New York

My sister Laura's wedding remains in my memory as one of those "unforgettable, beautiful days." The wedding and reception took place at her husband Randy Plimpton's family house, a turn-of-the-century Tudor-style home. Despite a shaky beginning—a misty, foggy morning—clear skies abounded in the afternoon, just as Randy had predicted.

SEPTEMBER 26, 1997 New York, New York

I spent an afternoon with Alexis shopping for her gray flannel wedding suit. I planned a wedding luncheon, ordered flowers and cakes, and hired, with Alexis's approval, photographer John Dolan, who captured the day she married John Cuti memorably.

A SPECIAL DAY

by Martha Stewart

In 1987 I wrote a book titled Weddings, a beautiful tome full of real weddings, how-to information, and hundreds of ideas for creating an extraordinarily important and momentous day.

This book is its sequel in many ways, but it is also important in its own right as a source of valuable inspiration and useful ideas for anyone involved in the creation of a wedding.

So much has been written about the subject of brides and grooms and weddings, but rarely has the subject been treated with such care, love, and loveliness. The staff of Martha Stewart Weddings continually comes up with special ways to celebrate and make your day more personal. The carefully researched way each aspect of a wedding is approached is unique to Martha Stewart Weddings, and we sincerely hope it is all that you need when planning your festivities—or even just thinking about the wedding you will have one day.

As you contemplate and design every detail, from the ceremony itself to the shoes specially dyed to match your gown, I hope you will turn to this book and its excellent companion website at marthastewart.com, where one can attain even more guidance. Using everyday language, our question-and-answer feature, askMartha, can address your queries immediately and direct you to related sources and suggestions. In this technological age it is exciting to have so many avenues to follow and so many good ideas to consider. But remember—your wedding day is yours and yours alone. It should be a personal reflection of your own taste and customs. What we can offer is inspiration in whichever form you find helpful.

INTRODUCTION

It's called the bride's day, and so it is. But all of us. Friends and relatives will laugh Passersby will see the bridal party, stop, and announcement with interest. Giddy children ritual of hope, promise, love and commitment.

the white dress, the veil, and flowers are for

and cry, eat and drink, rejoice and remember.

smile. Strangers will read the wedding

will dance around the floor, celebrating this

Every wedding day belongs to the world.

Our goal in the Best of Martha Stewart Living Weddings is to provide anyone planning a wedding with inspiration and ideas that will help her create an unforgettable day. Martha Stewart and the editors of Martha Stewart Living Weddings have played a role in hundreds of weddings as guests, caterers, editorial "observers," and consultants. In our magazine, we have featured a selection of these celebrations and many of the details that make them special. We have also created our own ideas for personalizing each of the elements of a wedding. On the pages that follow, we have organized, in three sections, the best of the best. For the Ceremony offers ideas about decorating the place where the marriage vows are exchanged; bouquets in every shape, scent, and size for the bride and her attendants; boutonnieres both classic and quirky; and decorations for the getaway car. For the Reception shows how to give the party its unique status as the celebration of a significant rite of passage. From indoor and outdoor lighting ideas, spectacularly set tables for four to forty, and a selection of the most requested wedding cakes to irresistible drinks and hors d'oeuvres and charming favors for guests, there are inspiring ways to personalize even the most by-the-book wedding reception. The photographs that capture and hold the day in sharp focus, and the guest books that become a record of all who witnessed the bride and groom become husband and wife, deserve as much attention to detail as every other element of a wedding. In Forever, we have created ways to elegantly tell the story of a wedding in framed photographs and to artfully chronicle the presence of every guest–in handmade books, boxes, even on a parchment scroll.

For all of the elements of a wedding that invite an original touch, there is essential information that applies to them all. The For Reference section features a wedding planner; information on wedding stationery, including how to choose and word invitations; planning the pace of the ceremony and reception; and music selections for both. A selection of recipes for cakes, drinks, and hors d'oeuvres and a directory of sources for the materials used to make the decorations, cakes, and favors are included in this section.

The planning of a wedding consumes a disproportionate amount of effort, time, and money compared with the few hours during which the actual event will unfold. But as deci-

sions are made about where to be married, in what kind of ceremony, whom to invite, and how to celebrate, the scales begin to balance: Planning can provide as much pleasure as the event itself and provides a chance to bank memories, not just of the wedding, but of the teamwork leading up to it.

Because the planning of a marriage consumes so much time and energy, we have come to understand that a cooperative team of planners and contributors, such as floral designers, caterers, musicians, and dressmakers, will create the perfect wedding. The result of all this excellent cooperation shows: in the relaxed beauty of the bride's and groom's countenances, in the photographs of the guests and other participants, and in the casual yet extremely carefully styled details of everything.

Organizing a wedding is a multi-stepped process that usually begins a year to six months before the wedding date. Use the Wedding Planner on page 207 to guide you. If less than six months remain to make a plan, don't panic; just get started as soon as possible.

Of the hundreds of decisions that will be made, determining the budget is the first; it will inform nearly every other decision. A couple should know how much they have to spend, and on what they have to spend it. In general, the reception accounts for 50 percent of the budget, then the gown and accessories, the music, the photography, the flowers, and any miscellany—invitations, favors, menu cards, bridal party gifts—will account for 10 percent each.

Once the budget has been decided, the site for the ceremony and reception should be chosen. While many couples are willing to start from scratch with a place where a wedding has never been held, those who choose locations that are often used for weddings have the advantage of working with experienced managers who can often raise questions a couple might not think to ask. A site manager may even know the local requirements for getting a marriage license. The more professional a wedding-site manager is, the more time a couple can devote to the creative details that will make their wedding memorable. Throughout this book, we have picked the most attractive sites—both traditional and unexpected—and shown beautiful ways to decorate them.

THE CEREMONY It is a combination of solemn and joyful sentiments; to express both of those qualities in a manner that is as beautiful as it is meaningful, we have created and documented romantic decorations for entrances, pews, aisles, and altars, both indoors and outdoors. We also show how couples have personalized a place that may have been used for thousands of weddings before theirs, or transformed a site at which they are the first to be married.

Of all of the elements associated with the wedding ceremony, the bridal bouquet is among the most iconic. A bouquet's life span is as brief as a butterfly's, but a bride will hardly feel married without one. The bouquets featured range from a tiny clutch of sweet peas to a voluptuous dome of 150 tea roses. There are examples of different shapes, styles, flower combinations, and stem treatments, edited from hundreds we have designed or documented. We also offer unexpected ways to design a boutonniere, the flower (or herb, or leaf) that the groom and his ushers wear just over the buttonhole on a lapel. And for the children who attend the bride, there are floral wreaths to wear in their hair, and baskets and diminutive bouquets to hold.

THE RECEPTION The bride and groom should be in the spotlight at the most elaborate party they will give, but it should not be forgotten that the festivities are planned for family and friends, too. In For the Reception, each site pictured lends itself to certain kinds of parties, and the decorative elements begin to fall into place from there. Learn how to illuminate a party to establish a setting as romantic as any movie set, make the most of every petal in a centerpiece, and enhance the glow of every guest. There are ideas for table settings, centerpieces, and place settings that make a dramatic impact when the guests enter the untouched, just-decorated space, but are also intimate enough to be appreciated when they sit down to eat.

If the bridal bouquet is the signature element of the ceremony, the wedding cake is the equivalent at the reception. And like the bouquet, it is evanescent, yet magical. We chose our favorite formal and not-so-formal cakes from the hundreds that have been created in the kitchens of Martha Stewart Living. Whether crisply covered in fondant and encrusted with gum-paste flowers, or loosely iced in swirls of buttercream and decorated with wild flowers, every cake tastes as good as it looks. All of the cakes are pictured to provide inspiration for structure,

decoration, and presentation. There are recipes on page 237 for some of our favorites: basic yellow wedding cake, chocolate chestnut cake, applesauce cake, and a croquembouche, the traditional French wedding cake.

What a host serves to eat and drink, and how it is served, are among the most important aspects of hospitality. We focus on drinks and hors d'oeuvres because they are the courses of a wedding meal that are most open to interpretation. Recipes for the hors d'oeuvres are written with the home cook in mind—they don't require special ovens or unusual equipment. In fact, many of them require assembly rather than elaborate cooking techniques. As for drinks, while the choices may seem straightforward—full bar, a smaller passed selection of cocktails, or champagne or sparkling wine and one soft drink—beverages lend themselves to reinterpretation, too. From the presentation, a glass rimmed with petal-pink sugar, for example, to the flavor of a wedding punch or regional specialty, we have suggested ways to custom-make cocktails that reflect the tone and style of a party. See the Recipes for a selection of drinks and hors d'oeuvres.

We do believe every detail counts, but we urge couples not to strain their relationships and pocketbooks in striving for perfection. If perfection lies anywhere it is in the intention, although we hope to help make the execution splendid, too. No matter how well planned, each wedding is apt to include an unwelcome surprise and a happy revelation. They may even be the same. At one ceremony, held at sunset by a river, the hosts set little ribbon-tied pieces of cloth saturated with insect repellent on each chair. The gnats were active that evening, and as the bride and groom turned to walk back down the aisle, they started to laugh when they saw their friends: the congregation had placed the cloths on their heads to keep the gnats out of their hair. Nature may have fooled the couple, but she also provided a mental snapshot that will always make them smile.

We have spent years creating and researching each of these areas so that we can offer excellent choices on every element of the wedding. We are thrilled to extend to the bride, her groom, and their families not only our ideas, but those of the wonderful floral designers, stationers, jewelers, musicians, caterers, bakers, dressmakers, event planners, and others who have contributed their expertise. Enjoy.

FOR THE CEREMONY

Kindly respond

The heart of every wedding is the ceremony. Its rituals are as old as romance and fidelity. Its roots spread deep to hold each couple's pledge that they will share the swales and swells of their lives forever. Its customs connect all who have ever joyfully crossed the border into the land of marriage. Yet each ceremony is unique, open to creativity, imagination, and tradition.

Whether the ceremony follows tradition or a unique and personal script, it will probably include elements of marriage rites that cross boundaries, languages, cultures, and centuries. Knowing about the ancient roots of traditions that are still alive can inspire ways to adapt the old and nearly universal elements of the wedding ceremony. These include a specially decorated, significant location; linking symbols like the wedding ring; a civil or religious official who presides; and attendants and witnesses. Among the first aspects of the ceremony to consider are the religious or secular nature of the service, whom the attendants will be and what the wedding party will wear, how many and which guests to invite, and where the ceremony will be held. From there, the bride and groom decide what kind of invitations, programs, and other printed elements to order; how to decorate a place that will only be used for an hour or so; and the design of the bride's bouquet.

THE SITE Some sites, especially those that resonate with nature, have always been considered auspicious for wedding ceremonies. Outdoor weddings have the longest history; early marriage ceremonies were often conducted in places that evoked spiritual feelings, or where spirits who could bless a union were believed to dwell. An arch etched into rock by aeons of battering waves, a hilltop with distant views, and a mossy clearing in a rustling wood all appealed to brides and grooms who lived close to the natural world. Even if the ceremony was as simple as taking each others' hands and walking through the rock vault to emerge on the other side reborn as a couple, such sites became associated with the formal joining of two people. Ceremonies held outdoors still reflect this instinct to identify with nature and the great cycles of rebirth.

Couples who are planning an indoor ceremony have more control over their surroundings, since they are not at the mercy of the elements, and also because houses of worship, hotels, historic houses, and private clubs are equipped to handle large gatherings. Home weddings, even when they are small, can require more ingenuity; wedding planners, caterers, and friends who have held weddings at home are the best sources for information and advice on how (and how not) to turn a private house into a place for a solemn ceremony, then quickly transform it into the site for a gala party.

THE SERVICE Once the place for the ceremony and the officiant have been chosen, the decision whether to exchange vows in a traditional service or to write or select passages should be made. Most couples choose to begin the service by reading the standard form in the prayer book of their denomination; they then look for further inspiration in poetry and prose, the files of the officiant, and from other weddings. Ideas for the service can come from unexpected sources; one couple based their vows on those spoken by that great romantic couple, Katharine Hepburn and Spencer Tracy, in *Woman of the Year*. But the ceremony can include more than what happens during the service itself: Kristin Quadland and Scott Egbert, who were married on her uncle's farm, planted a pair of maple trees to commemorate their wedding day, as other brides and grooms have done there since the eighteenth century. They included their guests in the ceremony by giving them handmade books that tell the story of the wedding trees.

DECORATING THE CEREMONY The architectural elements of a place and the kind of ceremony held there are often connected. Elisabeth de Tigny and Alexis Mourot, who were married in a Romanesque medieval abbey in France where the bride was baptized, chose a formal traditional ceremony; the decorations in the church and the formal dress of the bride and groom exemplified the mood. For Alexis Stewart and John Cuti, a sparely adorned ceremony suited their desire to emphasize the basics—their love and commitment—and they were married at City Hall. A bride of Jewish descent but not practice, who felt uncomfortable with a traditional Christian ceremony, and her Episcopalian groom were wed in a Quaker Meeting House in a particularly moving service performed by the father of the groom, who was the former headmaster of a Friends' school. The decoration was appropriately nonsectarian: smartly clipped evergreens in large pots. In traditional Jewish weddings, the huppah, the wedding canopy under which the bride and groom and the officiant stand, can be both religiously significant and decorative, with its posts wound with flowers, or the space it occupies rimmed with flowers (see page 38).

Wherever a ceremony is held, it is decorated to welcome and celebrate. Flowers have nearly always been included—it is hard to imagine a bride without a bouquet. The other flowers at a ceremony convey the same mood of freshness and fecundity, even when they are used sparingly. The only decoration in the early-nineteenth-century white clapboard church where Page Marchese and Adrian Norman were married (see page 23) was a heart-shaped gardenia wreath on the pulpit. Candles have a long connection with ritual, and couples find new ways to include them in wedding ceremonies: Annette Rocque and Matt Lauer provided candles for their guests to light and place in silver holders on the altar, where they cast a soft glow on the faces of the bride and groom.

CEREMONY AND SYMBOLS Certain symbols, most particularly those that indicate the joining of two people, have long been part of wedding ceremonies. Even when couples write their own ceremonies, they often adapt ideas that have been around for millennia. Couples in some primitive societies were tied to each other with reeds wound around their waists; certain African tribes bind the wrists of a bride and groom with braided grass. Hopi brides and grooms traditionally bent their heads over a basin so the elder women could join them by washing their long hair in a yucca solution.

In Western ceremonies, wedding bands are the most common linking symbols. The circle of the band represents eternity—for a bride and groom that means eternal love. The custom of placing the ring on the fourth finger of the left hand is convenient, since it dates back to the Ancient Egyptians, who believed that a vein connects that finger directly to the heart. The ring is not the only way to translate the idea of connection: Episcopal priests often wind a stole around the wrists of the bride and groom. A bride can tie Victorian "love knots" in ribbons that trail from her bouquet. And, as they did at the wedding of Sarah Ferguson to Prince Andrew, flower girls can hold flower-twined hoops, or wear a ring of flowers in their hair (see pages 84, 85, and 86), mirroring the eternal circle.

FRIENDS AND FAMILY Wedding guests are more than an audience; they are an integral part of the ceremony. They witness the union, and in many ceremonies they agree to support a couple's commitment to each other. One couple acknowledged their guests by setting out a bowl of stephanotis boutonnieres for them to wear. Others create keepsake booklets so guests can follow the order of service and reread the prayers and poems later (see page 203).

The most intimate of guests, of course, are the bridal attendants, chosen to honor friendship. Rules have become more fluid, and couples are comfortable inviting their closest friends to attend them. Some brides now ask male friends to be in their weddings; one groom, the only male sibling, chose his three sisters to be his groomsmen. Modern couples are so relaxed about including their most beloved companions that when Martha's friend Susie Tompkins was married to Mark Buell in San Francisco, she was accompanied by her Jack Russell terrier; and our design director, Eric Pike, stood up with his sister Amy as the "man of honor."

Attendants help with the preparations for the wedding, lend emotional support, remember the rings, and seat the congregation. Elizabethan bridesmaids often decorated the church with swags of flower-decked rope; in the same spirit, one bride asked her bridesmaids to join her early in the morning on her wedding day in a meadow near her house, where they gathered wildflowers to adorn the church. Whatever other roles they play, the members of the bridal party are charmingly decorative, none more so than the flower girl, a successor to children in the Classical world who scattered herbs and grains before a bride, offerings to the gods of fertility. This custom can be adapted by filling a basket with scented blossoms for a flower girl to toss, so the bride will release a slight fragrance as she walks along the carpet of petals (see pages 39 and 112).

To these fundamentals of ceremony—the special place and its decoration, the vows and the officiant, the witnesses and attendants—each bride and groom add their own singular, delightful notions. At one wedding the hymns were sung by the children's choir the bride belonged to when she was a little girl. A couple marrying for the second time included their children in the ceremony. One courageous bride walked down the aisle alone, a sign of love and deference to her father, who had died a few years earlier.

Some rituals have been performed since the human race was young; they seem to grow out of our very nature: We are creative and loving, jubilant and tearful—and also practical. Yet love is not just universal, it is also unique, and the many ways we embroider and embellish, or pare down, the marriage ceremony display our humanity and variety. ∾

A GLORIOUS STAIRCASE *provides a wonderful opportunity for embellishment. The steps leading up to this pillar-fronted church are lined with veiled privet topiaries placed in scallop-edged white-painted pots*

DECORATIONS
for the Ceremony

*I**t is quite short—usually less than an hour—but the ceremony is the one time during the wedding day when all attention is focused on the bride and groom, undivided. At the reception the decorations*

will be part of the panoply of a party. But at the ceremony, as the guests sit quietly, waiting for the bride, listening to the music or to the sounds in the garden, each decorative element must contribute to the moment.

Decoration should focus on the places where the eye is naturally drawn: the entrance, aisle, and altar. For centuries, flowering branches, fruits and herbs, and wildflowers have graced altars, doorways, and pews at weddings. How, and how much, to decorate them depends on the budget and the site, indoors or out, and its size.

When the ceremony and the reception are held in the same place, the decorations only have to be rearranged to do double duty at the party. But when the ceremony is in a room of its own, or at a house of worship, the decorations are used briefly, and many couples try to limit the cost. To decide how much a ceremony really needs to be dressed up, it helps to walk the space as a guest would, imagining what they will see, and when. When a couple thinks of their friends arriving all dressed up, and of the wedding party filling the aisle, they will realize that with a few well-placed flowers, wreaths, swags, or candles, the space will quickly look warm, pretty, and dramatic.

Before making any decisions about the decorations for the ceremony, talk to the clergyman or site manager about any restrictions. Can a nail be pounded into the front door to hang a wreath? Chances are, there will already be a nail there. Also ask what decorations will be in place at the time of the wedding; if it's close to Christmas, a church may be decked out in poinsettias and evergreens, which may or may not be a boon, depending on what you have your heart set on.

At most sites where a ceremony is held, the principal decorations are usually flowers, candles, and banners, and sometimes a carpet unrolled down the aisle to protect the hem of the bride's gown from being soiled. For indoor weddings, the first indication that something special is going on appears at the steps or doors. Topiaries wrapped in tulle welcomed guests at one church (see page 18); the bride and groom's initials shaped from flowers were hung from ribbons on the doors at another (see page 22). A plush wreath of white flowers tied with an extra-wide satin ribbon graced the wrought-iron gated entrance to an historic house; fresh flowers were tucked into the vines that framed the doorway at another. Where there are restrictions about tapping nails into the woodwork, garlands can be draped loosely over a church door or pew ends; wreaths can be hung from ribbons tacked over a door frame.

Floral arrangements, sometimes topped with lit censers, are often placed on the posts at the ends of pews, flanking the aisle (see opposite page, top left). When choosing tall pew decorations, it is important to sit and stand at different vantage points in the church to be sure the flowers will not obstruct the congregation's view. If the ceremony is held in a place where it's necessary to rent chairs, they can be personalized with tiny bouquets tied to the chairs closest to the aisle (see page 39). Or, for a small ceremony, the chairs can be adorned with simple slipcovers—not such an extravagance if the chairs will be used again at the reception.

Altar flowers can be arranged in urns or vases—most houses of worship, hotels, and clubs have serviceable ones—or they can be brought in their own containers. Some couples choose to spend money on special vases such as mercury-glass ice buckets or blown-glass fishbowls, for example, that can also be used at the reception.

Outdoor weddings often need the least decoration of all: The rugged oak under which Kim Stahlman and Michael Kearns were married was trimmed with buckets of flowers (page 41); the couple who was married on the Brooklyn Bridge couldn't have decorated it if they had wanted to. And when another couple held their ceremony on a dramatic seaside bluff in the Caribbean, the view—and the two of them—were the only ornaments.

As guests arrive, music will fill the space in a less tangible way. Its power to set a mood can't be overrated—but what kind of mood? When considering the music, a couple should acknowledge the distinction between the sacred and secular segments of the occasion: Popular tunes are wonderful for the reception, but not in church. The best professionals make it easy to translate a couple's taste and vision into song. (Some of our favorite songs for the ceremony are listed on page 230.)

The ceremony begins with the procession, and custom usually dictates the "marching order." The bride, often preceded by her attendants, is accompanied down the aisle by her father in most Christian weddings, while the groom and his attendants wait with the minister at the altar. Traditional Jewish brides and grooms both proceed down the aisle, accompanied by their fathers and mothers (see "Planning the Ceremony," on page 218). As with much else, adaptation can add personality: In some cultures a bride is accompanied to the church by a flock of friends and neighbors; modern couples have been known to parade to and from the ceremony on foot, in horse-drawn carriages, and in antique cars. But however a bride arrives, and wherever the ceremony takes place, she will be the central and most decorative element of any wedding ceremony. ❧

THROUGH THE DOORS, up the aisle to the altar and back; it will be over in minutes, but the ceremony—and the most subtle embellishments—will be remembered forever. Whether the wedding will be held in a house of worship or outdoors, the main spaces that have to be delineated with decorations are the entrance, aisles, and altar. Opposite, clockwise from top left: Lisa Ann Stewart and Von Manwell Hughes, who were married in Denver, Colorado, attached tall censers with bows at the bases to the pews. A paper cone filled with hydrangeas, scabiosa, tweedia, forget-me-nots, and blue lace flowers hangs from an existing nail outside a church door. At an outdoor wedding, the bride and groom use "borrowed scenery," the water's edge, to decorate their ceremony. An altar is marked by a skirted table with an abundant arrangement of oak-leaf hydrangea and 'Bianca' roses in a tall vase; the same flowers are also used in the bride's bouquet.

{ AISLES }

{ ENTRANCES }

{ ALTARS }

{ BORROWED SCENERY }

THE ONLY DECORATION *inside the church where Page Marchese and Adrian Norman (left) were married was the gardenia wreath at the pulpit (see instructions on page 29). Decorations cannot be nailed anywhere in this historic church in Edgartown, Massachusetts, so daisy initials (opposite) were suspended on fishing wire from the door tops.*

Indoor Ceremonies

HOW AN INDOOR CEREMONY IS DECORATED WILL DEPEND on the venue. A church or synagogue is usually the easiest to embellish, because the layout has already been designed for ceremonial occasions. Flowers and candles are the most effective materials; the ways in which they are used can be quite original. Heart-shaped and traditional wreaths are classic doorway decorations; the Victorians were partial to floral wedding bells. Because the flowers at a ceremony don't have to last for long, pew decorations can be arranged in lightweight ribbon-decked paper cones, or flower heads can be threaded into a garland and delicately swagged and hung over the sides of pews (see page 30). Sometimes a house of worship recommends that a couple work with particular florists who know the rules and the space; ask to see photographs of other arrangements they have designed when developing decorative ideas.

Exchanging vows in a ballroom, historic house or hotel, or private living room usually requires that the space be reconfigured to include an aisle, a seating area for guests, and an "altar" where the bride and groom, officiant, and attendants will stand. To establish the sense of an aisle, tall standing candelabra fitted to hold plants or flowers, paint-ed wood columns topped with baskets of flowers, or broad-based cylindrical candles can be placed down the center of the room. An aisle can be clearly marked with a carpet runner or an unrolled length of white cotton, and benches or chairs can be set on either side of it.

Architectural features such as a fireplace, Palladian window, or French doors overlooking a terrace are often natural focal points for a ceremony (be sure the light won't blind the bride and groom or their guests). Without a strong architectural detail to borrow, a screen or flower-decked trellis can be an effective backdrop. Or plinths topped with flowers or plants can stand sentry on either side of the "altar."

An important part of decorating any ceremony is the lighting. No matter the location, the aisle and altar should always be highlighted, and even if the ceremony is scheduled during daylight, it is wise to have a backup illumination plan for a dim day. Churches and synagogues usually have a range of options; try the possibilities at the time of day when the wedding will take place. Traditionally, candles are never lit before dusk. A house of worship is an exception; a candlelight ceremony can be held at any time of day, and candles can be the central element of the decoration.

MAKE A GRAND ENTRANCE *with a variety of door treatments. A lush pyracantha arch (above left) is embellished by tucking roses in water-filled tubes between its leaves to highlight a glamorous doorway with an arched glass overdoor; the roses at the top of the arch are ivory-hued, with darker peach roses on the bottom. The same technique can be used with bushes, small hedges, and potted plants; their leaves will anchor the flower stems. A delicate garland (above right) of dendrobium orchids and delphinium blossoms is strung with a needle and thread, then suspended in an airy arrangement around a doorway (see matching pew garlands on page 30). The strong architectural features of the historic house (opposite) where Rebecca Thuss and Patrick Farrell were married inspired the stately elegant decoration for their December wedding. A fragrant swag of California bay leaves and three varieties of eucalyptus was threaded through wreaths packed with pepperberries, miniature versions of the chocolate-beribboned wreath on the front door, which brings the eye up the stairs and invites guests inside.*

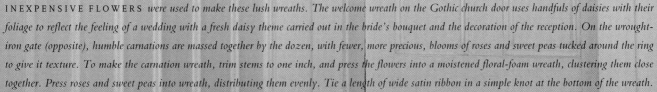

INEXPENSIVE FLOWERS *were used to make these lush wreaths. The welcome wreath on the Gothic church door uses handfuls of daisies with their foliage to reflect the feeling of a wedding with a fresh daisy theme carried out in the bride's bouquet and the decoration of the reception. On the wrought-iron gate (opposite), humble carnations are massed together by the dozen, with fewer, more precious, blooms of roses and sweet peas tucked around the ring to give it texture. To make the carnation wreath, trim stems to one inch, and press the flowers into a moistened floral-foam wreath, clustering them close together. Press roses and sweet peas into wreath, distributing them evenly. Tie a length of wide satin ribbon in a simple knot at the bottom of the wreath.*

ON CHURCH DOORS *(opposite), heart-shaped wreaths of roses, chamomile, stephanotis, and tuberoses are hung with satin ribbons tacked out of sight. Made on a base of floral foam (below, available from floral-supply stores) with a cardboard backing, this decoration is not difficult to construct, but it is time-consuming. Since the foam holds water, it can be made the night before the wedding. Make a hole in the form for a ribbon using an awl or Phillips-head screwdriver. Spray foam with water to saturate it. Trim flower stems to 2½ to 3 inches. Starting at center of heart, poke flower stems into foam; continue adding flowers until form is filled. Empty spaces will be filled in as the flowers open.*

IN FULL BLOOM, *shaped like a heart, stephanotis and gardenias make an opulent wreath (above). First determine how large you want your wreath to be. Then cut out a heart shape in these dimensions from two pieces of white foam-board. Cut a piece of satin ribbon to form a loop from which to hang the wreath. Join the two pieces of foam-board together with spray adhesive, with the satin-ribbon loop sealed between them. Snip off the stem of each flower as close to the base of the blossom as possible. Then with hot glue, attach each flower base to the heart-shaped form, placing the flowers close together (below). Hang the satin loop from an upholstery tack covered with a gardenia blossom. Make this wreath as close as possible to the time the wedding will take place; spritz with water to keep it fresh.*

AN OPEN WREATH *is made using both the fragrant blossoms and leaves of the gardenia. Make the heart form from two pieces of corrugated cardboard as you would for the full wreath (left); cut out center. Punch a hole in top of form with an awl. Thread filament through it, and knot, making a loop for hanging. Wrap form in green self-adhesive floral tape. Hot-glue leaves to form. Cut the blossoms as close as possible to their base, and hot-glue on top of the leaves.*

PEW DECORATIONS *don't have to last long, so they can be more whimsical than practical. These swags are made of dendrobium orchids and delphinium blossoms, strung in an airy arrangement to complement the garland hung around the church entrance (see page 24). The flower heads are simply strung with a needle and thread.*

A DAHLIA ROSETTE *hangs from a length of ribbon cut so that it falls just inside the architectural detail of the pew. To make, fill a plastic "beehive" (available at floral-supply stores) with floral foam. Saturate it with water, and cut flower stems to about 3½ inches. Starting at the perimeter of the beehive (bottom), poke the stems into the floral foam, and continue, pushing the stems at the top into the foam a little deeper (cut stems shorter if necessary) until you have a lush semisphere. The rosette can be made the night before the wedding and refrigerated. Thread ribbon through hole at the top of the beehive. We used dahlias, but the decoration can be made with Gerber daisies as well.*

A PAPER CONE *disappears against the white wood of this pew, emphasizing the crisp pink bows and the lilies of the valley—a classic bridal bloom. To make, cut water-resistant waxed vellum into an 8-inch square. Bring two corners together and overlap them, so the third corner points up in back and the fourth becomes the bottom of the cone. Use a bit of tape to temporarily hold the cone together, and make pencil marks for the spots for the two sets of holes for the ribbons. Untape the cone, punch the holes, reroll the cone, and tape on the inside. Punch two holes in the back, about 1½ inches down, for the ribbon for hanging. Add two dainty bows in front, and string another ribbon through the holes in the back in order to hang the cone. Wrap the stems of a handful of lilies of the valley in a damp paper towel, then plastic wrap; place wrapped flowers in the cone.*

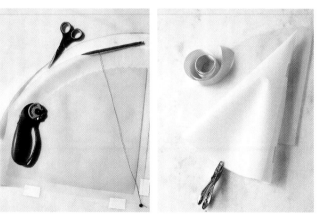

SWEET-PEA CLUSTERS
*are tucked into tropical ti leaves and suspend-
ed from handmade ribbon-covered hangers
attached to each pew. Ti leaves can be special-
ordered through a florist. To make the flower
pocket (bottom), bend a leaf into a cone, and
tack together with floral putty in between
the leaf layers. Make holes with a hole punch
⅝ inch from the top of the leaf, thread
ribbon from the inside of the cone to the back,
and tie the ribbon ends together. Place sweet
peas in tiny plastic vials with water (available
from floral-supply stores), and tuck into
cones. For the hangers: Wearing work gloves,
use metal snips to cut 28-gauge sheet
metal (available at crafts stores) into strips
that are ½ inch wide and about 10 to 12
inches long; the precise length depends on the
height of the pew. Bend each metal strip
into an inverted "U" shape with one end
longer than the other; it should fit snugly
over the top of the pew. Bend the long end up
in a small "U" shape. To cover the metal
strip with ribbon, run a piece of double-stick
tape along the entire hanger, inside and
out. Add ⅝-inch-wide ribbon on top of the
tape, overlapping the ends on the back.*

AT-HOME ALTARS *can be created with a runner, simple seating, and two arrangements—or just one. Kristin Quadland and Scott Egbert were married at Kristin's uncle's 1787 house. The ceremony was held under the barrel vault of his forty-by-twenty-foot ballroom, with a Palladian window as the "altar" (opposite). In keeping with the scale of the room, enormous arrangements of fall foliage and flowers placed on simple white-painted tables flanked the window. A dramatic arrangement (above left) of tulips, pomegranates, and roses, in shades from cream to blush, creates a makeshift altar at the foot of a grand staircase. Exuberant shell-pink dahlias (above right) are anchored in an unusual container: an ordinary aquarium. Cut a piece of vellum to cover the sides of the tank, wrap it around, and tape in back. Add a wide ribbon around the base, then center a skinnier ribbon over it.*

BALANCE AND SCALE *should always be considered when choosing arrangements for the altar. Exceptionally lavish and lush, this antique fishbowl bursts with hydrangeas, sweet peas, and viburnum. The woody stems, visible through the glass, add to the drama. By using a spherical-shaped vase, the stems can be crossed, allowing the flowers to move in every direction. Supremely simple, small mercury-glass ice buckets (opposite) are brimming with mono-chromatic arrangements of garden roses, providing a romantic backdrop for the bride and groom as they exchange vows. Rosebuds are tucked among the blooms.*

A RAVISHING WATER VIEW *(opposite) was the major decoration when Allison Muench and J. Phillips Williams were married in a small ceremony held in East Hampton, New York; two sets of flowers in tall frosted-glass cylinders marked the front and back of the aisle. Elizabeth Eubank and Randall Stern (left) were married at his family's country club, on a raised platform where the officiant and attendants stood during the ceremony and the guests danced during the reception. The altar cum dance floor was backstopped by potted trees brought in on casters, set in a semicircle.*

Outdoor Ceremonies

NATURE, WILD OR CULTIVATED, IS ONE OF THE FINEST decorations for a wedding. Unless the ceremony will be held in a walled garden, it is important to delineate the open space. Dramatic settings can be overwhelming; by establishing a foreground intimate enough for the wedding party to feel cohesive, the view of mountains, the sea, or rolling farmland will hold the background. A feature of the near landscape can be a focus—a magnificent tree, bower, or canopy can become an altar; stone walls and picturesque outbuildings are effective backdrops in the near distance. Those using a tent will have—literally—a blank canvas on which to lay out their theme.

At an outdoor wedding, nearly everything must be brought to the site, so the ceremony is usually minimally decorated. When Gillian Wynn and Peter Early were married by a river in a meadow in Idaho, they draped garlands of roses over a split-rail fence; and Josephine Sasso and Peter Callahan defined an outdoor aisle using potted dogwood trees. Laura Billingham and Albert Navarro said their vows under a willow arch in the thick grass behind a stately barn.

The principal concern for an outdoor ceremony is how to ensure against the vagaries of weather. Even in a dry climate, the day can be uncomfortably hot. Rather than leaving guests to fan themselves, furnish them with white umbrellas, or pleated Chinese paper parasols to use as sunshades. One Arizona couple gave guests straw hats with ribbons on which the wedding date was embroidered—the hats were original favors, as well as effective sun-protectors. Another hazard of the outdoors is poor acoustics; unless a wedding is very intimate, portable microphones are a necessity, set up where the bride and groom and officiant will stand, and near the musicians.

To stack the odds at an outdoor wedding, a marquee or tent can provide shelter from the elements (see "Tents," page 225). A marquee, which is an awning on poles, can be attached to a house or to a full tent. Marquees don't require much decoration, perhaps just vines and flowers wound around poles, and guests can enjoy the view from the open sides. A tent promises the best protection, and its flaps can be left up to create an indoor-outdoor environment if the weather is good. Even a winter wedding can be held in a snow-sculpted garden, with a tent heated by generators or natural gas, the cathedral-style clear vinyl windows softened with sheer fabric so guests can look into the soft winter dusk.

ALTARS AND AISLES *can be created outdoors (opposite). Two lush arrangements of 'Bianca' and 'Vendela' roses, Casablanca lilies, stephanotis, and yarrow flanking the aisle prompt guests to take their seats from the outside, leaving an untouched aisle for the bride; the tall arrangement marks the altar, and the same white ribbon that hangs from tent poles adorns nosegays of Casablanca lilies, stephanotis, yarrow, and sedum tied to chairs at the ends of rows (this page, bottom left). Clockwise from top left: Laura Billingham and Albert Navarro were married in front of a Pennsylvania barn that stands like a Shaker cathedral in the wood; an arch of willows became a kind of clerestory. The aisle at Amy Dedrick and David Roseman's wedding in Annapolis was marked by a scattering of petals. At Kristen Quadland and Scott Egbert's wedding, saplings lashed to a bridge formed an arbor where the bride and groom greeted guests after untying a ribbon.*

TREES ARE NATURAL ANCHORS *for decorations at an outdoor wedding. When Amy Dedrick married David Roseman on the grounds of an historic home, a wreath made of freesia, white dahlias, and yellow-and-mustard-colored roses (opposite) hung on a tree created a focal point for the outdoor altar. Kim Stahlman and Michael Kearns's wedding ceremony in a California vineyard (above left) was held under a majestic ancient tree; flowers in buckets were tacked onto the trunk high enough so the guests could see them during the ceremony. As the light dims, an evening wedding (above right) is illuminated with a romantic, glowing wreath; it lights up the garden, but would also be suitable for an indoor holiday reception. The base is a heart-shaped wire wreath form with two strands of tiny white lights twisted around the form. A brown extension cord blends with the trunk and ground.*

A CLEARING IN THE WOODS *becomes an exotic outdoor setting for a ceremony when a splash of color is introduced: A tropical pink banner inscribed with the initials of the bride and groom and a parade of trees define the background. The trees are made with bamboo for the trunks and an arrangement of dahlias, maidenhair fern, and astilbe for the foliage. The bamboo guest chairs are fitted with pink cushions, and a hot-pink peony is tucked under the seat at the end of each row. When Josephine Sasso and Peter Callahan (opposite) were married at her family's old stone Pennsylvania farmhouse, they created an aisle with dogwood trees in terra-cotta pots.*

JUST MARRIED! *To send a newly married couple on their way from the ceremony to the reception, there are plenty of creative variations on rice, which is discouraged as harmful to birds. Kristin Archer and Glenn Tatham leave their ceremony in Manchester, Vermont, under a shower of hydrangea blossoms (opposite). Allyn Magrino and Per Holmberg were feted with bubbles (this page, top left) by her sisters Sara and Jane. The small bubble bottles (top right) are made specifically for weddings (see the Guide); dress them up by hot-gluing a fabric flower to the top of each one. To give guests petals to toss, make cones (center left) by cutting paper doilies into quarters, rolling the paper into cones, then sealing them with a sticker or tape; stand the cones in a tissue-paper-lined box, and set out for guests to take as they leave the ceremony. Daisy heads (center right), popped off the flowers left over from the site decorations, were given to guests to shower Page Marchese and Adrian Norman as they emerged from the church. For an evening wedding, sparklers are a festive send-off to the reception (bottom left); these are taped to the back of matchbooks printed with the couple's names and the date of the wedding, then tied with a ribbon. Birdseed (bottom right) is the avian-friendly alternative to rice; each guest gets a handful, packaged in glassine envelopes that are sealed with the bride and groom's names.*

THE GETAWAY CAR *is the key to crossing the border into the state of holy matrimony. It should be beautiful, a shining sculpture adorned with ribbons and flowers, ready to whisk the newlyweds away. It is easily done, with a few decorations that integrate the vehicle into the style of your wedding.*

A CONVERTIBLE *shows a newlywed couple off to the world. Silk delphiniums and ribbon adorn this modern sports car; garland and ribbon are taped under the hood, with the ends secured to the wipers and mirrors. To make the garland, the flowers are strung with heavy thread (bottom).*

VINTAGE CARS *Vintage cars can be both quirky and classy, and the same can be true of the decorations. A theme of hearts makes this vehicle's purpose perfectly clear. On the back, spell love with a monogrammed heart (above). To make the heart, cut half-inch-thick white foam-board to the size and shape you want, paint it to match the color scheme of your wedding, and trim the exposed edge with a ribbon. Lightly trace your letters onto the heart with a pencil, then place silk petals along the initials and border; pin petals to the board with sequin pins (below). The final touch is the trailing bow, which is made of double-faced satin and attached to the bottom point of the heart with sequin pins.*

WILDFLOWERS *adorn the front of the vintage car that Elisabeth de Tigny and Alexis Mourot stole away in from the Romanesque abbey in the Dordogne Valley, France, where they were married. Silk flowers can be used in place of fresh flowers or mixed into a fresh-flower decoration. They can be chosen to match the flowers in a bride's bouquet or the floral decorations at the ceremony. Silk flowers are an especially good choice on a hot day or if the drive to the reception is more than a few miles.*

FLOWERS FROM THE CEREMONY
*were dramatic enough to serve as the only
decoration for this convertible. Collected from
the church while the wedding party posed
for pictures, the calla lilies were plentiful
enough to fill the space behind the seats of
this two-seater Mercedes convertible.*

A DOME OF ROSES *announces the bride. Martha Stewart made this spectacular bouquet from dozens of wired champagne and massage roses, as well as lilies of the valley. She formed the flowers into several clusters, then combined them. For streamers, a wide ribbon was dotted with spray roses by cutting off their stems then wiring and taping the roses, folding the ribbon around the wire stems, and stitching from the back (see page 81).*

BOUQUETS

for the Ceremony

*T*he wedding ceremony will probably be the only time in a woman's life when the way she looks and feels is so closely identified with the flowers she holds. At first the bouquet seems to be the most

ephemeral part of the ceremony, but when the music announces the bride and the congregation rises to watch her walk down the aisle, her flowers literally precede her. They help define her style, complement her dress, express the theme of the decorations, and can still be chosen for symbolic reasons, as they were in earlier times. Brides in Ancient Greece carried herbs that were thought to repel bad spirits. Elizabethan brides often held evil-dispersing garlic and chives. Orange blossoms were the flowers the goddess of the earth gave to Zeus' bride, Hera, on her wedding night, perhaps because orange trees bloom year-round, at least in temperate climates. Sometimes a bouquet incorporated plants that herbalists be-

lieved would fortify love or bring luck to the bride and groom.

Designing a bouquet can require delicate and elaborate technical skill, but it can also be as simple as gathering flowers and tying them with ribbon. Passionate gardeners might arrange their wedding to take place at the best moment for a particularly glorious border, from which the bouquet can be plucked. One family, who has cultivated a glamorous allée of spirea bushes, hosted a wedding to coincide with its blooming: The "aisle" was defined by the white-flowered shrubs, and the bride carried spirea blossoms, along with a profusion of other flowers. But generally, choosing the components of a bouquet requires more thought than using just what is in bloom.

Humans recognized the allure of flowers even before there was a word for beauty, so it is not surprising that bouquets are an integral part of weddings. The gown sets the mood, but a bouquet can underscore it. The effect of a bias-cut dress with thirties overtones is heightened by calla lilies bound in a tailored sash; tulle might call for lilacs and hydrangeas. A formal gown suggests a more structured bouquet, perhaps roses with a ribbon cascade. A casual afternoon ceremony in a striped tent is a natural setting for herbaceous border flowers like hollyhocks, lilies, and peonies in a bouquet that looks casually arranged.

Color, pale to brilliant; size, from nosegay to cascade; shape, symmetrical or loosely gathered; scent, fresh or sultry; and texture, crisp, silky, or sinuous; and what is in season: These are the principal ingredients to coordinate.

The color of bridal bouquets for much of the twentieth century was predictable: white or the palest pastels. Now nearly any hue is suitable. Flowers can be the sole note of color—an armful of coral roses in an all-white wedding or soft-petaled purple anemones with a cream velvet gown. Arrangements can complement a pastel-colored gown: An assembly of pinks with an apricot organza dress; deep-hued peonies, tulips, and lilacs to enhance embroidered cotton.

How big a bouquet should be is based on style, convenience, and cost. The size of the bride should also be taken into account: The bouquet should not overwhelm a delicate figure or seem too small for a tall bride. For some women, bountiful is the order of the day, but beware the unwieldy, especially if the ceremony is going to be long. The delicate nosegay is easier to handle, and small is not necessarily insignificant. A packed bunch of lilies of the valley or sweet peas will add fragrance, which is an accessory, too.

Before deciding on the shape of the bouquet, a bride should think about how she will carry it. A large arrangement must be held with both hands and can provide a sense of balance; a smaller bouquet allows the bride to place a hand on her father's arm. Stems influence the shape of a bouquet, too; long-stemmed roses lend themselves to a sheaf, while violets make a natural nosegay.

Elizabethan and Victorian brides often designed their bouquets to send messages in the "language of flowers" used by lovers (see "The Meaning of Flowers," right). A bride can use the old-fashioned meanings to express the way she feels, too. Or she can follow another Victorian custom and make a bouquet of flowers whose first letters spell out a word. Why not spell "love" with lilac, orange blossom, verbena, and euonymus?

Flowers may be invested with personal or historical significance, but they are also distinguished by certain qualities—the rose thorn that pricks, the lily pollen that stains—that are unfriendly to a bride in white. Some flowers must have their stamens clipped so they don't mark a dress, and others must be ruled out, or propped up, because the stems are too limp. Some wilt quickly, while others still look fresh after a day out of water. The flowers on the following pages have been chosen for their beauty, appropriateness, and resilience.

Flowers in a bouquet reflect affinities, hopes, and memories. Some brides have always imagined themselves carrying the daisies of the field; others associate gardenias with romance; and who would deny an arrangement of evergreens to a bride who met her husband cross-country skiing? While each bouquet is different, they all have this in common: Like the umbrella a tightrope walker carries for balance, the flowers a bride holds firmly as she walks down the aisle still a trembling hand; and the smell of the flower will always remind her and her groom of their wedding day. ✆

THE MEANING OF FLOWERS

ALLIUM *luck*
ASTER *beginnings*
CAMELLIA *honesty, excellence*
CHRYSANTHEMUM *hope*
CROCUS *youthful happiness*
DAISY *innocence*
FORGET-ME-NOT *remembrance*
FREESIA *calm*
GARDENIA *gracefulness*
GERBERA *purity*
GLADIOLUS *grace*
HELIOTROPE *devotion*
HONEYSUCKLE *the ties of love*
HYACINTH *young love*
LILY (WHITE) *innocence*
ORCHID *ecstasy*
PANSY *lovers' thoughts*
PINE *compassion*
RANUNCULUS *charm*
ROSE (RED) *passion*
ROSE (WHITE) *purity*
SUNFLOWER *power*
SWEET PEA *lasting pleasure*
TULIP *a declaration of love*
VIOLET *fidelity*
WATER LILY *unmatched beauty*

THERE IS A BOUQUET SHAPE *to suit every bride. Opposite, top row from left: Laura Billingham carries a bouquet finished with streamers of flowers. A cascade of peonies, lilies, foxglove, lilac, roses, astilbe, and alliums. Chosen for subtle differences in color and size, 'Peach Surprise,' 'Renate,' 'Timeless,' 'Sensation,' and 'Creame Gracia' roses are tied with a striped ribbon. Middle, from left: Diminutive replicas of a bride's bouquet are for the bridesmaids—the bottom is 'Magic Silver' roses; the top is peach 'Romy' and English garden roses. Alabaster tea roses and spiky astilbe have a satin "leaf" collar. Rachel Bold and her attendant carry satin-piped collared yellow flowers. Bottom, from left: For a sophisticated bride, a sheaf of miniature calla lilies. Elizabeth Eubank's bridesmaids carry handfuls of hydrangeas. Yellows and oranges meet in a gathered arrangement of parrot tulips, hyacinth, 'Acapulco' roses, stock, and miniature amaryllis.*

{ CASCADE }

{ DOME }

{ NOSEGAY }

{ COLLARED }

{ TAILORED }

{ GATHERED }

*PURE AND SIMPLE white bouquets
are among the most bridal. Newly married
Allison Muench and J. Phillips Williams
(left) clasp hands as they walk up the aisle,
her delicate bouquet held effortlessly in
one hand. She carries a small nosegay of
Eucharis (opposite), designed to suit a
petite bride. Popular in the forties, these
fragrant blossoms remain true to their
name, which means "very graceful."*

White Bouquets

IN ALL ITS INFINITE VARIATIONS—CREAMY, MILKY, AND barely blushing—white has been the hue of choice for bridal flowers since Queen Victoria married Prince Albert in 1840. Theirs was the most publicly romantic match of the nineteenth century, and millions of young women on both sides of the Atlantic followed the young queen's example. Of particular note was her choice of an unusually simple wedding, at least in comparison to other royals who had been married before her. She displayed her preference for a lack of ostentation by carrying a bouquet of white snowdrops and wearing orange blossoms twined among the diamonds twinkling in her hair; orange blossoms have been a staple of Windsor weddings ever since.

White is among the easiest colors for a bouquet because there is such an abundant choice of white flowers, regardless of the season (see glossary, page 54). All sorts of whites mix well together: Among the variations are the traditional combination of roses of different sizes and hues; the more exotic snowberries with dahlias and tea roses; or Casablanca lilies, looking surprisingly supple against the curving flowers of gooseneck loosestrife. For the matches to work, the flowers should be compatible in shape, size, and scent. Flowers such as ripe roses with blowsy blossoms look best with a crisper complement; those like lilacs, whose heads are composed of tiny buds, are set off by more massive petals and are often paired with peonies because they bloom in the same season. White flowers are a perfumer's delight. There are fragrances for every preference—lilies of the valley gathered in a pungent nosegay; a spill of roses from tart to luscious; the deep, sensuous aroma of lilies. Usually one scent should predominate, while the rest of the bouquet simply smells fresh.

A white bouquet can be as nonchalant as a plump clutch of sweet peas, or as dramatic as a single spray of precious orchids. It can focus on one kind of flower, finding variation in the degree of openness, from bud to full-blown. Or the flowers can be so densely packed that the whole arrangement almost seems to become a single bloom. Another possibility is to use the greens and browns of stems and leaves to set off whites and creams in the bouquet. White flowers are most gracious about the company they keep: A white bouquet can be dressed up in a collar of lace, taffeta, or tulle, and festooned with satin or velvet ribbons, and it will look just as pretty if it is bound in a trail of ivy or grapevine.

{ CLASSIC WHITES }

PEONY

RANUNCULUS

HYDRANGEA

CATTLEYA ORCHID

CALLA LILY

FRENCH TULIP

TUBEROSE

CASABLANCA LILY

TULIP

LILY OF THE VALLEY

HYBRID TEA ROSE

SWEET PEA

GARDENIA

STEPHANOTIS

GARDEN ROSE

FREESIA

CLASSIC WHITE FLOWERS *make simple and formal bouquets. They can be self-effacing (baby's breath, lily of the valley) or proudly starched and frilled (orchids, calla lilies). Crowd your bouquet with dense buds, or leave room for the butterflies, but gather some of the classics. The elegant Art Deco favorite, the* CALLA LILY, *is especially chic with slim, satiny gowns.* CASABLANCA LILIES, *ruffly and starlike, are fairly new in the florist trade, though lilies have been beloved by brides since ancient times. Highly scented* FREESIA *is graceful and long-lasting; its smallish, tubular buds open successively along arching stems. The* FRENCH TULIP *is larger, taller, and tulipier than the homegrown sort; the white variety, however, can be fragile and may droop. Elegant and high-centered in bud, the long-stemmed hothouse rose, or* HYBRID TEA ROSE, *is roseate perfection in flower. Hybrid teas differ from old-fashioned* GARDEN ROSES *in form; garden roses might have anything from a single row of petals surrounding a starburst of stamens to hundreds of overlapping petals in multiple sprays.* GARDENIAS *were once the classic corsage, but their waxen petals have to be fresh and protected from handling, as they bruise and yellow easily. Mophead* HYDRANGEA *blossoms are best known in blue, but the white form is a fresh, snowy ball. The nodding bells of* LILY OF THE VALLEY, *the most popular of small white blossoms, create traditional nosegays, full of perfume.* ORCHIDS *were once the definitive hothouse blossom, but flamboyant cattleya orchids, like those in our bouquets, can be grown in sunny rooms. The satiny petals and clean fragrance of* PEONIES *are reminiscent of old-fashioned gardens.* RANUNCULUSES *have countless petals arranged in a goblet form; they resemble roses, without perfume. The small, starry* STEPHANOTIS *is a flowering vine; it is a good mixer and a bridal favorite.* SWEET PEAS, *brought to England from Sicily in 1699, weren't extensively hybridized until Victorian times.* TUBEROSES *are feathery, fragile-looking, and hard to find, but the highly fragrant variety we're familiar with are tough natives of Mexico and can be grown in a warm garden.*

A CASCADE of about eighty sweet peas, an old-fashioned favorite for early summer brides, is interspersed with dots of "something blue," tweedia, and bound by a ribbon embroidered with the bride and groom's initial and wedding date.

W

5·24·98

STEPHANOTIS *makes a pure-white,*
snowflake-fragile nosegay. Pearl-topped
corsage pins are inserted into the bell of
each flower, either a teardrop or three small
round-headed pins in each. A row of the
same pins finishes the satin-ribbon-wrapped
handle. A single blossom is fashioned into a
simple matching boutonniere for the groom.

SOFT AND FEATHERY, *ruffled and lush, or bold and elegant, bouquets made from combinations of different white flowers set the tone of a wedding. Clockwise from top left: Waxy snowberries, available after the first frost, are mixed with icy dahlias and snowy tea roses, wrapped in pale-green satin around the stem and tied in a bow with scallop-ended streamers. Fragrant white Casablanca lilies in a softly gathered bouquet include opened and closed flowers, mixed with long curving gooseneck loosestrife. This dainty nosegay of "Stephanotis-in-the-mist," equal parts baby's breath and starry stephanotis, looks like a ballerina in its starchy faux-horsehair cuff. The white of gardenia blossoms on branches, lilies of the valley, and sweet peas is freshened by bright greens in this cascading bouquet, designed to be cradled in the bride's arm; a lemony-green satin ribbon binds the stem and is tied in a bow with streamers.*

USING ONE TYPE OF FLOWER *can have impact if the balance and scale of the bouquet is in proportion to the shape and size of the flower. The soft ruffles of this ethereal ball of yellow-touched white cattleya orchids (above left) trail off into curls of pale-yellow ribbon that emphasize the buttery hearts of the flowers. The classic nosegay (above right) is made of hundreds of stems of fragrant lily of the valley, nestled among their own green leaves and wrapped in white satin with the streamer ends cut with pinking shears. Cold-weather whites (opposite) are perfect for a winter wedding. Some of these Casablanca lilies are a hand-span wide. They are wired into a plump and ruffled lily "ball" intermixed with twenty silver-mesh leaves, some of which are tacked in a drift onto its silvery ribbon. Mixing real flowers with ribbons and even faux leaves enhances the beauty of both.*

A CASCADE *of peonies floats on a*
tender foam of lilac sprays in this fragrant
spring bouquet. It is tied with a white
taffeta ribbon, and can be held over one arm.

PURE-WHITE *stephanotis blossoms have long been a wedding tradition. This bouquet is made from about 225 blossoms. First cut off the stems, leaving a hole at the base of each blossom. Attach each flower to a stephanotis holder (available from floral suppliers). We wired about 150 blossoms, gathered them together, wrapped the holders with floral tape, and bent the wires so the blossoms formed a dome. The streamers are made by stringing about seventy-five remaining blossoms along white satin ribbon. Knot the end of each ribbon, and tie tops of streamers to bouquet handle.*

RED AND RUSSET *are among the many colors that can make a rose bouquet. When Agnethe Glatved (left) married Matthew Septimus at the Picnic House in Brooklyn's Prospect Park, she carried a nosegay of red garden roses and was accompanied by her dog, Lucy, who wore a red grosgrain ribbon. The range of rose colors is barely tapped in an autumn bouquet (opposite) made of bronze roses: 'Orange Unique,' 'Leonidas,' and 'My Lovely,' paired with golden oak leaves and hypericum berries, and tied in a russet velvet ribbon.*

Rose Bouquets

ROSES ARE AMONG THE MOST POPULAR CHOICE FOR A bridal bouquet, perhaps because the rose has long been a symbol of romance, whether it is the white rose of purity—pure love is the more precise meaning—or the red rose of passion. But roses are considerably more varied in color and shape than the standard white, cream, pink, and red suggest. Roses come in an astonishing array of colors, from hot pinks and oranges to subtle greens and peaches (see glossary on page 64) and can make a vivid or richly dark bouquet. Among the thousands of rose varieties, a bride can choose to carry a single perfect bloom, a lavish bouquet, or to mix roses with other flowers. Roses are often a practical choice in any season because such a variety is now available year-round.

The height of luxury is the all-one-color bouquet—there is a hue to suit every bride. An all-rose bouquet can blend several shades of compatible colors or can mix varying sizes and types for a voluptuous crush of rose upon rose that creates a look of sheer abundance.

The variety of roses is so extensive that there is likely to be one that works well with most other kinds of flowers. Surround roses with velvety chocolate cosmos for a textural sensation. Punctuate a dome of lavender roses with glistening viburnum and hydrangeas, or fill out a nosegay of tea roses with dahlias and snowberries (see page 57). With their stems stripped, roses can also be nestled among greenery of all sorts. Asparagus fern, pine, euonymus, and ivy are among the classic complements, but roses are so agreeable they can be juxtaposed with banana leaves or collared in satin ribbon (see page 51).

Bouquets made of roses can be sweet and feminine, like those in the baby varieties, but they can also be chic and sophisticated. Some are arranged in an understated way, others are richly elegant, like the lush heart-shaped bouquet of hybrid teas on page 69.

In selecting roses, as with any other flower, a bride should determine whether the varieties she is partial to are well-suited to a long day. Although some are too fragile to survive more than a walk down the aisle, they can still be used as long as the bride is aware that her bouquet may wilt before she is ready to throw it.

A bouquet of roses is only the beginning: This supremely versatile flower stands unchallenged in vases on an altar or as a centerpiece, tucked between the layers of a cake, nestled inside paper cones for guests to toss, and adorning a flower girl's basket or crown.

{ CLASSIC ROSES }

VANILLA
Peach

SENSATION
Orange

VERSILLIA
Peach

PAPILLON
Yellow

STERLING SILVER
Lavender

RED DEVIL
Red

BRIDAL
Pink

BLUE BIRD
Lavender

BARCAROLA
Black Red

PINK TANGO
Pink

RAVEL
Hot Pink

KELLY GREEN
White

IVORY
Off-White

BIANCA
White

EMERALD
Green-Yellow

ROSES GROW IN A SPECTRUM *of colors ranging from the deepest red to the brightest white, with countless shades in between. Most often the word "rose" brings to mind the tapered buds and sculptural elegance of the modern hybrid tea rose, but this is but one of the flower's many forms. Intense cultivation of the rose peaked in the nineteenth century, when mauve-toned European roses mingled with glowing, tea-scented Chinese roses, producing more than twenty thousand varieties that are available today. Not only can they be found in every color—except blue—but rose blossoms can be as big as oranges or as tiny as the tumbling sprays of cluster roses and thimble-sized miniatures fit for the most delicate bouquet.*

HARMONIZING *shades of several
different roses are combined in this dome of
fragrant flowers. Old-fashioned garden roses
like these, in hot and soft pink, off-white
and cream, and vanilla and gold peach,
bloom from early spring till late fall. English
varieties, each of which has a memorable
fragrance, are mixed with white ranunculuses.*

ROSES COMBINED WITH OTHER FLOWERS *or embellished with decorative trims neither disappear nor dominate. A pink ribbon (opposite) edged in brown blends seamlessly with garden roses. This page, clockwise from top left: Jewel-toned roses, 'Black Magic,' 'Red Devil,' and 'Black Beauty,' are combined with astilbe and pepperberries; the stems are wrapped in brown satin. A thirty-blossom spring bouquet is made from four types of peach roses— 'Versillia,' 'Mystique,' 'Oriental Curiosa,' and 'Singing in the Rain,' studded with eight blush-tipped tuberoses; the stems are bound with peach velvet ribbon. Fragile 'Sally Holmes' garden roses lasted only two hours after wiring—but they were a bride's favorite, and her florist was willing to make the bouquet minutes before the ceremony. Shiny Viburnum tinus and soft mophead hydrangeas are tucked between lush 'Blue Bird,' 'Delilah,' and 'Sterling Silver' roses.*

A CUFF of smooth chocolate cosmos surrounds lavender 'Paradise' roses and demonstrates how effective a mixed rose bouquet can be. Inspired by fifties haute couture, the bouquet is finished with a satin-ribbon wrapped handle and tiny chocolate velvet bows. GREENHOUSE ROSES, like the 150 hybrid teas that Martha Stewart used to make the heart-shaped bouquet (opposite), are available year-round from florists. For a lush and well-shaped bouquet like this one, roses should be wired with new "stems," wrapped in floral tape in clusters of twelve, and then gathered into several clusters. Wrap the handle with ribbon.

GATHERED *and ribbon-wrapped, peonies make a lavish bouquet. When Martha Stewart learned that her friend Allyn Magrino (left) was to be married to Per Holmberg, she offered to make the wedding bouquet, an enormous cascade of forty peonies, forty sweet-pea blossoms, and assorted French lilacs and roses (left and on the cover). Three shades of the 'Silver Lining' peony (opposite) blend beautifully in one luxurious bouquet. The shell-pink, apricot, and creamy yellow blossoms range from wide open to tightly closed. The flowers are densely packed, but room has been left for the buds to unfurl.*

Pastel Bouquets

MORE LIVELY THAN WHITE, SOFTER THAN RED, BLUE, OR purple, a pastel bouquet, made of complementary shades of one color or a range of hues, suggests overtones of spring and new beginnings. For the bride who wears a dress in a tint of pale pink, yellow, or blue— or who would like to add a hint of color to a white or cream gown— the pastel bouquet provides just enough color. The softest possible pastels—pale yellow, celadon, and cream—never compete with a softly colored wedding dress, or the bride wearing it. And a pastel color scheme can be carried through to the ceremony and reception.

The choice to use pastels opens a broad spectrum of flowers for consideration. One approach is for a bride to look for close cousins in the color family she likes best. Often, a pastel bouquet is most effective when it is composed of only one variety of flower in subtle variations: If it's not clear whether the petals should be called apricot, shrimp, or peach, the flowers will probably blend well.

The bouquet with the most gardenlike feeling is one in which a few complementary pastels, along with different shapes and varieties of buds and blooms, are artfully mixed. Greens can be incorporated in a bouquet to the same effect, or a bow and streamers of the right color can visually bridge the various tones. Lavender lilacs, striped apricot-and-raspberry tulips, soft-blue delphiniums, and blush-and-green ranunculuses are among the flowers that mix as though they had grown together. When choosing pastel colors, the intensity can be balanced by using flowers in subtle, nearly cream shades with others that are deeper. The shapes and sizes of the flower heads can be varied to set each other off, too: Hyacinths, with their big blossoms composed of tiny individual flowers, complement the small, tight, round ranunculus and the oval of a partially opened tulip. One way to play off a bride's mixed pastel bouquet is to give each bridesmaid a nosegay made of one color of the bouquet.

The pastel bouquet can convey a fresh-from-the-garden feeling, but pastels can also be quite formal, depending on the flowers and the way they are arranged. A handful of sweet peas in an up-turned collar of organza is decidedly streamlined; a dome of eighty sweet peas wrapped in satin ribbon is loose and luxurious. There is this, too: Flowers, like jewelry and makeup, are meant to emphasize a bride's natural beauty, and a bouquet of soft pinks held close to her face will cast a subtle blush on her cheeks.

NOSEGAYS *are well-suited to petite brides, and also to bridesmaids and flower girls. These lilac-pink cousins (opposite) of the traditional white lily of the valley are available only in May. Here, fifty stems, cuffed with their own leaves, are wrapped in a spiral of silvery lavender ribbon. A quartet of brides-maids' nosegays (above) are made of sweet peas in four different shades. Organza collars match the flowers in the nosegays. Each bouquet requires one square yard of fabric. The organza is basted twelve inches from one selvaged edge; the seam is then pulled taut, creating a loose cone of organza around the bouquet, with the selvage on the outer edge. The bottom half is wound around the stems, tucked in place, and secured with pearl-headed straight pins.*

ONE FAVORITE FLOWER *can make a dramatic bouquet if the proportion is right. Clockwise from top left. Unopened wood hyacinth buds make stunning bridesmaids' bouquets since the flowers' plump heads give a sense of anticipation; the stems are wrapped with double ribbons: A green grosgrain band is glued to mauve silk or lavender satin, with ends folded under and finished with ribbon-covered buttons. Crisp, star-shaped Astrantia burst forth from a ruff of gathered silk ribbon. This slender clutch of miniature calla lilies has elegance to spare; each flower hood is streaked with shades of lavender, and the long, graceful stems are cuffed with a dusky-purple taffeta ribbon held in place with glass-topped floral pins. Perfect for the late-summer bride, a bouquet of 'Cafe au Lait' dahlias could easily be culled from a garden; tucked away among the pink, salmon, and yellow blossoms are a few green-tinged buds.*

PALE GREEN *is a pastel shade, too. Here, a bouquet of viburnum and a Queen Anne's lace look-alike appears to be a bunch of soft, puffed snowballs.*
A close look reveals tiny blooms. Like real snowballs, viburnum needs to be kept cool. The stems should be kept in water and the blossoms misted every
half hour until the bride picks up her bouquet to walk down the aisle. The stem is wrapped in white satin ribbon and tied with a generous bow and streamers.

IF COLOR DICTATES THE CHOICE *of a bouquet, explore different flowers in the same hue. The tight, tiny buds of lilacs and willowy sweet peas (above left) provide a pretty backdrop—and room for the luxurious heads of multipetaled 'Magic Silver' roses to blossom in this beautifully blended bouquet; the stem is wrapped in picot-edged taffeta ribbon. A rosy hue (above right) unites these ranunculuses, sweet peas, and 'Rosario' tulips; an assortment of textures gives the bouquet its character. Stalks of pink astilbe reaching out from it echo the detailing on a beaded bodice, while the pink satin bow falls gracefully against an organza-skirted dress. A glorious early summer bouquet (opposite) with a just-picked look combines purple lilacs, parrot tulips in apricot and raspberry, fringed 'Aladdin' tulips, green hydrangeas, green-eyed ranunculuses, purple scabiosa, purple hyacinths, and 'Belladonna' delphiniums. Fifty blooms in nine different varieties make up this bouquet, but careful choice of color and scale and a subtle ribbon hold the color scheme together.*

IMAGINATIVE COMBINATIONS
of the palest pastels use only cream, yellow,
and greens for these bouquets. A hand-
tied bouquet is composed of ladies' mantle,
green hyacinth, and Achillea, collected
as though they were just picked and loosely
gathered. A bouquet of spring flowers
(opposite) has the glow of pale sunshine.
Its subtle colors are complemented by rich
fragrance. Ranunculuses lend solidity to ethe-
real poppies and dainty narcissi; 'Cream
Perfection' tulips are as sleek as the buttery-
yellow satin ribbon used to tie the stems.

THE STEMS OF A BOUQUET *can be liter-
ally overshadowed by the flowers above, but they should be
just as beautiful as the blooms. Much as you choose the right
shoe for a dress or the right tie for a suit, give careful consideration to the stems. Whether a bride walks down the aisle
with an elaborate bundle of peonies or outfits herself and her
bridesmaids with modern sheaths of calla lilies, a thoughtful treatment of a bouquet's handle or stems will complete the look.*

*The ideas here illustrate basic techniques—classic, square
end, exposed stems, fabric collar, and streamers—but are by
no means the only choices. A bride can re-create them for her
own bouquet, or use them to inspire more personal designs.
The first step in planning a stem treatment is to think about
the flowers the bride will carry, since particular flowers are
more suited to particular dressings. A large rose bouquet will
require a full wrapping of ribbon or fabric to hide the hardware of wired roses underneath. But an elaborate wrapping
needn't be based on function. Even the most delicate posy
can be complemented by lengths of ribbon encircling its stems,
finished with an extravagant bow.*

*Simple wrappings, like a single band of ribbon fastened
with a button, or fabric held in place with decorative pins, are
perfect for flowers with long, elegant stems. Exposed stems
should be trimmed neatly with a sharp knife so they look fresh.*

*What wrapping should be used? A piece of fabric that
echoes the bride's or bridesmaids' dresses, an antique handkerchief for "something old," or the prettiest lengths of ribbon
available. Select embellishments that will make a statement
all their own—just as a bride and her bouquet should.*

A BEAUTIFUL HANDKERCHIEF *becomes a collar
for a bouquet with a few stitches. The stitching is easily
removed, and a wrapping of floral tape protects the fabric from
stains. To make, fold a handkerchief into a triangle. Leaving a generous portion of thread at either end, hand sew 1-inch
stitches across fabric, about 2 inches below fold. Arrange
bouquet; wrap stems with floral tape. Place arrangement on
handkerchief so tops of blooms lie below fold (bottom left).
Pull fabric along thread to create gathers. Fold in left side
of gathered fabric (bottom middle); tuck thread ends inside.
Fold up bottom edge of fabric so point hits base of blooms
(bottom right). Wrap right side of fabric over left and around
stems; pull taut. Fasten with decorative pins; adjust collar.*

CRISSCROSSING RIBBON *is a simple, yet beautiful
way to finish off the stems of a bouquet. First arrange the
bouquet, with the stem ends cut neatly. One posy (below)
has pale-yellow daffodils ringed with paper-whites; the
second posy is arranged the other way around. Starting at
the top of the stems just below the flower heads, make a
knot in the ribbon. Continue down half the length of the stems,
crisscrossing the ribbon and knotting as you go (above).
Be sure that the ribbon knots are on the side that will be
facing out. Leave the remaining ribbon in long streamers.*

A TIGHT DOME OF ROSES *is made even more beautiful when finished with an opulent satin ribbon and bow. A few more rosebuds are sewn in the trailing ribbon ends. To make, first strengthen the rose stems and support the heavy blooms by wiring 24-gauge wire to each stem then wrap with floral tape (top right). Taper the stem cluster by trimming the stems on angles at varying lengths; tape the stems together. Place the stems on a length of ribbon a few inches left of center—we used 2 yards of 3-inch-wide satin ribbon to make a 5-inch-long handle. Wrap the long end of the ribbon around the stems, spiraling downward (second from top); the short end will tie into the bow. At the bottom, the last spiral will over hang the stems. Fold the overhang up, covering the stem ends; wrap the ribbon back to the top of the stems. At the top, tie the ends in a bow (third from top); cut the long ends on a diagonal. Wire and tape the rosebuds; pinch the trailing ribbon around one stem. Stitch each bud in place (bottom); repeat.*

STREAMERS *give a bouquet an added dimension. Cut varying lengths of ⅜-inch-wide double-faced satin ribbon. Collect leftover florets from the bridal bouquet; cut the stems of the florets short. Tie one end of each ribbon around a floret's stem (above left). Some streamers can dangle from the center of the bouquet; tie the free end of a ribbon around the stem of a flower cluster. Other streamers can drape from the bouquet's base or handle. Once all streamers are in place (below), wrap the stems with complementary ribbon or fabric, using a square-end technique (see instructions at right).*

TO MAKE A FABRIC SQUARE END, *first arrange the bouquet; wrap and tape the stems together. Center the stems on a piece of fabric (below left); cut the material so it extends 3 inches on either side of the stems and 2 inches below the bottoms. Fold the bottom of the fabric up over the stem ends. Slide the bouquet to one end of the fabric. Wrap the stems, continuing along the length of the material (below right); fold the edge under, and secure with decorative pins. To complete the look, tie a bow with a coordinating ribbon at the base of the blooms (opposite page, left).*

TO MAKE A RIBBON SQUARE END, *choose a ribbon that's a little wider than the bouquet stems' circumference. In the back of the bouquet, about one inch from the bottom of stems, secure one end of ribbon with a pin (above left). Bring ribbon under stems and up from side; pin to secure. Fold ribbon back over itself diagonally, and wrap stems, spiraling upward to base of blooms (above right). Fold edge under, and secure with two decorative pins. Millinery flowers are a nice addition to this gingham ribbon. Using thin ribbon, make crisscrosses down the length of the handle, and tie, leaving enough ribbon at ends to make streamers; tie on two additional streamers. Attach flowers at points where the ribbon intersects and at the ends of the streamers (opposite, right).*

Good Things for little girls

PERHAPS THE ONLY SIGHT MORE SIGH-INSPIRING THAN the first appearance of the bride at a wedding is the debut of an adorable flower girl, walking down the aisle in her own white dress, haloed in flowers, and sprinkling rose petals in the bride's path. Including children in weddings is a tradition that dates back thousands of years. At ancient Greek and Roman services, young girls strode ahead of the bride, littering her path with herbs and grains to represent the hope for fertility. By the Middle Ages this practice had barely changed: Two girls, often sisters dressed identically, would walk down the aisle carrying armfuls of wheat. The concept of the flower girl was born during the Elizabethan era when wealthy families would import exotic flowers for young girls to carry down the aisle. Flower girls have also worn rings of flowers on their heads to symbolize both innocence and eternity.

Today, having children take part in a wedding has less to do with highlighting a woman's fertility or a family's wealth than with including loved ones of all ages in a special day. It's common in European weddings for the entire bridal party to be composed of children. In the United States, depending on their ages and maturity levels, youngsters are often asked to fill one of several spots on the wedding day. A flower girl typically ranges from 3 to 8 years old. She directly precedes the bride in the processional, carrying a basket of petals that she scatters down the aisle. A bride with a long train might also have two to four young children as pages whose sole job is to maneuver the skirt. A couple having an evening service might include candlelighters—slightly older children who can light the candles in the church or hall just before the processional begins.

Whatever their role, part of making little girls feel comfortable and underscoring their importance in the pageantry is to give them something to wear or hold that has been specially made for them. A flower girl will feel like a princess—and walk with her head held high—with a crown of flowers on her head. Or she can hold a basket decorated with silk or real flowers that echo the bride's bouquet and filled with petals and herbs to be scattered ahead of the bride. A bride who is nervous about slipping on the petals might prefer that the flower girl simply march down the aisle, clad in a dress chosen just for her, clutching a tiny nosegay or pomander and tossing nothing more than smiles from side to side.

A POMANDER OF ROSES *is an alternative to a bouquet. To make the pomander (below) make a base using a utility knife to carve a piece of floral foam into a 4-inch ball. With needle-nose pliers make one dime-size loop, then another at a 90-degree angle to the first, at one end of a 12-inch piece of heavy-gauge floral wire. Insert wire through axis of the ball, which will rest on the horizontal loop. Make a dime-size loop at top of the ball and snip off remaining wire. Soak ball for ten minutes. Choose any fragrant flower with a sturdy stem (roses are a good choice because the stems dry well), and cut the stems to one inch. Remove the sepals and outer petals. Poke the stems into the foam, covering the ball. The empty spaces will be filled once the blooms open. Store the ball in the refrigerator. Just before the ceremony, create a ribbon handle (carefully, so as not to get them wet): thread a 12-inch-long ribbon through the upper loop. Knot ribbon ends. Thread another length through the bottom loop and knot. Cut the ribbon ends at an angle.*

FLOWERS IN HER HANDS *and in her hair make a young attendant feel extra special. A flower girl (above) wears a wreath of roses and carries a wicker basket filled with petals and trimmed with roses at the base of the handle. To make a floral wreath, wire blossoms with five inch stems, then wrap floral tape just beneath the flower heads. Tape the flowers together, two inches apart, overlapping stems and clipping excess wire. When you reach the desired length, weave the last stem onto the first and twist the wire closed.*

COVER A BASKET *with flowers that echo the bride's bouquet. Page Marchese carried oxeye daisies on the day she married Adrian Norman. At the reception, the flower girl carried a basket trimmed with the same flowers (opposite) filled with favors for guests. To make the daisy or rose basket (above) wrap a basket handle with seam binding, securing it with hot glue at the ends. Cut the flowers to the bases of the bud and attach them to the basket with hot glue. Fill the rose basket with rose petals, or use whole roses so ripe they will tumble apart into petals when thrown.*

THE FINISHING TOUCH *to a man's attire is a small sprig of flowers or herbs known as the boutonniere. For a formal evening wedding, the groom and his ushers wear full dress, or "white tie." This ensemble is named for the white bow tie made of piqué—a crisp, textured cotton—accompanied by a black tailcoat with peaked lapels worn unbuttoned, black trousers, a white wing-collar shirt, and a white piqué vest. A boutonniere of lilies of the valley perfectly matches the tone.*

BOUTONNIERES

for the Ceremony

*T*he plumage of the male of most species may be gorgeous, especially during the courtship dance. But the male of our species usually selects subtle, and extremely becoming, gray, white, and black

coloration for his wedding clothes. Still, don't count out an atavistic attraction to a bit of decoration on the part of the groom and his attendants—and that is where the boutonniere enters the story. *Boutonniere* is a French word that refers to the buttonhole on a lapel, where these small garnishes—usually, but not always, flowers—are pinned. *On* it, not *in* it, is the most common arrangement, since men's suits and cutaways are not usually made with a pair of buttonholes to hold the stem of the flower in place, as they were in the eighteenth century.

The boutonniere had its heyday in the nineteenth century—the era of the "language of flowers" (see page 50)—when the bud a man wore was often a "word," to be answered by a woman in the same flower vocabulary. Today this seems like a bit of delightful nonsense, but it can add some whimsy to one of the little details of a wedding—a bride or groom might choose a red rose, signifying passion; or an aster for "beginnings." To add a touch of originality, the principal flower can be combined with less predictable elements—a rose can be pinned on a fan of hydrangea leaves, or have its stem wrapped in striped satin. A boutonniere can also be composed of elements with personal meaning: Flowers are part of nearly every courtship and those with private resonance convey a message the bride and groom will both read clearly.

Plucking a flower from a handy arrangement at the church, then poking it through a buttonhole is one approach to the boutonniere, but it is a pleasant creative enterprise for a bride and groom to choose the flowers for him, his ushers, and other men in the family. Getting the flowers into shape requires some forethought—stems are often wrapped, bows attached, and pins selected—but there are plenty of stylish ways to pull boutonnieres together that don't require a lot of work.

The elements of the boutonniere are its centerpiece, generally a flower, leaf, or herb; the stem, usually bound in ribbon; a pin; and sometimes a small bow for a finishing flourish. When choosing boutonnieres for the wedding party, consider the style and season of the wedding, the flowers the bride and her attendants will carry, and those that will decorate the ceremony and reception. Most important, the flower and its wrapped stem should coordinate or contrast with the groom's attire. On a tuxedo, a chocolate cosmos stem might be wrapped in black satin ribbon to match the stripe on the trousers; on a seersucker summer suit worn with a yellow-striped tie, the boutonniere could be a daisy tied with a cream satin ribbon. A pinstriped navy suit would be complemented by a lisianthus bud with lavender ribbon; a white dinner jacket is a handsome background for a creamy tulip bud held in place with a glass-headed pin.

A boutonniere can be unscented or fragrant; at an outdoor wedding, stronger-smelling flowers will drift sweetly in the air; indoors the gentler scent of a magnolia blossom or lemon geranium will carry. Some flowers provoke allergies, not just in the groom, but in the best man or the officiant, so avoid them, as well as those with overpowering scents.

Boutonnieres don't have to be floral: Herbs, leaves, and berries used alone or in combination can add symbolic meaning. A boutonniere made of small sprigs of rosemary and thyme bunched with a lone viburnum blossom and pine needles sets the tone for an outdoor wedding and holds special significance. The rosemary stands for fidelity and remembrance; the thyme means courage; viburnum represents a sweet disposition; and the pine is for compassion.

A boutonniere should not be perched on the edge of a buttonhole, partially hidden behind the lapel, but shown off in front. Nor do the flowers have to be worn stem-down; an attractively wrapped stem and bow might look more interesting set at the top; and wearing a flower upside down is said to extend its freshness. Like a bride's bouquet, a boutonniere should be finished to prevent the stem from leaking on a suit; wrapping the stem is the usual precaution.

The pin used to secure a boutonniere to the lapel of a suit can be as decorative as the arrangement itself. A pearl-tipped pin can be used to hold the flower head in place, with the pearl emerging from the center of the blossom. The ordinary corsage pin is usually best hidden behind lapels. Antique stickpins can add a classic touch to modern boutonnieres, and they also make wonderful gifts for groomsmen. Stickpins, once used to hold ties and cravats in place, are still worn as lapel ornaments; they can be found in every design imaginable—golf clubs, animals, fish hooks, books—and should be chosen to reflect the interests of the men who will receive them.

Above all, a boutonniere should look fresh throughout the wedding, a big task for a little flower that is likely to be pressed into innumerable hugs and jostled on the dance floor. Choosing a flower that starts as a bud and opens as the reception progresses is one approach; avoiding those that droop quickly, like open tulips, is wise. And having a second boutonniere waiting in the refrigerator is a good idea, so photos taken at the end of the party don't feature a wilted gardenia.

Any finishing fillip—and the boutonniere is, perhaps, a small detail—may only be noticed by those most closely involved. But paying attention to even the smallest element adds to the satisfaction and confidence that comes from putting a personal stamp on every part of a wedding day. ✎

FOUR LAPEL TREATMENTS *all coordinate with elements of the grooms' attire. Opposite, clockwise from top left: A navy pinstriped suit dressed with a pale-purple tie is trimmed with a lisianthus bud, and a wrapped stem is enhanced with a purple satin bow. Chocolate cosmos petals add to the drama of a tuxedo jacket; the stem is wrapped in black to match the lapels. A tulip cradled in its leaf is elegant against a white dinner jacket; an insect pin topped with a glass bead holds the boutonniere in place. A blue delphinium is cool and crisp against a gray cutaway; the stem, wrapped in black ribbon and a grosgrain bow, disappears into the suit. The groom who wears less formal attire may want to wear a less structured, unusual boutonniere like those on pages 94 and 95.*

{ LISIANTHUS }

{ CHOCOLATE COSMOS }

{ DELPHINIUM }

{ TULIP }

A WHITE BOUTONNIERE *exists to complement every white bridal bouquet. Above, clockwise from top: A gardenia with a white wrapped stem and bow; a mini-spray garden rose with a polka-dot stem; a tuberose set against a eucalyptus leaf; a mimosa blossom wrapped with shell-pink grosgrain. Stems can also be wrapped to blend with dark lapels. Opposite, clockwise from top: A green-ribbon-wrapped rose and bud; a chaste sprig of snowberries; three tuberose blossoms and buds; two acorns and stephanotis; ranunculus bound in baby blue; lily of the valley on its own green leaf; one gardenia on its gleaming leaves.*

FLOWERS, BEADS, NUTS, *and leaves can make the groom's boutonniere as surprising as the bride's. Buy the freshest flowers you can find, and make the day of the wedding; refrigerate until needed. From left: Snip a single blue hyacinth floret from stem; insert a pearl-tipped pin through the center and out the bottom. To attach two white hyacinths to bay leaves, insert end of 10-inch-length of 24-gauge wire through 6-millimeter pearl bead; use round-nose pliers to turn wire into tiny loop (below left), keeping pearl from slipping off; insert wire through hyacinth floret; wrap wire "stem" in green floral tape (below right), and repeat with another floret; hold end of 5-inch length of wire against back of stem of California bay leaf, and with floral tape, bind together and cover wire; repeat with another leaf; use floral tape to join two flowers; add leaves as you wind down stems. To make a pearl-centered lavender hyacinth, join four florets using technique described above. To make acorn-and-oak-leaf boutonniere, use acorn with cap and stem, and a 2- to 3-inch oak leaf; glue cap in place with wood glue; wire acorn and leaf as described for leaves above using brown floral tape; glue 2-millimeter pearl to tip of acorn. The rose-leaf-and-pearl-flower boutonniere is made by threading five 2-millimeter pearl beads to center of 10-inch length of 28-gauge wire; twist wire so beads form a circle; bind double-wire stem with light-green floral tape; position flowers on rose leaf, curving leaf around stems; bind with dark-green floral tape, and tie ribbon at base.*

BEAUTIFUL BOUTONNIERES *can be made with traditional flowers presented in new ways, with unusual flowers that speak for themselves, or with no flowers at all. Among the most desirable flowers are (top left, clockwise from top left): tweedia blooms; a 'Sexy Rexy' antique garden rose; an African violet leaf with two blooms; a single pink hydrangea flower. Flowers and leaves can be plucked from the bride's bouquet, as we did here (top right, clockwise from top left): lily of the valley and a tiny fern; viburnum and 'Bluebird' rose; hypericum and golden oak leaves; a 'Black Magic' rose and astilbe. It doesn't have to be a flower to be a boutonniere (bottom right, clockwise from top): dusty miller; Berzilia; California live oak leaves with acorns; and a bud of mature ivy. Beauty goes beyond roses (bottom left, from top): Australian kangaroo paw; a lavender gladiola bloom; a blushing bride bloom; and a bunch of Eryngium (blue sea holly).*

Mr. and Mrs.
Siegel

Stephanie Thorne

Harold

Spring

FOR THE RECEPTION

April

Spring

Eleanor Townsend

Mr.
Sam

Of all the parties a couple gives, as long as they shall live, their wedding reception will be the most memorable. More than any other, this party must be gloriously decorated and flawlessly organized. But it will be the spontaneous moments— the stolen kiss, the poignant embrace, the tearful toast that cannot be planned— that will forever define the day.

 *This celebration* of one of life's happiest events is the occasion for the most delightful of parties; it will linger in the memory of every guest—the little flower girl up past her bedtime, the great-grandmother who has been part of four generations of family nuptials, and the friends who have traveled from afar. A bride and groom and their behind-the-scenes team will work for months so the wedding will run so smoothly that even missed cues won't throw off the pace of the party—or the couple's composure. The collaboration of family, friends, and professionals is as much a part of the wedding as the event itself.

STYLE AND BUDGET Most couples start with a feeling about the mood they want to achieve—formal or informal, urban or rural, indoors or out. These thoughts lay the groundwork for decisions about the site, its decoration, the size of the guest list, and what kind of drinks, food, and wedding cake to serve. The style of a wedding is as much a matter of taste as it is of budget. Simplicity has its own sort of glamour. But a full-blown formal wedding can have its informal moments, as Tricia Trask and Joseph O'Leary demonstrated when they conveyed their guests from the ceremony to the reception on New Orleans' famous streetcars, then paraded into the party behind a jazz band.

When working out a budget, estimates from professionals will help refine the plans. Don't give up on an idea that seems too costly before thinking about whether it can be scaled down or adjusted, and still create a similar effect. And remember to include the little details that can add up: favors, bridal-party gifts, tips, transportation, and valet parking.

THE SITE A successful reception can be held almost anywhere, from a castle, to a backyard, to the "back forty." Some couples know exactly where they want to be married; others get ideas from wedding planners and caterers, books and movies. Newport, Rhode Island's Rosecliff mansion can be rented for a formal dinner dance, or an empty barn can be decorated for a square dance. If a couple loves the country but lives in the city, they can usually get a permit to hold their reception at a botanical garden or a lovely dell in a park. Just be clear about the rules; some places impose a curfew, others don't permit the preparation of hot food, the lighting of candles, or the serving of liquor.

Destination weddings, with the reception the culmination of a weekend's festivities far from home, have become more common. They are usually smaller and more intimate because of the travel involved. Since much of the planning will be done long-distance, the reception is likely to be less formal. That leaves space for improvisations that add charm and flavor by taking advantage of local resources. Alison Frye and Douglas Foregger, who live in New England, were wed on the Caribbean island of St. Bart's. At the ceremony the bridesmaids were inspired by the lush tropical foliage to tuck oleander blossoms in their sandals. The groomsmen wore island flowers for their boutonnieres. Guests rolled into the reception in a convoy of mokes, the local open-air cars, danced to calypso music, and feasted on barbecue.

A site that pleases the bride and groom should be comfortable for their guests, too. A plantation house in Georgia might be so popular that it is only available on a midsummer Saturday when most people won't enjoy dancing as the thermometer climbs toward one hundred degrees. If the ceremony will be held in a church a half-hour's drive along winding country roads from the reception, it is thoughtful to provide maps for those who don't know the lay of the land. And sometimes getting to an out-of-the-way site becomes part of the experience. That's what Molly Sweeten and Spencer Boggess did: They were married on Maine's remote Squirrel Island, and transported friends and family to the island chapel and back to the mainland reception by boat.

DECORATIONS Even the most beautiful places for parties—indoors, outdoors, or in a tent—call for some decoration. How much can be difficult to gauge when you look at an empty space. If possible, preview the place where the reception will be held when it is set up for someone else's party, or see pictures of the room as it has been decorated in the past. Concentrate on lighting and the arrangement of tables and chairs. Lighting can make a tremendous difference in mood; it should be soft and flattering, but strong enough so guests can see each other and the food. Consider how the space will look during each phase, from the time guests arrive in the pristine room, through the time they circulate during the cocktail hour, on to dinner and dancing, until the band announces the last song.

FOOD AND DRINK The wedding feast has always been a way for couples and their families to share their good fortune, symbolized by special party food. The most flexible reception is a cocktail party featuring an assortment and quantity of hors d'oeuvres that can be as extensive as a buffet. Food and drinks can be passed, or stations can be placed around the room, along with small tables and chairs.

A seated dinner is usually more expensive and logistically complex, but at a large wedding, especially if many of the guests don't know each other, tables with place cards make everyone feel included. It's possible to combine an all–hors d'oeuvres meal with organized seating, which permits guest to circulate informally, but also gives them the chance to have dinner partners they might not otherwise have met. Greeting guests on the receiving line and the tradition that the bride and groom will see everyone during the reception—as Prince Edward and Sophie Rhys-Jones did—also helps to integrate the party.

Even a seated meal doesn't have to be formal; it can be as casual as the dinner Kimberly Stahlman and Michael Kearns held in a vineyard, with Dixieland music and tables set under the trees. And formal references can be mixed into a countrified atmosphere, the way a couple of pros, designer Josephine Sasso, who is known for her bridesmaid dresses, and Peter Callahan, a New York–based caterer, did at their wedding at Josephine's family's farm in Pennsylvania. While the rustic setting included a corncrib, the canvas dance floor was painted black and white to look like marble tiles.

The three elements of food and drink that most readily lend themselves to being personalized to reflect the style of a wedding are drinks, hors d'oeuvres, and the wedding cake. Some couples invent a special drink for the reception, or coordinate drinks to reflect the decoration or theme of the party. Hors d'oeuvres don't require the same kind of commitment to a particular style of food that a main course does: A couple can choose a dozen favorites, from inventive canapés to Caesar salad in bite-sized shells. The cake, the reception's equivalent of the bridal bouquet, is grand and glorious—and if it tastes as good as it looks, it vanishes quickly. MUSIC Sound draws guests into a party: The tinkle of glasses, the buzz of conversation, and the beat and melody of music can be irresistible. While music for the ceremony is usually traditional, the reception can feature dance tunes, background sound, or a showcase performance. Before hiring a band or deejay, listen to their tapes, and if possible, watch them perform. Ask for a guarantee that states particular musicians, like the piano player whose style made you choose the band in the first place, will be playing at the wedding. Once the band is booked, request a list of the songs in its usual repertoire, then check tapes and CDs to make a list of additional titles. Our guide to reception music on page 230 will get you started. Once all lists have been made and discussed, edit the deejay's or musicians' list, and ask for a final rundown of what they will play.

Music should not overwhelm or undermine conversation, especially while the meal is being served. To be sure guests are delighted, not assaulted or out of range, test the sound system in advance. No guest should be seated too close to a loudspeaker; and if the music is too loud for conversation, be quick to ask the band or deejay to lower the decibel level. The best bands and deejays also know how to set the pace and gracefully move the party from one stage to the next.
TEAMWORK Caterers, florists, and wedding planners all have a role in the organization of a reception. Friends do, too, and in many communities, pitching in is a tradition. At one elaborate wedding party, held in a tent attached to a big house in Florida, friends of the bride's mother brought their own silver bowls and lace tablecloths, and arranged the flowers on each table. Their participation was a gesture of friendship, not a matter of frugality; but sometimes it is necessary to be frugal. A bride who was to be married in a small ranching community in Wyoming invited the whole neighborhood, ranchers and townspeople, to her wedding. In turn, her neighbors volunteered to bring their special dishes; that bountiful wedding feast was based on a pioneer custom, the potluck supper.

A wedding reception is a mixture of the visual: pageantry and still-lifes; the romantic: intense conversations, whirls around the dance floor, quiet moments at the edges of the party; and the sensual: delicious food and drink, glorious fragrance, and wine. What pulls it all together is a combination of meticulous planning and the story behind the party: the reason every couple has invited close friends to eat, drink, and dance together, to celebrate the start of "something new."

A BUFFET TABLE *can be a focal point of the decoration. The table for this Tuscan feast is covered with a simple linen cloth, topped with a runner, then dressed with garlands of Russian olive branches and decorative bread bows. The branches are strung together with 28-gauge floral wire; the bread bows are attached with fishing line. The branches of an old maple tree shades the table from sunlight. As evening settles in, pillar candles in old and new canning jars, hung from the branches, cast a warm glow.*

DECORATIONS
for the Reception

*T*he most romantic and dramatic moment of a wedding—the heart-stopper and tear-starter—is, of course, the first glimpse of the bride walking down the aisle. But there is another moment of drama

that comes when guests arrive at the reception. The decoration of the space, and the tables that inhabit it, are like a theater production. But the scenery for this play must be designed on a large enough scale to be viewed from the back of the house, yet also intimate enough to be appreciated close up, at a table or on a buffet.

When considering the big picture, keep in mind that the space in which the party is held is likely to be decorative in itself, whether it is a tent with a scalloped overhang or a room with plaster moldings, high ceilings, and French doors. Wherever the reception will take place, the focal points for decoration are likely to be the buffet, bar, and

dining tables; doorways; walls; and, in a tent, the tent poles. Decoration is not just how a space is dressed; its effect depends on how it is arranged for appearance and traffic flow. The placement of tables and chairs, and the siting of the dance floor, if there is a choice, are integral parts of the decoration, too. The dance floor should be readily visible, as should the bride and groom's table, and wherever they cut the cake. Visit the site when it is empty, and sit and stand at various points before deciding how to arrange it.

The mood and theme of the party establish the style of the table settings. The first decision is about the most basic pieces, the tables and chairs. For a seated dinner, round tables are the most common choice, preferably seating no more than eight or ten, as guests can't talk across tables that are too wide. Tables can also be rectangles (each one usually seats about a dozen guests) or set up in banquet formations— long rows or a "U." The size and shape of the tables dictate how to handle covering them; find out if ready-made rental cloths will fit. If not, choose a fabric and have it hemmed to fit, then keep the cloths for future parties. Caterers and party-rental services now have quite a selection of fabrics, colors, and patterns for tablecloths and napkins; often a bride will rent a plain cloth for the underskirt, then order toppers or runners in a complementary pattern or color. Simple white or colored hemstitched linen or cotton napkins can also be ordered. Some rental companies will embroider them with the couple's initials, a lovely and useful keepsake for a couple to use again and again. A bride whose reception had a Western theme bought bright bandannas for napkins. Ten years later she still takes them out for summer buffets.

Party chairs can be attractive just the way they are; the most popular choices are ballroom and folding chairs, usually in gold-tone metal with velvet seats or white-painted wood. For smaller weddings, slipcovers can customize the chairs, and specially made cushions can soften the seats.

When thinking about table settings, imagine laying out a garden in which the overview and vignettes play against each other. Keep traffic flow and conversation in mind: Be sure to set tables far enough apart so guests and waiters can move around comfortably, but place chairs close enough together so dinner partners can talk easily, though not so close that elbows bump when neighbors try to cut their food. Design centerpieces that have a strong impact without overwhelming the tables, and make sure that the centerpieces are low enough to allow guests to talk over them. Flowers are the most popular choice, but other ideas include fruit, candles, herbs, candelabra, or sculptures.

For those who prefer flowers, there are many ways to treat them. Lavish arrangements, filled with exotic blooms, can be arranged by a floral designer. And centering the flowers is only one approach. They can be set at each place, or in a row across the table. One bride placed silver cups with red-and-orange tulips and red ranunculuses down the middle of a long table to echo the festive red Chinese lanterns overhead. Another created centerpieces of roses, hydrangea, and freesia in silver Revere-ware bowls, then set miniature versions in julep cups at each place. Plants are another alternative; they can be transplanted into silver or china bowls, or terra-cotta pots, left plain or spray-painted.

It may seem as though once the tables have been dressed and arranged, it's time to move on to the other big elements of wedding planning. But the details at a reception really count, separating your party from any other. A little surprise, whether a handmade place card or a sprig of rosemary tucked into a napkin, will seem as if it was specially designed for the guest who unfolds her napkin and catches a little whiff of an herbal scent, or slips her place card into her handbag to save because the card is so pretty.

Table numbers, menu cards, and place cards have a practical function as signposts, but they can also be handsome, whimsical, and even edible. It is acceptable to be traditional or completely original when designing them. At one wedding, each table number was beautifully calligraphed and placed in a silver picture frame. For another, the bride made heart-shaped doily place cards filled with sugared almonds.

As the song says, "the sentimental things apply"—but so do the aesthetics. Every wedding is a series of visual experiences, and while many of them feature the bride and groom, dining tables in particular are designed for the guests' comfort and pleasure. Most of all, when decorating the reception, a good host is sure that all the guests feel as though they are sitting at the most interesting table at the party. ❧

THE ELEMENTS OF DECORATION *include lighting, place settings, table settings, and seating details. Opposite, clockwise from top left: At Elizabeth Harrison's wedding to Keith Schwebel, the tent glows with lights layered behind organdy, with a chandelier at the apex of the tent. Set each guest's place as if he or she is the most special; here, a fragrant bouquet of roses is set at each place, the plate set with a simply folded napkin and a favor for the guest; sugared almonds are rolled up in embroidered handkerchiefs collected at tag sales and flea markets. Centerpieces don't always have to be flowers; here, country loaves are wrapped in parchment paper tied like a ribbon and stacked one on top of the other; unwrapped and broken into pieces for sharing, the bread can be dipped into bowls of olive oil and eaten. Simple tented table cards, arranged in alphabetical order, have calligraphed numbers inside to guide guests to their tables.*

{ LIGHTING }

{ PLACE SETTINGS }

Ginny Edwards

{ SEATING DETAILS }

{ TABLE SETTINGS }

Lighting

IT'S CERTAINLY A BONUS WHEN THE MOON IS FULL AND the stars are bright, but don't count on just natural light or even standard indoor lighting alone to brighten a reception. Lighting should be both practical and magical. When a party is held outdoors, paths must be marked; lights need to be placed at floor level so no one trips; tables, bars, and buffets must be illuminated so guests can see the food; and ambient and spot lighting of just the right tone and intensity must be adjusted so everybody will look their best. Lighting also subliminally influences the sound level. Bright lights encourage chatter and noise; soft lights and candlelight call for whispers and romance.

Some party lighting is purely decorative: a heart-shaped wreath outlined in fairy lights, for example, or "borrowed scenery" that doesn't illuminate, but does decorate. Summer Tompkins and Brooks Walker III were wed on an island in San Francisco Bay, where the lights of the Golden Gate Bridge acted as their backdrop. Not every wedding is so spectacularly sited, but sunsets and moonlight are free, and any reception can be scheduled for the most beautiful time of day.

To create a mood, think first of ambient lighting—the overall tone, color, and intensity established by overhead fixtures like chandeliers, fairy lights in a tent, or paper lanterns. How much light is shed is only part of it. The quality of light can be modified by changing the color of the bulbs: Pink tints are flattering indoors; yellows look better in a garden. Weddings held outdoors and in tents have special power needs, sometimes from a generator. But whether there are plenty of outlets or special accommodations need to be set up, talk to the site manager, tent rental company, or an electrician to be sure not to overload the circuits.

When a reception begins, natural light is often enough, and may even need to be filtered with curtains. As the light fades, artificial sources come into play. Some lights, like strings of vellum-shaded bulbs in a tent, blend romantically with the dusk, and are bright enough when darkness falls. Others should start low, then be adjusted as the sky dims, so there isn't a sudden jump from dark to dazzling. (Assign someone to lighting detail, and try it out before the party.) When it is time to switch on the overhead lights, light the candles on tables, including bars and buffets. And remember that as surely as one of the most important ingredients of a successful party is the injunction "Let there be light," the qualifier is "But not too much."

PAPER LANTERNS *are both pretty and economical and can be used indoors and out. The tent (opposite) comes alive in the fading afternoon light when strings of lights covered in shades made of vellum, pierced with two holes each and strung with wire, were lit at dusk. Strung from tree to tree, Japanese lanterns (above left) illuminate Kim Stahlman and Michael Kearns's vineyard reception. At Annette Roque and Matt Lauer's more formal tent party (above right), Chinese lanterns are clustered over tables covered with rich red silk; trays of pillar candles surround the centerpieces of orchids, dahlias, roses, sweet peas, and chocolate cosmos, which are mounded in antique silver bowls.*

CANDLES *can stand on their own, or in simple hurricanes or votives that shield them from the wind. This page, clockwise from top left: Cylindrical vases make protective hurricanes for pillar candles of different sizes set in sand and shells at the seaside wedding of Hayley Richmond and Stuart Boesky. Pillar candles of different heights are clustered in a bed of red berries on branches to decorate a mantel at Agnethe Glatved and Matthew Septimus's autumn reception. Candles in glass vases are held in place by a cluster of brown nuts; stones would serve the same purpose. At Annette Roque and Matt Lauer's wedding, cylindrical candles in frosted hurricanes are placed around the edge of the pool to reflect in the water. Candles (opposite) provide the only light during dinner at the reception of Allison Muench and J. Phillips Williams, casting a romantic glow and creating an ambiance of warmth as the sun goes down.*

FLOATING ON WATER *or on air,
candles are undeniably romantic. An afternoon
buffet (see page 100) moves gracefully toward
dusk, with dozens of candles in canning jars
suspended like fireflies; the hangers are made
by attaching four pieces of hanging wire to
another piece of wire, which is then twisted
around the rim. Large hurricane vases containing floating candles (opposite) are placed
like beacons on either side of a path strewn
with large pieces of confetti mixed with
rose petals in shades of pink and yellow.*

A TWILIGHT DINNER *at an outside reception (opposite) is served on the lawn under tall maple trees strung with romantic lanterns hanging randomly on chains from strong branches—small and large, these lamps hold ivory tapers, their bases disappearing in a layer of rose petals; votives in clear and frosted-glass containers adorn the tables. A candle-and-blossom-filled lantern before it is hung for the night (above left). The tables are set with simple white and ivory china and linen (above right); each setting is adorned with a glass compote filled with a floating candle, mixed rose petals, and phlox blossoms. Candlelight at each place setting creates glowing rings on every table.*

FRUIT AND FLOWERS *can be mixed to create an original tablescape. In this sculptural centerpiece (left and opposite), a rented silver compote is filled with Rainier cherries, peaches, golden raspberries, silk leaves, and stephanotis; a sage-green satin ribbon folded into a bow sits atop a yellow silk square, which was fringed by pulling the threads from around the edges. Cherries prop up the place cards (see page 133), and yellow napkins coordinate with the silk square.*

Table Settings

SETTING A TABLE USUALLY BEGINS WITH A CLOTH AND napkins, china, silver flatware, and glasses, but what holds it together aesthetically is the centerpiece, which doesn't have to be placed in the center at all. And while an artfully arranged, fresh bowl of flowers can be the focal point of a decorative tablescape, flowers are only one option. Arrangements can be made of almost any material; a compote can be filled with sugared fruits, a "garden" of fresh herbs can be planted in silver-painted pots, or a sheaf of grains sashed in silver ribbon can be set on a bed of raw rice in a silver tray. Candles, votives, and candelabra can also be integral parts of table settings, especially for after-dark receptions. Sometimes, candles need be the only table decoration. But what guest wouldn't appreciate sitting at a table decorated with both candles and flowers? At the waterside reception of Allison Muench and J. Phillips Williams (see page 109), small arrangements reflected in the glow of pillar candles.

When flowers are the central element of table decoration, it's natural to think of favorites first. Then think about how the flowers can enhance the mood of the party. A couple whose reception had a fiesta theme, with bold-colored tablecloths, used the brightest zinnias they could find for centerpieces. Types of flowers can be mixed, or the centerpiece can be made from just a single variety. Arrangements can be large and full, or a single dramatic stem can capture the spotlight. The ways of arranging flowers and the containers they are displayed in are enormously varied. An expensive profusion of blossoms can be formally organized in an heirloom silver container; a smaller, less costly bouquet can be enhanced by setting it under a glass bell jar. Flowers of the field can be left to sort themselves out, or arranged as minimally as greenhouse orchids. Containers can also serve more than one purpose, like the painted metal bucket that was decorated with a table number on its side, then filled with chrysanthemums.

Potted plants can be used inventively, too; the display down the center of a narrow table in a conservatory alternated mushroom baskets planted with grass and three-foot-tall delphiniums in painted terra-cotta pots. A fitting tablescape for a garden reception was made with roses in a large silver-painted pot, surrounded by smaller satellite pots, each planted with fragrant herbs. To be sure the centerpieces would have a life long after the party, guests were asked to take the herbs home, to keep memories of the wedding fresh.

CENTERPIECES *can include flowers, potted plants, and stalks of grain, but they must be designed so they don't impede conversation. Clockwise from top left: A dozen roses are tucked in a glass vase, the table number and arrangement elegantly covered with a glass cloche. Metal pails become planters for small trees with hydrangea petals scattered over the soil; to make the striped buckets, sand and prime, coat with water-based enamel, and let dry overnight; for stripes, tape pattern, paint exposed areas in contrasting color, and remove tape while paint is still wet. A classic spring arrangement of pink peonies, deep-purple lilacs, and ivory roses is loosely displayed in a glass vase; the table number is framed in silver, and votive candles shed light at the level of the plates. A bouquet of wheat, rye, and oat grasses become a handsome table decoration; the stems, cut flush at the bottom and tied with a silver ribbon, stand on a bed of brown rice.*

A FOOTED FISHBOWL *is a dramatic container for a few full rose blooms floating in clear water. The theme is echoed in votive holders filled with water and a single rose. The fish-bowls make lovely gifts for the wedding party; guests can take the votives home as favors.*

A LONG, NARROW TABLE *can accommodate guests and centerpieces, only if the decorations are long or tall. White mushroom baskets (opposite) are planted with grass and set in a row down the center of the table in this greenhouse; place cards are tucked into the baskets on either side to make the most of the tight space. Delphiniums in white pots are placed in between seats so that guests can talk across them. The pleated paper lanterns, like Elizabethan collars, are delightful during the day, and softly illuminate the party when dusk falls (this page).*

CANDLES AND FLOWERS *enhance each other to create intimacy. Clockwise from top left: Annette Roque and Matt Lauer chose orchids, dahlias, roses, sweet peas, and chocolate cosmos in silver bowls; trays held pillar candles. For Summer Tompkins's San Francisco wedding to Brooks Walker III, center-pieces of roses, grapes, hydrangeas, and persimmons were surrounded by tall candles and votives. Debbie Felderbaum and Glenn August were married at New York's Pierre Hotel, where Parisian florist Christian Tartu decorated the tables with flower-bedecked epergnes, with candles perched above the roses and hy-acinths. At Rosanne Cash and John Leventhal's reception, domes of roses, ranunculuses, and delphiniums were topped by candles with soft, gathered shades and tall pillars. The arrangement opposite is nearly transparent; candles in the candelabra illuminate roses, sweet peas, scabiosa, freesia, and lisianthus in bud vases.*

FRESH OR SUGARED, *mixed or all the same, fruit can make lovely a centerpiece, no matter the season. At Rebecca Thuss and Patrick Farrell's Christmas wedding reception, sugared lemons and eucalyptus leaves were casually arranged into generous white ceramic compotes (opposite and above left), each propped with a glass-beaded ornament. A paper-covered box, filled with pâte de fruits and bound with thin ribbon, awaited each guest. The table decorations were kept to an elegant minimum to allow the beauty of an ornately decorated Christmas tree and the majestic architectural details of the historic house—the high ceiling, French doors, double Palladian window, and brass sconces—speak for themselves. At the summer reception of Shannon McClean and Brian Andrew Townsend, a long, narrow banquet table (above right) set under a pitch-roofed white marquee was decorated with glass-footed compotes piled high with quinces, figs, and pears; the rose-filled silver julep cups, engraved on the bottom with the wedding date, were given to each guest.*

A GARDENSCAPE *in the middle of each table (this page) reflects the setting, a pretty walled garden (opposite). Silver spray-painted pots are filled with tarragon, oregano, mint, sage, and roses. The hill-and-dale height variation is achieved by using upside-down pots for stacking. A white paint pen transforms metal garden stakes into table numbers and place cards. After the meal, the centerpieces will be dismantled and the guests invited to take the herbs home as favors.*

SIMPLICITY *works best when every detail pulls its weight. Martha (left), a guest at Allison Muench and J. Phillips Williams's wedding, sits among friends at the dinner table where the only decorations were pillar candles of varying heights and a compact arrangement of anemones placed in front of each guest. A rimmed white soup bowl, glass charger, and white piqué tablecloth (opposite) provide the setting for bursts of yellow like a simply folded napkin and a lemon-marzipan favor; the centerpiece of fresh lemons and lemon leaves placed on the table is intertwined with a pale-yellow ribbon, lightly curled and trimmed at the ends.*

Seating Details

DECIDING WHO SITS WITH WHOM CAN BE A CHALLENGE, but felicitous seating is an important element of hospitality, giving families and friends a chance to mingle, and old friends who haven't seen each other for a while a welcome opportunity to catch up. Reception cards are both decorative and functional, beginning with table cards, which assign each guest to a table; then continuing with place cards and table numbers that help people find their seats; and ending with menu cards that describe the meal.

For a buffet or seated dinner, a host may assign guests to the tables, then allow them to choose their own seats—and seating companions. This tactic is more successful if the guests are likely to know one another. Many couples, however, choose to use place cards as a way to help guests meet each other, even when the food service is informal. Either way, a table is usually set up outside the dining area to display the table cards, often placed in envelopes with the guest's name written on the outside. A seating chart may be placed near the entrance to the room where the meal will be served, too, so guests can easily find their way around.

Seating details can carry through a color scheme or a theme, like maple leaves glued to table cards at an autumn wedding, which make an attractive display when guests arrive. Place markers don't have to be the traditional tented cards; they can lie flat or can be written on more flexible paper to be wrapped around a napkin or the outside of a menu scroll. Usually, place cards are printed with the couple's initials or names or a tiny symbol, and the guest's name is written in calligraphy.

Often a favor, incorporated into the place setting, is set at each seat: an attractively presented bag of seeds or bulbs, a clutch of candies, or a beautifully wrapped piece of soap. Each place at the seated dinner for the reception of singer Rosanne Cash and John Leventhal was set with a guitar pick with "Rosanne & John" written on it and a chocolate guitar made by the bride's mother. A decorated cookie in the shape of a watering can awaited each guest at the summer reception of Amy Dedrick and David Roseman.

Guests don't always know whether they're meant to dismantle the beautiful tablescapes or not, so a sign saying "Enjoy" or "Please pick a bouquet" near the centerpiece will make it clear that you want them to take home a memento from the party.

David and Amy
June 21, 1997

Bruschetta with Red Pepper and Basil
Sauteed Jumbo Lump Maryland Crab Cakes
Roasted Medallions of Lamb

Spring Field Salad with Tomatoes
Nasturtiums, and Chevre

Dauphine Potato and Garlic Custard

Roast Atlantic Salmon Fillet with
Kalamata Olive, Basil, Lemon Butter

Spring Asparagus Bundles

Wedding Cake
Iced ... Mint

Rose Martin

Eleven

RECEPTION CARDS *make the day go smoothly. A simple ecru reception-card set (opposite) is tied together by a delicate fritillaria motif and formal Venetian script; the table card, which is slipped into a pale-blue, tissue-lined envelope, is sealed with an adhesive fritillaria sticker. The folded (or "tented") place card indicates only the name of the guest, and the menu highlights the calligrapher's fluid writing. A matched set may not be easy to find, but putting one together is easy if all of the pieces share a common theme. Clockwise from top left: A letterpress set, with a pale-green-flower emblem, is elegantly understated. Blue ink on a stiff white card is soft and elegant; the cards all have round, gilded edges. Handmade table cards stamped with the table number are placed in handwritten vellum envelopes. An oak-leaf hole punch embellishes place and menu cards; glue punched-out leaves to cards of a contrasting color.*

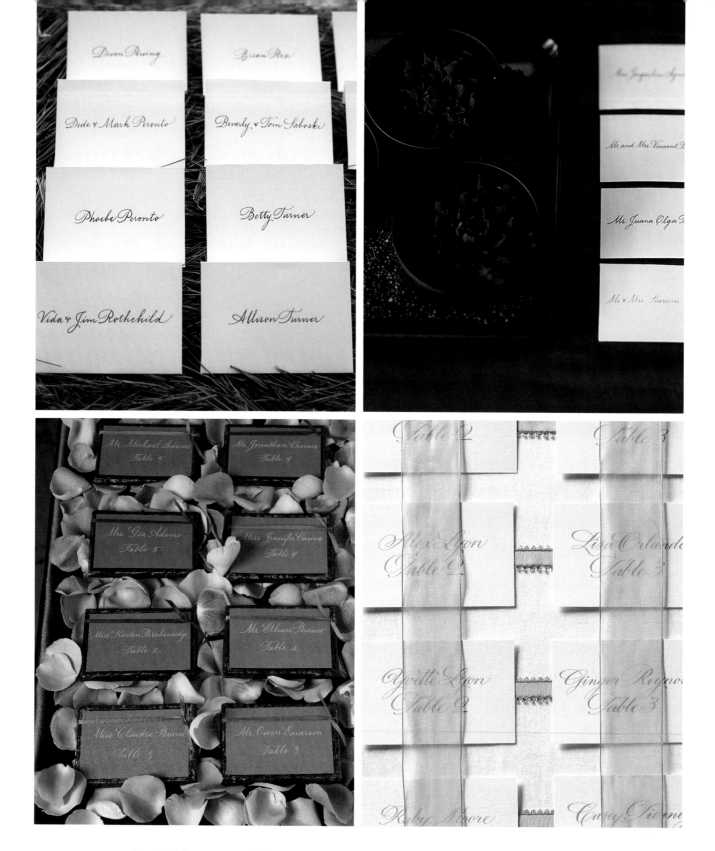

TABLE CARDS *can be original, fragrant, even edible. Clockwise from top left: At a Christmas wedding, table cards in envelopes are propped on a bed of pine needles on the table where guests find their seating assignments. When trimming a table that displays table cards, choose decorations that are low and stable so they won't tip; here, dahlias float in black glass bowls set on a black ceramic tray in a bed of gravel. At an outdoor wedding these table cards, set over a decorative grid of ribbons, are held in place with organza so they won't be blown away. Wrapped chocolates with each guest's name written on a chocolate-colored card are placed on a bed of rose petals. Dried autumn leaves (opposite) are arranged over a plain white cloth, then held in place by sheer organza; the autumnal theme is carried through with oak leaves glued to table cards. To dry leaves, place in a telephone book between paper towels for a week; change towels every few days.*

SETTING A BEAUTIFUL PLACE *for guests can be as simple as folding a napkin in a special way, using typography, or creating a favor to establish a theme. Top row, from left to right: At the garden reception of Josephine Sasso and Peter Callahan, each place was set with white cotton piqué napkins custom-edged with chartreuse China-silk piping, gathered loosely and tied in a matching silk ribbon. Silk flowers on wire stems are loosely tied around cone-folded napkins; at each table there is a different flower at each place, all of them echoing the flowers in the centerpiece. On a minimalist table, a pair of chopsticks, tied with silver thread and resting on a silver dragée almond, are offered for an Asian-inspired first course; they can be given to guests as favors. Cut sweet peas are kept fresh in tiny florist's vials of water, then tucked into a napkin; to replicate the fold, lay the napkin on a flat surface, and fold in half widthwise so the folded edge is near you; fold the top layer back down halfway, and turn the napkin over and fold the edges into the center, then fold the napkin in half. Center row, from left to right: The beautiful calligraphy on the menus at the dinner reception of Annette Roque and Matt Lauer is set off in a folded hem-stitched linen napkin decorated with pepperberries; the crimson berries and the colored seal on the menu card tie the place setting together. A napkin wrap can be pretty and practical; the band securing this napkin serves as a place card, and the sprig of rosemary tucked into the ring is fresh, fragrant, and a symbol of fidelity. The cherry*

couplet, which complements a fruit centerpiece, is an edible device for holding a place card. White-painted mushroom baskets planted with grass are arranged down the center of a narrow table; folded place cards are tucked along the rim to save space. Bottom row, from left to right: Some seating details can fulfill several jobs. A moss-mounded miniature terra-cotta pot is pierced with a twig on which a place card flies like a banner; the potted moss is a favor for the guest. A children's table is set with toys to keep young guests entertained; each child is greeted with little wooden brides and grooms used to prop up place cards with lettering early readers can make out—a generous selection of crayons is placed at each child's fingertips for instant entertainment; the craft-paper tablecloth awaits decoration. Two heart-shaped paper doilies are stitched together, filled with candy, and tied with ribbon; with a name written on the center, they combine favors and place cards. A little bag of nuts tied in a café au lait ribbon does double duty as a favor and a holder for the place card.

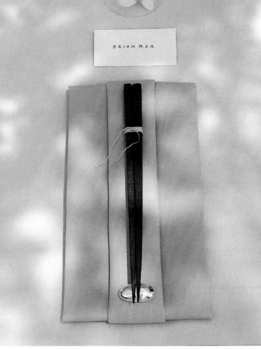

BRIAN REA

Montgomery

Mr. Winthrop Pike

MAGGIE

Sara

Kathryn

Amy Hunter

ROLLED, FOLDED, KNOTTED, OR GATHERED, *napkins finish a table setting. On a pale-blue-and-white luncheon table (above left), blue sugared almonds, a hydrangea centerpiece, a menu card calligraphed in blue, and crisscrossing ribbons that peek through an organza overlay carry out the theme; the finishing touch is the rolled blue linen napkins, each tied with a blue gingham ribbon attached to a small truffle box. On a formal table (above right) in colors of silver, pink, and white, a casually knotted damask napkin softens the style. The peony centerpieces in silver Revere bowls are echoed by miniature bowls, each holding a single bloom; silver-rimmed place cards and plates, set on silver chargers, unify the theme; the napkin's knot serves as the place-card holder. Color can dramatically change the look of a place setting; two different china patterns were used for the setting above and on the opposite page; the color of the centerpieces, napkins, and tablecloths reflects each host's style.*

YELLOW CAN BE QUIET AND INNOCENT, *or hot and bright. A yellow cloth (above left) coordinates with a daisy theme that was executed throughout Page Marchese and Adrian Norman's wedding, from wreaths to bouquets to favors; the simplicity of the table setting is carried out with plain-white china, a table number wrapped around a tall cylindrical candle, and the luxurious pure-white hemstitched linen napkins. Yellow when paired with pink gives an energetic tropical look (above right). Pink and yellow roses are arranged with freesia and pink hydrangeas in a silver Revere bowl; a small cluster placed in a silver mint-julep cup at each place setting mirrors the centerpiece. The apricot place cards are made of printed yellow vellum, which is tied to bright-pink card stock with two colors of satin ribbon and then attached to the napkins. Vellum can go through a home printer, and sheets printed with several names can be cut into individual place cards.*

MODERN FLUTES *of Champagne and
fresh, uncomplicated seasonal flavors set the
tone at the fall wedding reception of Agnethe
Glatved and Matthew Septimus. Hors
d'oeuvres included chicken quesadillas and
lahvosh-bread pinwheels with grilled eggplant,
roasted red pepper, basil, and hummus.*

COCKTAIL HOUR

for the Reception

*C*ouples meet, court, and celebrate over food and drink, combining romance with the sensuous pleasures of eating—surely one reason that weddings in nearly all cultures are commemorated with feasts.

Most wedding receptions in our culture include a lively opening phase when guests talk and circulate: the cocktail hour. Of the many stages in the sequence of the party, this is one not to skip. Pretty cocktails and beautifully presented hors d'oeuvres set the stage for the party. And guests are peckish after the ceremony. Hors d'oeuvres will help assuage their hunger and act as a buffer to the cocktails. In this chapter, we have concentrated on cocktail-hour offerings because they are such fertile fields for originality and creativity, both in what can be served and how it can be presented. The choice and presentation of hors d'oeuvres and drinks can easily enhance the theme of the reception, through color,

the style of food, the types of platters and plates used to serve it, and the way the serving pieces are decorated.

Drinks may include Champagne and a full bar, but can also feature a special cocktail created for the wedding or one that is specific to the region where the wedding is held or even a traditional family recipe. As for hors d'oeuvres, even if they are followed by a formal seated meal, they lend themselves to the most personal and inventive variations. Wedding food should be suited to the time of day, the season, and regional dining customs, and it should be connected to the bride and groom. The cocktail hour might feature favorite hors d'oeuvres from places where they have traveled together, ethnic specialties that reflect their family histories, or might simply be a sampler of the foods they love most.

Unless the party will be small or the hosts are professional party-givers or chefs, a caterer or the staff at the reception location will most likely develop the menu. When interviewing caterers, ask to see examples of proposed menus and photographs of their work, and ask for references from other clients. These menus will indicate a price range and specialties, but most caterers are willing to try new recipes and presentations, especially when they will be preparing an assortment of hors d'oeuvres. Some caterers offer a tasting that allows clients to sample the dishes on the menu.

The caterer should provide a staff to accommodate the service needs for the cocktail hour. When guests arrive, waiters often greet them with Champagne, soft drinks, or a special drink requested by the host. As the party progresses, waiters continue to pass an assortment of drinks, take orders, and clear away empty glasses; guests can also place their own orders at the bar. To be sure everyone has been offered enough food and no one is standing around with an empty glass, it is best to provide waiters to pass trays of hors d'oeuvres, set out the food on buffet tables, replenish the food, and keep the platters and trays looking attractive.

A good hors d'oeuvres menu features a balanced variety of foods. Do not serve a selection of all meat and bread, or of all vegetable dishes and tea sandwiches. Always include food for vegetarians, for those with shellfish allergies, and for anyone on a low-cholesterol or low-fat diet. Complement strong flavors with mild; caviar is assertive, for example, and should be served with something gentler, like salmon or crab. In the same way, it's important to offset spicy food with something refreshing, such as cherry tomatoes filled with herbed goat cheese. Choose hors d'oeuvres of varying temperatures, from hot to room temperature to cold. Some couples choose a single theme or cuisine, like Asian or Mexican, while others mix different food styles and types. An advantage of hors d'oeuvres is that guests can choose whatever they like. At most, an hors d'oeuvre is one or two flavor-packed bites, easily dispatched with no mess or fuss. Generally, if hors d'oeuvres precede a substantial meal, offer five to six different hors d'oeuvres, each yielding one or two per person. Most guests are happy to eat a few rich, decadent hors d'oeuvres, particularly if they are also offered crisp fresh vegetables at a crudité station and the pure, clean flavors of raw oysters or boiled shrimp.

Whatever style of food is offered, it must be delicious and plentiful, and presented so it is easy to eat and looks appealing. Except at the most formal reception, it is best to have both passed hors d'oeuvres and food stations. Passed hors d'oeuvres are ideal, since guests may keep conversing and enjoy their food without moving. This requires extra hands in order to keep the food flowing from the kitchen onto the trays and out to the guests. Arranging a few food stations around the reception space assures that every guest's appetite is whetted before dinner. Plan to have enough food stations or buffet tables to avoid long lines, and keep space issues in mind, so that food is placed where guests can easily see and get to it. If hors d'oeuvres can't be eaten neatly in a couple of bites, provide small plates, and perhaps even a fork. In any case, be sure there are plenty of pretty napkins. Guests need a comfortable place to eat, too, so arrange small tables and chairs where people can sit and still be in the midst of the party.

When the reception is over, many couples realize that the wedding cake is the only food they have tasted; they were so busy greeting guests, talking, and dancing that they forgot to eat. To ensure a satisfying end to a wedding day, ask the caterer to pack a sampling of hors d'oeuvres for the bride and groom to enjoy once the guests have left, or to take home to savor over a romantic replay of their cocktail hour. ∽

A LIVELY COCKTAIL HOUR, *however formal or casual, requires delicious food, special drinks, and space for guests and waiters to circulate. Opposite, clockwise from top left: Guests were served lemonade sprigged with mint at the seaside wedding of Amy Dedrick and David Roseman. Vermont's Green Mountains were the backdrop for the cocktail hour at Kristen Archer and Glen Tatham's reception. A traditional display blurs the boundaries between hors d'oeuvres and a light buffet: Inspired by the garden, San Francisco caterer Paula LeDuc made salmon roses and leaf-shaped scones, gingered prawns with minted papaya salsa, and rare beef on herb bread; pedestals display blueberry pinwheels, calla-lily cookies, asparagus with a basil-tarragon sauce; a cake stand holds meringue mushrooms and shortbread violet nosegays. Kim Stahlman and Michael Kearns, surrounded by a California vineyard, enjoy a cocktail and a quiet moment together.*

{ DRINKS }

{ HORS D'OEUVRES }

MARTHA *was among the three hundred guests who gathered on the terrace outside the tent to raise a glass of wine to friends Susie Tompkins and Mark Buell at their San Francisco wedding (left). There's no need to sacrifice creativity when offering guests the variety of a fully stocked bar (opposite). Two tables are covered with white cloths and laid out facing each other horizontally, with a space between them for the bartenders. Extra bottles and glasses are hidden below. The back table, covered with a pale-green runner, adds depth and a resting place for bottles, carafes of juice, shakers, and garnishes. Garlands made of daisies, sedum, astilbe, mums, and stock hang from the front table to separate the glasses and create distinct serving lines.*

Drinks

GLASSES AND GOBLETS, BOTTLES AND SHAKERS, LITTLE bowls filled with lemons and limes—all the tools for toasting, drinking, and celebrating—can be found in one convenient spot: the wedding bar. The bar should be planned with as much attention to detail as the menu, with carefully chosen ingredients, measured, blended, and garnished just right, then displayed in a beautiful setting.

For any wedding, a traditional, fully stocked bar is always a generous option. If, however, the expense exceeds the budget, serving one well-chosen drink, or a small group of them, can be an equally expressive way to toast the day. A wine and Champagne bar, for instance, can cost significantly less than a bar with mixed drinks. A punch bar can capture the quaint hospitality of an at-home wedding and will be the least straining on a budget. A favorite wine or spirit can also become the theme of a party. A wine lover might serve a tasting of precious wines. A couple married in Denver, who were partial to fine beers, served a selection from Colorado microbrewers. Regional preferences can also distinguish the selection: mint juleps in the South, Long Island iced teas on the East Coast, or sazeracs in New Orleans. Climate enters the picture, too. At an outdoor summer wedding, drinks should be refreshing: fruit daiquiris, perhaps. Another possibility is to serve cocktails that echo the color scheme of the wedding. The garnish, too, can tie in with the decorations. See the Recipes section for selected drink recipes.

Every one of these ideas opens up a world of decorative possibilities. Create an inviting space, utilizing any natural backdrop your setting provides, such as two trees for festive posts at either end of a table. Next, dress the bar itself: Place simple votives and flowers on the table, or suspend elaborate fabric panels from above. Carry over colors and themes of the table settings. The key is to keep it simple, enabling bartenders to attend to everyone with ease and efficiency.

Drink service follows a simple formula: For a full bar, one bartender can serve thirty to fifty guests. If the bar features a specialty drink, a waiter can take care of as many as one hundred. A caterer can advise as to what glasses are needed; but as a rule, it is not necessary to have more than one all-purpose glass for wine; Champagne requires flutes.

Whatever drinks are served, they should be of the finest quality. When guests toast the bride and groom, with freshly squeezed papaya juice or Champagne, they should hoist a glass of the best.

A WELL-DRESSED BAR TABLE *can help to prime your reception. Two organdy panels, suspended from bamboo bars, create a dreamy backdrop for a wine and Champagne bar (above left); inexpensive planters filled with ice keep the Champagne and white wine cold, and keepsake carafes, engraved with the couple's initials, are placed on either side of a tall, flowering orchid, which divides the U-shaped bar into two serving lines. Oranges and lemons (above right) are loosely arranged around the rim of a white-clothed table, the ring filled in with kumquats and their leaves; pitchers of white-wine sangria are set out for guests to serve themselves. Inexpensive glass-storage jars (opposite) are paired with heirloom ladles and rows of cups at a punch bar; chosen for their complementary tastes and palettes, the punches (from left: pineapple-apricot, cantaloupe, honeydew, and strawberry Champagne) are garnished with fruit slices or frozen juice ice cubes; the couple's initials, made of individual stock blossoms, are pinned to runners draped over a white linen tablecloth.*

THERE IS A DRINK *to match every season and level of formality of a wedding. Top row, from left to right: Our version of a Bloody Mary is perfect for a wedding brunch; called an Afternoon Delight, it is a mix of tequila with tomato, orange, and lime juices, and gets its spice from cumin and Tabasco; float a cucumber wedge and chile pepper in the glass for a garnish. Generous glasses of Champagne were served at Kimberly Stahlman and Michael Kearns's wedding reception. An afternoon wedding is the perfect time to serve Orange Blossom Nectar, a blend of orange juice with bourbon and papaya; it is served in glasses rimmed with sugar and orange zest, with tiny buds and leaves for garnish. Stems of snapdragons are dramatic stirrers for rose-pink cocktails; with a length of monofilament (clear fishing line), attach a flower's stem to a glass stirrer: Wrap line around bottom of stem and bottom of stirrer, wrap line up to top of stirrer, then back down to bottom; tie off, and trim. For the cocktail, mix one and a half ounces of vodka, four ounces of grapefruit juice, and one ounce of cranberry juice; serve over ice. Center row, from left to right: A bottle of icy vodka can decorate the bar if it's encased in a frozen layer of colorful flowers and fruit; to make one, place bottle into a fully opened half-gallon cardboard milk carton; insert flowers or thinly sliced fruit (we've used nasturtiums, lemons, and limes) around the bottle, filling one-third of the carton; pour water into the container, just covering the fruit and flowers; place upright in the freezer; when completely frozen, add another layer of fruit and very cold water, and freeze; repeat, filling a third at a time—so that fruit and flowers do not float to the top—until the water reaches bottle neck; remove from the freezer just before serving; cut away milk*

carton with a utility knife, and wrap a dinner napkin around the base; serve with slices of lemon zest tied in knots. The Rasmopolitan, a twist on the popular Metropolitan, combines flavored vodkas with lime and cranberry juice; serve it straight up, garnished with red raspberries. A good punch can be the only drink served; made from Champagne, rum, dry sherry, and peach schnapps, this one is garnished with slices of fresh, ripe peach and will please both wine and spirits drinkers; the silver serving tray is garnished with a single peach blossom. During the cocktail hour at the reception of Rebecca Thuss and Patrick Farrell, guests were offered cranberry martinis with sugared rims and swizzle sticks made from the fresh berries. Bottom row, from left to right: Pimm's Cups are garnished with strawberries, lemons, limes, and cucumbers. The Mint Vodka Gimlet asks for nothing but a summer afternoon; a variation on the classic gimlet, it is a mix of vodka, lime juice, and fresh mint with sugar syrup. Fruity Caribbean Love Punch uses dark and spiced rums, fresh pineapple, freshly squeezed orange and lemon juices, and various aromatic island spices; serve it in a punch bowl garnished with star fruit and slices of lime. Don't forget color: Darker drinks feel more fitting during the fall and winter; evening is the ideal time for the Bicycle Built for Two, a mix of brandy, port, and orange juice; sanding sugar colored with food coloring coats the rim of the glass.

A WEDDING CAKE OF SEAFOOD *(opposite) is an appropriate start to the reception. These simple yet striking ice sculptures will easily survive the cocktail hour of an outdoor party in any climate. Three tiers of chilled shrimp serve as the centerpiece of the table, its linen cloth pressed into squares. Ice pillars on either side hold caviar, which will be at the perfect serving temperature. Lucite trays catch drips from pillars. Square votive candles complete the theme; they fill in the rest of the tabletop and create a magical glow at dusk. Spicy cheese twists (left), a miniature Caesar salad in an edible bowl, and a hominy square are served on a six-inch plate.*

Hors d'oeuvres

HORS D'OEUVRES, "OUTSIDE THE WORK" IN FRENCH, refers to the food that precedes the "opus" of the main course. But in fact, a bountiful selection of hors d'oeuvres, attractively and imaginatively presented, can be a full meal. Even if more food will be served later, hors d'oeuvres are an intrinsic part of the cocktail hour, satisfying the cravings for something delicious to eat after the ceremony.

When deciding what to serve, remember that preparing hors d'oeuvres can require a lot of space; consider whether there is adequate preparation room—stove burners and ovens, refrigerator shelves, and countertops. This is important for a home wedding and also when using a space that has limited (or no) kitchen facilities, like an historic house or a tent. If the space is too small, it is best to focus the menu on room-temperature foods and items that can be prepared in advance.

The size of the guest list is also an important factor. At a party for more than two hundred, it is easier to control the quality of the food if at least some of the hors d'oeuvres don't require complicated preparation: poached salmon, served on plates, for example, is simple to make and present. It is also a good idea to combine more exotic offering with traditional foods like salmon, so less adventuresome eaters are

well provided for. See the Recipes section for selected hors d'oeuvres.

How much to serve depends on the time of day: Guests at an evening reception are likely to eat more than they would at lunch time. A good rule of thumb for a cocktail hour before a meal is to provide five or six selections, and estimate one or two of each per person. When hors d'oeuvres are the main course, eight to ten choices are reasonable, and assume that guests will eat two or three of each.

For presentation, classic serving pieces can be decorated in new ways, perhaps by creating a bed of fresh coconut shreds or rose petals. Hors d'oeuvres can also be served on unusual platters that reflect the mood of the party. At a garden reception, tea sandwiches can be laid out on a soil sifter lined with parchment paper; warm herb muffins can be served in baskets with vine-trimmed handles.

When creating buffet tables, concentrate the decoration on the front; swag garlands across the skirt of a tablecloth, or edge the tables with flowers, leaving plenty of room for food. An evening buffet should be illuminated with candles or subtle overhead lighting so that guests can see what is being served. And, if the assortment includes exotic selections, place cards identifying them next to each platter.

HORS D'OEUVRES *should be as decorative as they are delicious. The classic English tea sandwich (opposite) is reinvented with ingredients from the sushi bar. Smoked salmon, poached chicken, cucumbers, dill, watercress, and cream cheese are mixed with the unexpected: wasabi, shiso leaf, salmon roe, black caviar, and sesame seeds. Above, clockwise from top left: Pale-pink quail eggs are arranged with fresh bay leaves to create a trailing vine. The power of pattern is displayed in an arrangement of asparagus tartlets: creamy goat cheese, asparagus, and lemon zest are baked in an open pastry tart, then cut into bite-size pieces. Miniature Caesar salads in crispy cups are nestled in shaved Parmesan; croutons and cheese crisps add crunch. The geometry of a tray is heightened with the linear arrange- ment of cubes of hominy; roasted red-pepper, yellow-pepper, and portobello-mushroom toppings give variety; fresh tarragon and capers hug the side of the tray.*

AN ATTRACTIVE PRESENTATION *can be as simple as a single silver tray or a selection of white ceramic platters. Clockwise from top left: Monica Mahoney and Paul Adler included a tapas station at their reception: prosciutto with fruit; grilled-vegetable antipasto; smoked salmon and fennel salad; prawns and asparagus; and goat cheese with toasts and tomato. Smoked salmon-and-caper petits fours are garnished with fresh herbs and edible flowers. Savory napoleons are made from layers of flatbread filled with salmon, hummus, and olives; they're topped with golden caviar and salmon roe. Heart-shaped finger foods—filled with melted cheese and topped with a mango salsa—make a delicious snack. At an afternoon tea reception (opposite), hors d'oeuvres and cake are served together; savories include endive filled with seafood salad, deviled eggs with caviar, and cucumber and dill-butter canapés; the fondant-covered cake is decorated with marzipan lilacs.*

CAKES
for the Reception

The symbolism of the wedding cake dates back to the ancient Romans, who broke a thin loaf of bread made of wheat, representing fertility, over the bride's head. Guests picked up the crumbs and

kept them for good luck. The modern custom of packaging pieces of cake for guests to take home was inspired by this rite; it is said if a woman sleeps with a single slice under her pillow, she'll dream of the man she'll marry.

Over the centuries, the cake has evolved in other ways: Towering tiers, for example, which distinguish wedding cakes from all others, actually date from the late Middle Ages, when the bride and groom stood over a cluster of little cakes and kissed. And the cake continues to change with the times. It used to be that the bride and the cake could be clad only in white. These days, though, when a bride may consider anything from oyster gray to shell pink for her gown, her

choice of cake may veer from the traditional as well. Whatever the design, the wedding cake should be awe-inspiring, though the trick is to be sure it tastes fabulous, too.

The elements of a wedding cake are the cake itself, the filling, the icing and the decorations. Rather than considering only the style (the look) or the substance (the way the cake tastes) think of the two together. The design and flavor should reflect the style of the wedding as much as a couple's taste. If froufrou doesn't appeal, a cake with clean, architectural lines and graphic details may be the perfect choice. If excess is best, this is the day to go for something dramatic.

The cake can be nearly any flavor, not just yellow or white

but chocolate, spice, lemon, carrot, chestnut, or hazelnut, among others; and can be filled with jam, lemon curd, whipped cream and strawberries, or passionfruit purée to name a few. Most cakes are iced with either buttercream; fondant, a paste of sugar, water, and corn syrup kneaded like dough until it takes on a satiny texture; or marzipan, a mixture of almond paste and sugar. The icing is partly a matter of preference, but also a matter of practicality, especially as it relates to climate and season. The soft simplicity and edibility of buttercream is never more appealing than on a wedding cake, but if a wedding is outdoors in July, the cake must be refrigerated up to two hours before serving. Fondant and marzipan are ideal for keeping cakes fresh when they are too large to refrigerate. Fondant holds up especially well, and even helps to preserve a cake.

When the flavor, fillings, and icing have been chosen, the focus should turn to the fanciful: what the cake will look like. Both the decorations and the structure of the cake will help determine its personality, as will the style of the wedding and the time the reception is held. Is it a daytime or evening event? Formal or casual? A formal dinner is a natural environment for an elaborately iced, multitiered confection like the couture-inspired cakes in this chapter. A simple tiered coconut cake with swirls of old-fashioned seven-minute icing would be just right for a low-key country reception.

Decorations can be made of marzipan; royal icing, which dries very hard and is the best material for delicate, long-lasting decorations; or gum paste, which is thick and malleable and ideal for the most realistic edible reproductions of fruit and flowers. Meringue can be used for beautiful, airy decorations, and complements almost any flavor cake. A cake can be embellished with sugared or plain fresh fruit, flowers, and nuts, too. If using flowers, think about color and texture rather than deciding on specific flowers. Remember, too, that expanding the field from the small number of edible flowers to the entire range of nontoxic blooms (the caterer, cake design-

er, or florist can advise) provides much more opportunity for expression. If there is any doubt about whether the flowers are edible, arrange them so they don't touch the cake.

The internal structure of a cake also influences its appearance. With each layer, more support is needed: dowels that prevent the upper layers from crushing the lower ones, foam board under each layer, and a base, which can be found at a baking-supply store. One role of decoration is to hide the inner workings; real or gum-paste flowers can mask dowels, while piped icing, moss, or nuts and fruit conceal the rim of a base.

The hotel where the reception is being held or the caterer will usually be responsible for making the cake. Some couples, however, choose to have their cake created by a specialty cake designer. In some cases, making the wedding cake may truly be a labor of love: Some couples are lucky enough to have an ambitious novice baker take the project on (see "Wedding Cakes 101," page 233) as his or her gift to the couple.

Don't forget to include the price of the wedding cake when establishing a budget. The cost is calculated per number of servings. And, of course, the more elaborate the cake, the more expensive it will be. Prices range from a couple of dollars per slice for a simple cake to as much as $15 per slice for an exquisite cake from a designer. To reduce costs, order a smaller cake to display, then feed the majority of guests from sheet cakes, which will be sliced discreetly in the kitchen.

The tradition of the bride and groom cutting the cake originated because the early multitiered cakes were so heavily iced that a bride alone could not cut a slice. Today the cake-cutting symbolizes a couple's commitment to nurture each other. While the cake is meant to be eaten immediately, the top tier is often removed, then frozen. This custom dates from the early nineteenth century, when the saved portion was eaten to celebrate the christening of the couple's first child. Now many couples keep it for their first wedding anniversary—as a reminder of the sweet finale to the most romantic day. ∽

THE CAKE DEFINES THE STYLE *of a wedding almost as much as a bride's dress, whether from haute couture or casual chic. On page 152, a daisy cake is displayed under netting. Opposite, top row from left: A dress encrusted with fabric flowers was the model for these gum-paste dogwood blossoms. Sugared pears, crab apples, and candied chestnuts grace a chocolate chestnut cake. Food editor Susan Spungen tucks hydrangeas between the tiers of a buttercream cake. Center, from left: A summer's berry harvest fills the tiers of a basket-weave cake. A grape-arbor cake is adorned with white-chocolate grapes and gum-paste leaves. Crewelwork used by dressmakers inspired this cake of fondant and white chocolate. Bottom, from left: "Crottin" cakes in the shape of goat cheese are stacked to mimic a tiered cake. Rebecca Thuss and Patrick Farrell cut their chocolate wedding cake. A classic wedding cake is circled with wild rose hips and dahlias in bold colors.*

{ FORMAL }

{ FRESH FRUIT }

{ LESS FORMAL }

{ SUGARED FRUIT }

{ FONDANT }

{ GUM-PASTE FLOWERS }

{ FRESH FLOWERS }

Citrus Basket Cake
for 100

FLOWER GIRL *Katherine Hadinger ponders a three-tiered cake for one hundred (opposite). A slice (left) reveals an orange-chiffon cake layered with three different citrus curds, served in blood-orange sauce with candied orange peel adorning the plate—a combination dreamed up by Stacie Pierce, pastry chef at Union Square Café in New York City. The decorative elements of the cake include sugared fresh kumquats and their leaves, and realistic gum-paste orange blossoms in various blooms. Constructed with hexagonal tiers, the cake is supported by a central pedestal, then covered with "wicker-work" piping in buttercream, created like a basket-weave pattern but with a plain Ateco #7 tip.*

Formal Cakes

A WEDDING CAKE COMPLEMENTS THE RECEPTION MUCH the way a bride's bouquet is designed to enhance her dress. A formal dinner dance is best suited to a formal cake, but what does "formal" mean? It's not too different from the way we think of formal fashion, which is characterized by structure, materials, and decoration.

A multitiered cake, with intricately designed icing and fresh or iced flowers arranged in a strict pattern, typically conveys formality. Certain icing applications are more formal than others: buttercream piped in a precise basketwork pattern; scrolls that suggest fabric appliqués; tiers wrapped in fondant "ribbons"; white-on-white flowers and ribbon rosettes, finished with buttercream dots. Details from a wedding gown—a single bow, a row of buttons or pearls, a swatch of lace—can inspire a grand cake and can set the tone for the entire event. Many of the cakes in this chapter, for example, borrow dressmakers' details; they reinterpret millinery flowers, dotted swiss, and grosgrain ribbon.

Ornamentation will also convey a cake's style, as surely as jewelry is a glorious accent to any ensemble. A good wedding-cake designer can weave the sparkle of precious metals—gold or silver dragées, or edible gold leaf—into a multitiered masterpiece. Or a cake can be studded with marzipan fruit as perfectly rendered as those in a botanical drawing. Gum-paste flowers, tinted jewel tones, will glisten against the porcelain finish of a fondant-covered cake.

Some formal details are especially appropriate for an evening reception; others have a daytime elegance, like the daisy cake on page 152, with royal-icing petals and fondant that has been "quilted" with a dressmaker's wheel. The cake is as traditional as a child's smocked dress, but its whimsy makes it suitable for a garden-party wedding.

The way a cake is presented can underscore its formality, too: A footed silver cake stand, a Chippendale cake table, or a table covered with embroidered organza are fitting formal displays. Think, too, of accessories: An antique silver cake knife, fluted caked plates, and lace dessert napkins all add to the ceremonial atmosphere.

Although any kind of cake can be structured, iced, decorated, and presented formally, one type is more innately dressy than any others. A multitiered cake, white both inside and out, will evoke the formality of the past, and is always the appropriate gastronomic gesture if you want to pay tribute to tradition.

FRUIT AND FLOWERS, *real or silk, are among the prettiest ways to decorate a cake. Early summer is the time to choose a cake piled with the freshest and most varied assortment of the season's best berries (above left); tiny strawberries, red currants, gooseberries, raspberries, and blueberries look beautiful jumbled together on a basket-weave tier; the ruffly basket-weave effect is created using a nontraditional tool for the job: an oversize leaf tip; the three tiers of pound cake are supported by wooden dowels—most of the berries are arranged before the dowels are inserted, which helps hide the supports, and the remaining fruit is added after the tiers are assembled. Fresh hydrangeas, violas, thyme, and scabiosa (above right) bring romance and color to a cake decorated with buttercream and piped leaves; the monogrammed cake topper is made from small sprigs of thyme wired to twenty-four-gauge wire. A tower of roses (opposite): Each tier is frosted with ivory buttercream and alternated with several types of roses, such as 'Sahara,' shaped in tiers of the same height; the flowers are anchored in a central core of oasis, which keeps them fresh for hours. The oasis is shielded from the cake by plastic separators and camouflaged by the flowers.*

SEASHELLS AND STARFISH *adorn the outside of the wedding cake made for Hayley Richman and Stuart Boesky's seaside reception (opposite); the chocolate layers are covered with white buttercream decorated with sugar-dough sea treasures tinted gold, copper, and mother-of-pearl. Set in a latticed gazebo with curtains to keep out the sun and curious birds, guests can admire it before it is cut. The tops of this button cake's three stacked boxes (above left) are covered with fondant and marzipan buttons; some are painted with a pale shimmery coloring to simulate a pearly finish, and at the base of each box is a fondant ribbon, made by pressing strips of fondant into ribbed elastic for the look of grosgrain; a gum-paste bow serves as the cake topper, and for the cake table, grosgrain ribbons are woven together to cover a board. Fabric-coiled appliqués used to embellish dress bodices inspired the lighthearted details on this scrollwork cake (above right); to make these decorations, gum paste is fed through a pasta machine, then rolled into curls and attached to the fondant-covered cake with water.*

CHOCOLATE AND CREAM, *two favorite flavors, make strikingly different formal cakes. A chocolate cake was the focal point of the dessert table at the Christmas reception of Rebecca Thuss and Patrick Farrell; each square glistens with ganache, and the sparkling decorations—sugared Seckel pears and bay leaves—soften its modern lines. Guests were also offered an array of sweets; glacéed fruits, rose biscuits, marzipan candy, lady fingers, spiced nuts, and foil-wrapped candies. Though intricately decorated, a monochromatic cake (opposite) is dramatic in its simplicity; flowers and rosettes that any couturier's seamstress would be proud to have made are applied to each side of the hexagonal layers. The icing is white-chocolate fondant, and the decorations are gum paste; made in advance, they must be dried overnight and can be held in an airtight container for several weeks. The flowers are applied to the fondant with small dots of stiff royal icing.*

PASTEL ICING *in barely tinted hues emphasizes the dressmaker details on these cakes. This sky-blue swag cake mimics the color of Wedgwood Jasperware; it is touched with bits of buttercream icing that recall dotted swiss; the pole was inspired by a scene in the movie "Sense and Sensibility." The New Look cake (opposite) was inspired by Christian Dior's groundbreaking 1947 fashions, trimmed with bows. Ideas for cake decorations can come from almost anywhere: a wedding-dress detail, a favorite intricate lace, a cherished china pattern, or an inherited piece of jewelry.*

FRUIT, NUTS, AND JUST-PICKED FLOWERS *adorn these cakes, or so it seems. The just-ripening strawberries and their leaves on the wild-strawberry cake (above left) are molded from a mixture of white chocolate and corn syrup, the same confection that covers the cake layers of white-chocolate mousse and fresh strawberries; the blossoms are made from gum paste, and the swags of tiny leaves are piped white-chocolate ganache. A botanical print come to life, the stately woodland nut cake (above right) displays pistachios, almonds, and filberts as they appear in their pods, as well as almonds and pecans in the shell, all crafted out of marzipan; more marzipan seals the cake, and ledges in the front are created by setting the four-inch-high tiers flush in the back. A four-tiered primrose cake (opposite) takes its fanciful spirit from the colors and designs of Majolica; the cake's gum-paste flowers and leaves appear to support the tiers, but they actually hide the dowels that are doing the work.*

ON A DESSERT TABLE *set in a four-square carpet of flower petals under an airy white swag, sweets are stacked to mimic the croquembouche—a mass of tiny profiteroles, and the traditional wedding cake of France; pineapples, symbols of hospitality, are set atop each pole. A garland of leaves and apricots frames the apricot tree cake (opposite). Beneath the elegant swags of icing is a homey almond cake filled with apricot jam; the cake sits on a foam-board base that was wrapped with green floral tape and is hidden by fresh leaves that have been pinned in place. Whole apricots are arranged simply around the base. A china cake stand elevates the top tier; it must be supported, as any cake layer would be, with a piece of cardboard hidden under the base of the stand; dowels are driven through the tier to keep it from sinking into the cake—the cardboard should be removed just before serving.*

A WEDDING IN THE WOODS *inspired the marvelous woodland cake (opposite) made of smooth buttercream-frosted tiers, piped with sprawling green buttercream ferns, then adorned with acorns and oak leaves; to make the velvety moss pedestal, place the bottom tier on a foam-board round and frost both; place the frosted tier on a larger polystyrene base, pin pieces of moss around the perimeter, then pin live clovers into the moss just before presenting. Celia Barbour and Peter Weed (left) strolled through a woodsy glade after their ceremony on Squam Lake in New Hampshire.*

Less Formal Cakes

IF THE MOOD OF A WEDDING IS INFORMAL OR A BIT unconventional, why not choose a cake that is unexpected, too? An informal cake can be as whimsical as the day will allow.

The elements of all wedding cakes are the same; it's how the icing, structure, flavor, and decorations are combined that dress it up or down. A formal cake may be structured in many tiers and elaborately displayed, but it will take on a rather informal feeling if the icing is swirled and the decoration applied casually.

Many of the cakes in this chapter are decorated with buttercream, icing that lends itself to all kinds of casual interpretation. It can be applied with a wide spatula for a rough texture. Or it can be piped in playful designs such as stripes, polka dots, and ruffles. As open to translation as it is, buttercream is never pure white. It is made with butter, which makes it the color of ivory. For brides who have their hearts set on an informal all-white cake, snow-white seven-minute frosting can be applied in broad strokes. Or the cake doesn't have to be iced at all; a dusting of powdered sugar is all it needs if adorned with lush decorations such as glossy caramel-coated lady and crab apples.

If a less formal tiered cake isn't informal enough, a sheet cake, spe-cially decorated, has its own charm. For an afternoon reception, one with buttercream flowers won't make too much of itself. Less height does not necessarily mean less impact; two slim sheets can be stacked and still maintain a low profile—the drama comes from the size of the sheets.

A wedding cake can be almost any flavor; an informal one expands the possibilities the furthest. White or yellow cake is always appropri-ate, but a homespun flavor such as applesauce is perfect for a wedding at home or in the garden. The fillings can be straightforward—cream cheese or black-currant preserves—and the decorations simple, too.

Even if the decorations are intricate, they should grace the cake as if they were casually strewn: plump sugared pears and crab apples that appear to have fallen from trees onto the tiers of a chocolate cake; sugared rose petals floating on the tiers of a buttercream cake.

Though it may look unstudied, an informal cake requires as much attention to detail as a formal cake. The cake stand can be made from humble materials—polished wood, beaded milk glass, a plant stand; and the cake table dressed in cotton or linen cloth. No matter how informal, the cake must be displayed with as much care as it was made; it will then be perfectly dressed for the occasion.

FRESH FRUIT *sparkles when dipped in slick caramel or fine sugar crystals. Caramel-dipped lady and crab apples glisten atop a moist spiced applesauce cake with cream-cheese filling; the top tier is supported with walnut dowels, and apple-tree branches fill the space between the tiers. The chocolate chestnut cake (opposite) has a round platform, topped with square layers; the sugared-fruit decoration is plentiful enough so when the cake is cut, each slice can be served with a Seckel pear, crab apple, or candied chestnut— any small, seasonal fruit can be used.*

DISGUISED BY ITS FROSTING, *a wedding cake can be anything inside: The only rule is that the icing, filling, and cake complement one another. A light, fresh pound cake (above left) is sprinkled with rose water and filled with black-currant preserves; the tiers are neatly set back rather than centered, creating large surfaces of rough-textured ivory meringue butter-cream on which to scatter the soft-toned crystallized rose petals made by Toni Elling of Meadowsweets. No special talent is needed to create this luscious-looking confection (above right)—just swirls of fluffy seven-minute icing applied to a snow-white cake; freshly shaved coconut falls where it may. Tiny fresh mums adorn the cake, while sweet peas and ranunculuses dress the table.*

A LOW PROFILE *can be just as dramatic as a towering silhouette. The two-layer chocolate cake (above left), with piped icing around the rims, is decorated with pink spray roses, chocolate cosmos, and hypericum berries, perfect for a winter wedding. Martha made the spring-garden sheet cake (above right) with layers of almond genoise, dacquoise, and buttercream filling. It is frosted with meringue buttercream, which uses egg whites to produce a fluffy, but stable icing, and is decorated with edible spring pansies, violas, and grape hyacinths set in four "flower beds" at the corners. The center of the cake is dusted with confectioners' sugar and piped with a tinted buttercream "M," for marriage, or for Martha, who suggests that a bridal couple entwine their own initials on their cake.*

TIERED WEDDING CAKES *can be constructed from graduated layers balanced on uniform columns, or individual cakes arranged on a unique stand. Four tiers on Ginny Edwards and Thomas More Griffin's color-washed cake are separated by columns piped with buttercream; the fluted sides echo the interior of the shingled seaside club where they were married. The alternating layers of chartreuse and celadon were tied to the color scheme of the wedding, which included the bride's chartreuse dress. An antique wooden plant stand (opposite) is looped with young yellow tulips and white carnations, cone hydrangeas, clematis on the vine, white scabiosa, andromeda, and white lisianthus, then used to support ten 10-inch cakes, each piped in white buttercream with a different pattern.*

A CENTERPIECE *for the party becomes favors for the guests on their way home. Orchids are transplanted into terra-cotta pots painted white and arranged on a saucer; a butterfly-shaped tag on a thin wire hovers over each plant so guests know they are gifts as well as decorations.*

FAVORS

for the Reception

*M*ost are small enough to fit in the palm of your hand and can be as ephemeral as a tiny bunch of fresh flowers or a handful of sugar-coated almonds. But no matter their size or shape,

favors are among a wedding's most appealing elements and one of the easiest to personalize. Although favors are influenced by tradition, they are not beholden to it. In fact almost anything can be made into a favor as long as it is pleasing, portable, and available in multiples.

Edible favors are always well received—even after a formal seated dinner. Cake—usually not the wedding cake itself, but a different confection such as fruitcake or the groom's cake— is the most traditional sweet and easy to make in quantity. It used to be that only unmarried women at the wedding were given favors, pieces of the groom's cake to take home. When couples began to give all their guests a memento from the day, favors became anything sweet—cookies, chocolates, nuts, fruit, candy, and mints. Sugar-coated almonds, or dragées, are customary favorites. Because the almond is a seed, it represents fertility, abundance, and fruitfulness. When a bitter almond is used in a dragée, the hard sugar coating produces a piquant contrast of sweet with bitter; the dragée thus represents an important part of the wedding vow: "for better or for worse." Just as the couple has pledged to support each other in good times as well as in bad, those in attendance symbolically honor the marriage vows by partaking of the almonds. Though cake and almonds are traditional, there is room for creativity in their packaging and display. Cake slices can be tucked into wedge-shaped boxes, assembled in tiers and decorated with fresh flowers to mimic a wedding cake; sugar-coated almonds are often bundled in tulle, but tucked into tiny boxes embellished with silk blossoms and arranged on a tray, they become a field of flowers for guests to pick from.

Small tokens for guests can also be inspired by a wedding motif. The windmill that overlooks Hayley Richman and Stuart Boesky's summer rental house in Bridgehampton, N.Y. became the theme for everything from their invitations and bridal-party gifts to the boxed chocolate windmill they gave to each guest. Another couple used daisies—fresh in the bride's bouquet, embroidered on her gown, and gum-paste replicas on the cake—and carried the theme through to the daisy-seed packets passed to guests at the end of the party.

Among the best favors are those that double as decorations for the reception. A plant stand stocked with buckets of nosegays, for example, are an appropriate decoration for a spring wedding, and guests will be delighted to choose a bunch when they leave the party. And when arranged on a table surrounded by pillar candles, favors can brighten an entry hall, embellish a traditional table setting, or create impact in an otherwise bare alcove. Favors can be incorporated at the table, as place cards, part of the centerpiece, or even hanging off a chair. In fact, a side table or dinner table adorned with artfully arrayed favors can be so attractive, there may need to be a small sign to let guests know that the gifts are meant for them to take home when the party ends. The children's table is ideal for setting with favors—crayons and small toys keep little hands busy on a long day.

Some of the favors in this chapter are encased in bags and pouches, which vary in size, material, and construction in order to best display their small offerings. A simple glassine bag lined with colored paper is a charming container for cookies. And when wrapped in slender satin ribbon, pleated

cupcake linings make pretty cups for candy. One couple who was married in a cherry orchard gave each guest a bag brimming with ripe, juicy berries. Everyone left the party with a treat for the ride home—and no one was tempted to pick from the trees. Handmade bags crafted from felt, moire, or ribbon will take a bit more time and effort but can be made in advance, and designing and assembling favors can be fun, particularly if the bride invites her bridesmaids to help.

The bride and groom always make an effort to express their gratitude to guests for sharing the day by circulating at the reception, but a favor can be used to send a message, too. Matt Lauer and his Dutch-born bride Annette Roque gave each guest an elaborately wrapped box containing one chocolate and one vanilla fortune cookie. The fortune, written in English in one cookie and Dutch in the other, was Elbert Hubbard's quotation "The love we give away is the only love we keep." A message can be written in an unexpected place, too. The decorative paper wrapped around a votive candle can carry a note on the inside, the sentiment read when the guest removes the wrapping to light the candle.

Favors are often as memorable as their details, so take time to think about everything needed to make them well before the event. If favors require individualized tags or labels, ask the calligrapher who addresses the wedding invitations to make them, or ask a computer-savvy friend to print them out at home. If a presentation is a bit subdued, a florist can bring a few sprigs of flowers to provide the splash of color that's needed. And if the thought of arranging the favors before the party seems overwhelming, with a little guidance, the caterer should be happy to help.

Small gifts placed by an exit can act as a final farewell, but they can be an opportunity for a graceful bit of theater during the reception: Flower girls can pass favors out to guests. A flutter of flower girls circulating with baskets of gifts is a charming way to punctuate the events of the day. ❧

A WEDDING FAVOR MAY BE ALMOST ANYTHING; *the only thing it must be is symbolic. Opposite, clockwise from top left: A daisy theme was carried through to the favors at Page Marchese and Adrian Norman's wedding; daisy seeds were packaged in glassine and tied to a scallop-edged card with a slender satin ribbon. Cellophane bags, secured by cards with the bride and groom's names, contain flower bulbs and the glass, pebbles, and instructions needed to help them grow; a lush bouquet hints at the favor inside. A windmill was part of the borrowed scenery at Hayley Mills and Stuart Boesky's seaside wedding; boxed miniature chocolate windmills were stacked to mimic a wedding cake, and each guest helped themselves to a "piece" as they left. Favors at Allison Muench and J. Phillips Williams' wedding were stenciled with the wedding date: Mint candies were packaged in aluminum containers originally made for watch parts.*

CREEPING DAISY
HARDY ANNUAL
PLANT IN THE SPRING IN FULL SUN

HE LOVES ME, HE LOVES ME NOT, HE LOVES ME
WE TIED THE KNOT

PAGE AND ADRIAN, SEPTEMBER 7TH, 1996

{ PACKAGING }

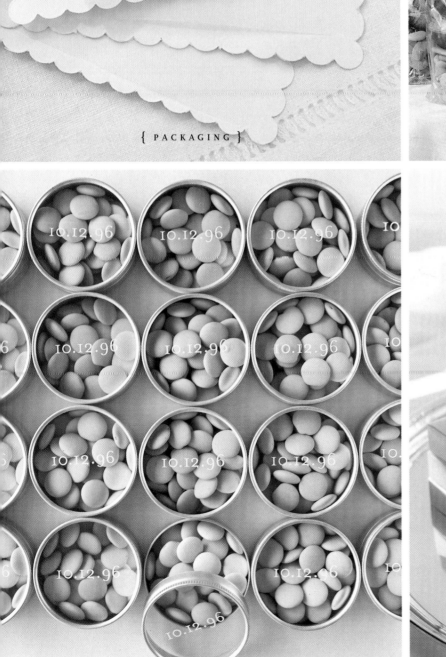

IO.12.96

{ PRESENTATION }

CAKE AND COOKIES *are traditional favors for wedding guests. Here, the groom's cake is assembled in white boxes stacked in the shape of a three-tiered cake; tucked between the boxes are ranunculuses, sweet peas, hyacinths, and lilies of the valley. Messages from the bride and groom are tucked inside fortune cookies (opposite; recipe on page 239, instructions on page 185). Present them to guests in brown-paper boxes elegantly wrapped in onionskin paper and tied with a slender ribbon; a sticker stamped with a fritillaria finishes each package.*

LITTLE COOKIES *make a big impact when packaged with care. For this favor you'll need a utility knife, a ruler, colored paper, a 4¾-by-3¾-inch glassine bag, a stapleless stapler, and cookies. With the utility knife, cut a piece of colored paper into a 3⅜-by-6-inch rectangle. Slip the piece of paper into the back of the bag, and add the cookies. The bag will hold one large, or two or three smaller cookies. Fold the colored paper over the front of the bag to form a flap; seal the bag in the center with the stapler (below). These favors are particularly attractive if you fill them with decoratively shaped cookies. Here, they are presented in rows along lengths of satin ribbon (above).*

CHAMPAGNE GUMDROPS *take on a decidedly elegant air when arranged in cupcake linings and bound in a delicate ribbon. These dainty pleated paper cups are available in lovely pastels and shimmery metallics and can be filled with a favorite small candy. Bind with a length of decorative ribbon attached to a handwritten tag.*

A GARDEN OF FAVORS *is created with fabric flowers set atop candy boxes filled with sugared almonds. To make them, snip fabric flowers from their stems, and hot glue a single bloom to the top of each cardboard candy box. They can be filled with any kind of sweets, then clustered on a tray or table for guests to take as they leave the reception. The note, "Please pick a flower," will let guests know that these favors are for them.*

HOMEMADE FORTUNE COOKIES

hold romantic messages for guests. Handwrite or photocopy lines from classic love poems onto strips of paper, or make up your own fortunes; the paper strips should be about 6 inches long and a little less than a half-inch wide. The cookies, French tuiles with cocoa powder (see the Recipes section), are only flexible enough to shape for a few minutes once they come out of the oven. Slide an offset spatula under a cookie, and flip it over. Lay a fortune across the cookie, and form into a loose cylinder with the fortune inside (below). Press your finger into the center of the roll, and bring the ends together with your other hand. Because you have to work fast, this is a good project to do with one or two friends.

MERINGUE KISSES *are as ethereal as a bride. Inspired by classic chocolate kisses, these pale-pink delicacies hold message for guests. In your best handwriting, spell out words like "love," "joy," "friendship," and "forever" on plain paper, then have them turned into rubber stamps (most office-supply stores can do this; see the Guide). Using pastel inks, stamp the word onto one end of a strip of ¾-by-8-inch onionskin paper. Place the meringue in the center of an 8-inch square of thin waxed tissue paper, arranging the blank end of the paper strip under the kiss (below). Pull the wax paper up and around the meringue, making sure the message peeks out the top. Twist the paper to close.*

CHERRIES *or any fresh fruit are inviting favors. Each of these pretty sacks holds a handful of juicy red cherries, a lovely snack after an outdoor summer reception. Buy a bunch of glassine bags; snip tops with scalloped scissors. Fill each bag with enough fruit so the cherries—or grapes, lady apples, miniature pears—peek out over the top. To ensure that the bags will stand, turn corners in underneath the bags. Display the fruit favors on wooden crates set on a table near the exit.*

TEA FOR TWO *is offered in these little bags. For each favor, you will need a 4½-by-7-inch glassine-lined paper bag; 12 inches of ¼-inch-wide satin ribbon; scissors; and loose tea (bottom). We used five varieties: Earl Grey, rose hips, jasmine, lemon, and green tea. Cut top of bag straight across about one inch from top to trim irregular edge. Fill bottom half of bag with loose tea; fold in half. Circle ribbon around back of bag so two strands are equal lengths at front. To tie a single-loop bow, pass one ribbon end under the other; pull snug. Pressing on center of knot, fold right end forward and to the left; form a loop. Fold left end around loop, then pass it beneath knot and loop. Tug on that end and the loop to tighten knot. Arrange loop and ends, trimming ends so they are in equal relation to the size of the loop. Be sure to label the displays so guests can choose their favorites (top).*

FRESH FROM THE MARKET, *lilacs, phlox, and sweet peas bloom in painted metal buckets calling to mind a French flower market (opposite). These bunches, wrapped in colored waxed tissue paper and displayed on a tiered metal plant stand, are decorative during a party, and then, with a little sign slipped onto the table to guide guests, can be taken home. Keep the posies fresh by placing stems into small water-filled flower tubes before wrapping in white waxed tissue paper (below).*

FRAGRANT SOAP PACKAGES *make practical favors. For each, you will need wool or other non-raveling fabric, such as felt; 14 inches of ¼-inch-wide satin ribbon; a genista sprig; and a soap-making kit (see the Guide). Make soap according to kit instructions. Cut fabric into a 7-by-3½-inch rectangle (below). Fold up 2 inches over longer length, pin, and stitch each side to form a pouch, leaving an ⅛-inch seam allowance. Slip soap into pouch; fold flap over. Cross ribbon over pouch to form an "X" at center of side with flap, pull ribbon to back, and tie a knot. Tuck genista sprig through crossed ribbons. Before our soap hardened, we sprinkled it with fennel seed, oatmeal, and almonds (above).*

For Our Guests

TO DISPLAY *the wool-sleeved handmade soaps on the preceding page, a trio of stacked ironstone compotes in graduated sizes are a centerpiece on a buffet table, as well as a repository for favors; the square pillar candles complement the shape and texture of the soaps. Votive candles (opposite) in three shades of white, are wrapped in corrugated paper and tied with waxed twine; written inside the paper are messages from the bride and groom.*

Keep the story of your wedding where it can be enjoyed every day, and whenever it seems as if it was only a dream, turn the pages one more time and revisit where your life together began. Catch a glimpse of those photos on your wall, or the picture on your desk, and for a moment, be there again, walking down the aisle, dancing the first dance, sharing the first kiss.

TO DISPLAY *and preserve wedding*
photographs and memories, the bride and
groom can create a hanging photo album.
On a bedroom wall, black-and-white photo-
graphs are unified by frames in two tones:
black and silver. Pictures on the bureau,
framed to coordinate with the wall display,
are of the husband and wife as children, along
with an unframed picture of friends.

KEEPING MEMORIES
Forever

Of all the wedding keepsakes, the ones we hope will last the longest are often made of the most fragile and fleeting materials. Beautifully bound guest books and elegantly printed programs presenting the order

of service, prayers, and readings are among the elements of a wedding that are designed to be saved. But many couples also make scrapbooks or shadow boxes to preserve their invitations, place cards and menu cards, lists of presents, and wedding announcements. And then there are photographs, the most likely mementos to be looked at again and again.

The tradition of the wedding portrait began in the mid-nineteenth century, when the first professional photographers suggested that couples come into the studio to sit for a photograph before a "romantic" backdrop to commemorate their marriage. And sit they did: Heavy cameras and long exposure times didn't allow for spontaneity, which is why the couples look so stiff—the subjects had to remain absolutely still, barely breathing for minutes, while their images were captured. By the 1930s, new, lightweight cameras gave photographers the freedom to roam, and more impromptu photographs were taken along with the traditional portraits. This is still the preferred mix today: formal, posed portraits; candid shots that reveal moments the same way an artist's quick sketches do; and still-lifes that document an overall impression as well as all of the details of the wedding ceremony and reception.

Choosing a photographer is one of the most important decisions when planning a wedding, because much of what is recorded depends on how the day was seen through his or her eyes. A photographer should be both a reporter and an artist, and like any artist whose work one lives with, the photographer's style should coincide with the "collector's" sensibility. Finding someone to take wedding pictures who quite literally sees the way the bride and groom do takes a bit of legwork. The first step is to get referrals from family, friends, or other wedding professionals, like a catering manager or florist. At an initial meeting, an experienced photographer will be able to show a couple a portfolio of his or her work, both from weddings and other kinds of celebrations or gatherings. Some photographers will send a disk or CD-ROM instead, so a bride and groom can view their work on a home computer and print out or even e-mail samples to solicit the opinion of a family member or friend.

An appreciation for a photographer's style is a necessity, but equally important is a couple's compatibility with him or her. Meeting with the photographer before the wedding day allows the bride and groom to see how they'll interact. It is also a time to discuss details, both big and small, such as the photographer's attire; a couple can request the attire blend into that of the guests—like a tuxedo for a black-tie occasion. It is also important for the couple to make a list of the people and the moments they want recorded; it's a good idea to assign a member of the bridal party to help the photographer determine who is who at the wedding. When making this list, a bride and groom should check with the officiant about photography at the ceremony. Some religious institutions do not permit photography during the service; others allow photos, but without using a flash.

It will also be necessary to discuss in advance the type of shots a couple wants—formal or casual—how they intend to display them, and the type of film that will be used. Some couples like black-and-white photographs, others prefer color, and many ask for both. The style of the wedding may influence the choice; color typically looks more casual; black and white more classic. But there are other considerations: Black and white printed on archival paper will usually last longer than color prints, which can fade, although correct processing and storage can substantially extend the life of a color print. Some images, like group shots, translate better in black and white, which brings different skin tones and the colors of clothing into balance: A single jarring tone can throw off the balance of the picture, for example, if one guest is wearing a very bright color and everyone else is in muted shades. But some elements of the wedding, like the flowers in a bouquet or a table setting, are better conveyed in color photographs.

As for videos, the cameras, the lights, and the videographer do not have to be as intrusive as they may have been in the past. Advancements in technology have given way to maneuverability, and the cameraperson, like a still photographer, can easily capture all the special moments requested by the bride and groom (be sure to provide a list of all events and people for them to cover, too).

By the time the newlyweds return from their honeymoon, the videographer should have a rough cut to view and the photographs should be developed. Some photographers organize the photos in a book; others send loose proofs. A couple will sort through the proofs, and instantly be brought back to their wedding day, and see the little details and expressions they would have missed without a professional on the job. Some of the pictures will be ordered for an album, others to display, and still others to send as gifts to family and friends. Photo albums and scrapbooks themselves can be small works of art; so can picture frames and wall arrangements for what one wedding photographer calls "romantic reportage." To save all the "works on paper" that have taken so much time conceptualizing, designing, and making, we have created guest books and album and frame ideas, along with guidelines for attractively displaying the photos. ∽

CREATE A LASTING RECORD *of a wedding with unique albums and guest books. Opposite, clockwise from top left: A bride is always beautiful, but a perfect portrait depends on a good photographer; Page Marchese chose New York photographer Andrea Gentl to take her portrait when she arrived at the reception. On a bracket, a gilt frame displays a romantic portrait; the silk mat matches the ribbon edging that was saved from the bridal bouquet. Page Marchese and Adrian Norman personalized their guest book with a card glued to the cover, trimmed with a daisy ribbon; a daisy was glued to the page marker. Photographers don't store their prints in albums; they use acid-free portfolio boxes: A blush-pink tray box holds fifty eight-by-ten-inch photographs, and a clamshell box holds eleven-by-fourteen-inch photos. Prints can be matted or left unmounted. To lift out photos, make a tab of double-faced ribbon; fold it in half crosswise; glue to inside edge of box.*

{ PHOTOGRAPHERS }

{ DISPLAYING PHOTOGRAPHS }

{ STORING PHOTOGRAPHS }

{ GUEST BOOKS }

BETH PAGE MARCHESE
AND
ADRIAN GATES NORMAN

MEMORIES OF A WEDDING DAY *are elegantly framed for all to see. Clockwise from top left: Wedding memorabilia, which might otherwise be stored away, is displayed and protected in a shadow box; the invitation, table and place cards, and program, along with flowers from the bouquet, are hot-glued onto gabardine selected to match the frame. A beautiful photograph of the bride striding through a field of sea grass is displayed like the art object it is; the wooden frame was made by a carpenter, then covered in velvet to reflect the color of the bride's gown; the easel is a simple brass plate holder that was silver-leafed to coordinate with other silver accents in the room. One frame tells the story of a wedding day: a portrait of the bride, the newlyweds, the bridesmaids, the groomsmen, and the church; a mat was cut to fit the photos and the silver frame. For bridesmaids, their photograph in silver frames is presented in moiré satin ribbon sewn into a reusable pouch.*

THREE PORTRAITS—*the groom's parents, the bride's parents, and the bride and groom—are displayed in white-lacquered frames; a tiny spacer holds the photographs away from the glass, and the pictures are tacked to the wall through a moiré ribbon.*

A LINEN PORTFOLIO BOX *(opposite) is a lovely and sensible way to store and display wedding photographs. Photographs last longest when stored in total darkness. For that reason, an archival-quality portfolio box is ideal. Inside, thirty to forty photographs are mounted with photo corners on acid-free watercolor paper. For additional protection, acid-free tissue is placed between the pages. The edge of each page was first deckled by roughly tearing it along the edge of a ruler (below left); three rows of satin ribbon are lightly glued to a large sheet of acid-free tissue, which wraps around the boxed photographs inside (below right).*

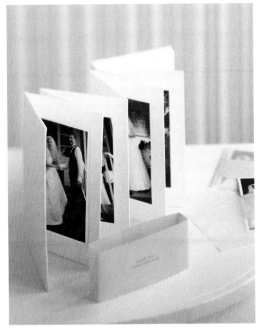

SAY THANK YOU *with special pictures from the wedding day. A creative alternative to a photo card—reminiscent of the traditional photo Christmas card—is an accordion-fold book that opens to reveal fifteen or so prints (above). When closed, the collection looks like a deck of cards. The "pack" is bound with wide silver paper cuffs (below) that were imprinted with the couple's name on a computer printer. The cuffs are secured in the back with glue.*

EXTRA PRINTS *of the wedding day can be stored in inexpensive boxes such as this one, which allow a couple to separate shots with file cards. Each separator is labeled by event: "Shower," "Rehearsal," "Ceremony," "Reception," and "Bridal Party." A photograph mounted on the top of the box makes a fitting label.*

A STORE-BOUGHT ALBUM *embossed with the couple's names on the front can be dressed up with a custom-made slipcover (bottom). Crafted from green Ultrasuede and tied with a sash of organza (below), the slipcover not only looks pretty but protects the album from fingerprints and dust that can build up over time.*

A PRESSED FLOWER *from the bridal bouquet is traditionally mounted on the last page of a wedding album. The sweet peas (above) were flattened under a pile of books for six weeks, then secured with a piece of ribbon from the bouquet. Make two vertical, quarter-inch-long incisions near the middle of the page, thread the ribbon through, and then tie a bow gently around the stems.*

A CUSTOM-MADE PHOTO BOOK
(opposite) uses eight-by-ten-inch prints with wide borders that are dry-mounted onto heavy acid-free paper and bound together; a sheet of acid-free tissue is bound between each page. Grosgrain ribbon with pearls sewn along the end serves as a bookmark. The wedding invitation is mounted into the well of the book's front cover. When closed, it makes a handsome display perched on a silver-leafed photo easel (above).

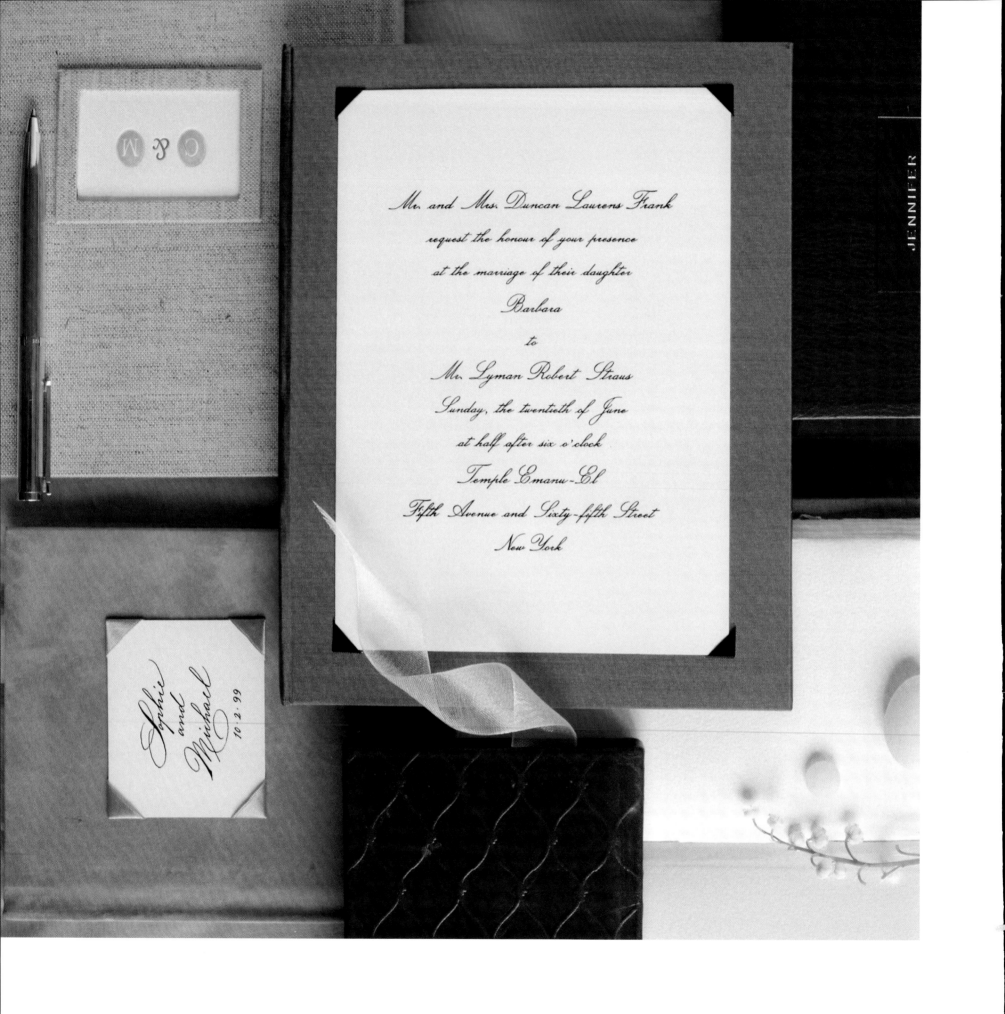

CUSTOMIZE A PREMADE BOOK *with little effort. Opposite, clockwise from top left: Fasten an engraved silver plate to a leather photo album. Emboss a card slipped into the front cover with initals. Affix a card with a design from the invitation, the invitation itself, or a calligraphed card with the couple's names and the date to the cover with ribbon or photo corners. Even a page marker of ribbon can beautify a store-bought book. Instead of placing one guest book off to the side, why not set these store-bought paper photo albums (above left) at the centers of each table; tied closed, they serve as table markers, but inside, each guest's name is inscribed at the top of a page—guests can pass the book, find their names, and write their wishes; have photos taken of each table, and afterward, glue photos over table numbers in fronts of books. A guest book can be as simple as thick cards and paper, with an invitation glued to the first page for decoration (above right): Front and back covers are thick cards lined with printed paper; a place marker is glued between the back cover and its lining. Score covers with a bone folder so they open easily; punch two holes through covers and white-paper pages, and bind together with ribbon: Feed it through from back, and tie in a bow. Place invitation on first page, and secure with ribbon corners: Make two forty-five-degree folds in a length of ribbon, forming a point; slip it over each of the invitation's corners; glue in back.*

A GUEST BOOK *doesn't have to be a traditional book at all; it can be a box, a photo album, even a single sheet of paper. Clockwise from top left: A rice-paper scroll (purchased at an art-supply store and cut to size), ink, and a dipping pen create an elegant keepsake. Shannon McLean and Brian Andrew Townsend set out note cards and asked guests to compose messages. Rather than written sentiments, this book is filled with pictures guests take of themselves with instant cameras; the cover is made of book board and cloth glued together with neutral-pH adhesive; the pages are 8½-inch pieces of paper taped together; clear photo corners affix photos. Small cards provide just enough space for sweet thoughts; after the wedding, envelopes can be glued in an album so the cards can be reread. Guests at Rebecca Thuss and Patrick Farrell's wedding (opposite) wrote a note, tucked it into an envelope, and placed it in the compote to be collected at the end of the day.*

Wedding Planner A SIX MONTH COUNTDOWN TO THE BIG DAY

DEADLINE	✓	TASK

SIX MONTHS OR MORE AHEAD

Arrange for your family to meet your fiancé's, if they haven't already.

Announce engagement in local newspapers.

Select date.
Have backup dates in mind, and be prepared to be flexible in case the site, caterer, or officiant is already booked.

Set budget, and establish priorities.
If you intend to splurge in one area, such as flowers or food, take that into consideration.

Buy comprehensive wedding planner, organizer, or computer program.

Hire bridal consultant.
It might seem like an indulgence, but the professional advice and access that a consultant offers can help save money in the end.

Reserve wedding and reception sites.

Choose a caterer.
If you have favorite foods or family recipes that you want to incorporate, discuss them with the caterer.

Compile guest list.
Begin to notify out-of-town guests of the wedding date, so they can make necessary travel arrangements.

Choose and book officiant.
If you plan to write your own vows, discuss them now with him or her.

Choose attendants.

Order dress and accessories, including veil, gloves, and shoes.

Book florist, and choose arrangements.

Book photographer.
Discuss whether you want black-and-white or color photography, and whether you prefer posed or

candid shots. Give the photographer a list of shots you think are important.*

Book videographer.

Book band for reception.
Attend a performance to be sure the band's style fits yours. Start compiling a list of songs you want—and don't want—them to play.

Book musicians for ceremony.
Think about what you'd like them to play when the guests are being seated, when the bridal party walks down the aisle, and when you walk down the aisle.

Plan and book honeymoon.

FOUR TO SIX MONTHS AHEAD

Reserve any rental equipment, such as tables, chairs, and tents.

Register for gifts.

Order wedding cake.
Design can reflect the theme, dress, colors, flowers, or reception space.

Arrange any necessary transportation.

Order stationery, including thank-you notes.

Purchase or reserve groom's attire.

Purchase wedding rings.

Book calligrapher.

Choose favors.
If you're making something or wrapping the favors, start as soon as possible.

Book room for your wedding night.

Purchase going-away outfit.

Choose gifts for bridal party and for each other.

Reserve accommodations for out-of-town guests.

TWO TO FOUR MONTHS AHEAD

If your state requires blood tests, make appointments.

Discuss details of menu and decor with caterer.

Discuss service with officiant.

Buy stockings and any special lingerie your dress requires.

Choose readings for ceremony.
Give copies to those you've asked to do the readings so they'll have time to practice.

If you are writing your own vows, do so now.

Schedule rehearsal time and rehearsal dinner.

ONE TO TWO MONTHS AHEAD

Buy guest book.

Have programs printed.

Mail invitations.

If you are going to change your name, complete proper documents.

Send wedding announcements to local newspapers.

Send change-of-address information to post office.

Practice hairstyle with headpiece.

Have makeup artist do trial run.
Schedule this on a day when you have another party or special event, so it won't go to waste.

Write thank-you notes as you receive gifts.

TWO WEEKS AHEAD

Have final dress fitting.
Bring along the shoes and lingerie you are going to wear on your wedding day.

Obtain marriage license.

Arrange seating plan, and write place cards.

Notify caterer of final guest count.

Write toasts for rehearsal dinner and wedding reception.

Address announcements.

Break in wedding shoes at home.

ONE WEEK AHEAD

Pick up dress or have it delivered.

Pack for honeymoon.

Confirm travel arrangements.

Confirm details with caterer.

Have facial or other beauty treatment.

ONE DAY AHEAD

Finalize seating chart.

Assign different responsibilities, such as handing out corsages and boutonnieres, to members of bridal party.

Confirm limousines or other transportation.

Have manicure and pedicure.

Give each member of the bridal party a gift along with a personal note.

Rehearse ceremony.

Hold rehearsal dinner.

YOUR WEDDING DAY

Have massage in the morning.
A massage will give you some time to reflect and relax before the big event.

Mail announcements.

Mail gift to your parents to thank them for their help and support.

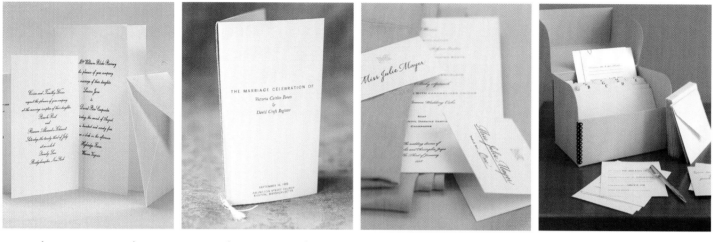

{ INVITATIONS }   { PROGRAMS }   { RECEPTION CARDS }   { THANK-YOU NOTES }

Stationery

Choosing wedding stationery is yet another way to set a wedding apart from all others. The wedding invitation announces a couple's new life. Its character—formal, informal, elegant, or amusing—reveals the new couple's style. Take the time to choose favorite papers, typefaces, colors, and symbolic emblems. But there is more to wedding stationery than the requisite invitation. Matching programs, and reception cards, ordered from the same stationer, can all carry an individual stamp. "At home" cards for later use and correspondence cards for writing thank-you notes should coordinate as well. It's a stationery wardrobe, so to speak.

INVITATIONS

Somewhere between traditional etiquette and creative expression lies the perfect stationery—invitations that tell guests what to wear, where to be, and when, all in a way that quietly reflects the bride and groom.

"The key is to make your guests feel that you really want them there, not that you were obligated to invite them," says Marc Friedland, president of Creative Intelligence, a Los Angeles-based design studio specializing in wedding stationery. The way to do that, he says, is with an invitation that sets the tone for all the festivities to come. And with today's relaxed rules of etiquette and expanded possibilities for design, it's easier than ever to do.

"The word 'proper' is a little outdated," says Joy Lewis, owner of the New York City engraver Mrs. John L. Strong Fine Stationery. "People should express themselves in a way that draws from the traditional continuum but doesn't stop the clock." And they do. Even in this cyberspace age, when engraving an e-mail address on a reception card is not unheard of, the bulk of wedding stationery remains classic.

The most formal of traditional invitations consists of an ecru sheet of high-quality cotton or linen rag paper, folded once. It measures either 5½ by 7½ inches (embassy) or 4½ by 6¼ inches (classic), and arrives in a double envelope, one inside the other, to protect the invitation. A high-quality engraver may offer more than eighty different typestyles, but most couples choose an English script, which is an idealized handwriting, or an antique Roman typeface, a warm, matter-of-fact style available either solid or shaded. If the reception is held at a different location, a separate card is usually enclosed telling guests where and when they are expected. And then there's the reply card. In the past, guests were expected to reply on their own stationery, but these days an RSVP card in a stamped, addressed envelope is often sent with the invitation.

For mailing, these elements are stacked in the envelope, face up, with the invitation on the bottom, the reception card in the middle, and the reply card on the top. If a direction card or map is necessary, it should be printed in the same style as the invitation; it should not be a photocopy. Directions can be sent together with the invitation, placed above the reply card, or sent under separate cover once the guest has given notice that he or she will attend.

In the past, a piece of tissue was used to prevent smudging, but with today's more stable inks, some brides choose to forgo the extra paper. However, to be sure the ink arrives intact, request "not for machine handling" at the post office. For peace of mind, some include the tissue.

Some brides prefer to address their own invitations, while others use calligraphers to write out the envelopes; ask the engraver for a recommendation. Couples often select commemorative stamps and ask at the post office that they be hand-canceled, an added touch that says no detail has been overlooked.

Although most wedding stationery follows this format, there are some variations. French-fold invitations are one alternative enjoying a bit of a revival. These are pieces of paper, folded in half twice—once horizontally, then vertically—to fit into either a classic or embassy envelope. The bride's information goes on the left, the groom's on the right, with the where-and-when information centered below both. French folds also work well when invitations are printed in two languages.

Four-ply cards, called flat cards, are also becoming popular. These heavyweight cards might have beveled edges, trimmed in gold or silver, with an icon or ornament at the top.

The majority of couples choose ecru wedding invitations engraved in black ink. Instead of ecru, invitations are sometimes engraved on white, particularly in Europe. Such printing processes as lithography, thermography (heat-sensitive powders that result in raised letters), embossing, and blind embossing can be employed. Unique invitations can be created with colored inks, die cuts, wax seals, silk ribbons, and floral inclusions—flowers embedded in the paper. "New Yorkers have traditionally

been more of the ecru-and-black mentality, but more and more there's a departure from that," says Friedland, whose range of colored inks includes eggplant, olive, burgundy, navy, and charcoal. "The West Coast, which traditionally was over-the-top, is now going more traditional."

Across the board, though, he detects a major change that's common to both coasts. "Weddings," he says, "are becoming really, really fun again." The right invitations hold that promise even before you open the envelope.

INVITATION WORDING

Considering the hundreds of decisions a bride will make before her wedding day, what could be more tempting than to let the invitations essentially write themselves? After all, parents of brides have been requesting the honour of their guests' presence in precisely the same language for more than a century. And it is hard to deny the security in knowing that these phrases have passed the etiquette test of generations.

Even if a couple intends to compose their own wording, it's important to understand wedding protocol before they deviate from it. Traditional invitations are formal, both in phrasing and format—line breaks instead of commas, numbers, dates, and times spelled out. British wording and spellings are also commonly used ("half after seven o'clock" and "the favour of a reply is requested").

A typical invitation includes certain elements: the host line, request line, bride and groom line, date and time lines, location line, and reception and R.S.V.P. lines. Although every invitation should have all of these, they can be worded and arranged in countless ways to reflect the style of the occasion and the changing times. "The trend is that you do whatever makes good etiquette sense and makes you feel good," says Jerome Brownstein, engraving consultant at Ross-Cook Engraving in New York City.

One line of the invitation that has been most affected is the host line. Traditionally, the bride's mother and

CONTENT *An exquisite invitation should also serve as a memento. Use a paper that won't disintegrate over time: 100 percent rag, made of cotton or linen, is best. Papers made with wood pulp, which is highly acidic, can discolor.*

WEIGHT *Stationery is usually measured in bond weight. A good letter sheet is made of thirty-two- or forty-pound bond. You may also come across offset weight. Hundred-pound offset is roughly equal to forty-pound bond. Heavy cards (common in Britain, where invitations to weddings of the aristocracy are called "stiffies") should be made of three-ply stock.*

FINISH *Traditional invitations have a smooth vellum finish. Less traditional papers may be laid, having a subtly ridged texture. Cards can have indented panels; edges can be beveled (cut on a slant) or deckled (rough).*

HANDMADE PAPER *An invitation can be personalized by using handmade paper, which tends to have interesting textures and colors. Good art-supply stores often have a varied selection.*

PRINTING METHODS

ENGRAVING *Letters are etched onto a metal plate, which is rolled with ink, then wiped; the ink remains in the etched lines. The paper is then pressed onto the plate, leaving a raised image and indentations on the reverse.*

LITHOGRAPHY *This is another old method, originally involving stone slabs and grease pencils. Updated, it is commonly called litho, offset litho, or just offset, and it produces a crisp, flat image.*

BLIND EMBOSSING *Plates are used to produce raised images without ink. This printing method is reserved for motifs, monograms, and addresses on the flaps of envelopes.*

LETTERPRESS *This used to be the most common form of printing. Raised type is inked and stamped on the paper, resulting in an effect almost the opposite of engraving. While large printing plants have almost all converted to offset print and computerized typesetting, small print shops using letterpress can still be found and can be the source of exquisite stationery.*

HANDWRITING *This is always correct and always charming. The most expensive copperplate engraving, after all, is simply mass-produced handwriting.*

4002 EAST BROOKHAVEN DRIVE
ATLANTA, GEORGIA 70296
Mr. and Mrs. Luther
1607 East Four
Charlotte,
MR. AND MRS. JAMES WILLIAM EDWARDS
REQUEST THE HONOUR OF YOUR PRESENCE
AT THE MARRIAGE OF THEIR DAUGHTER
HILLARY BETH
TO
MR. MICHAEL JOHN FOSTER
SATURDAY, THE TENTH OF APRIL
NINETEEN HUNDRED AND NINETY-NINE
AT HALF AFTER SIX O'CLOCK
SAINT JOHN'S CHURCH
ATLANTA, GEORGIA
BLACK TIE
HOST LINE
REQUEST LINE
BRIDE AND GROOM LINE
DATE AND TIME LINES
LOCATION LINE
RECEPTION
IMMEDIATELY FOLLOWING THE CEREMONY
FOUR SEASONS HOTEL
ATLANTA, GEORGIA
M
WILL ATTEND
THE FAVOUR OF A REPLY IS REQUESTED
BEFORE THE SEVENTEENTH OF MARCH

INVITATIONS *A formal invitation today typically includes separate cards for the reception and reply, and the language is prescribed by tradition: The bride's parents are hosting and inviting guests, the time is spelled out, and British spellings are used. Although appropriate for a black-tie wedding, such invitations would be out of sync with a more casual affair.*

father paid for the wedding and were the hosts. Over the years, however, as it has become acceptable for the groom's parents to contribute to the event, their names also began appearing on the invitation, often on the line directly after the groom's name, preceded by the words "son of." Today they even may be elevated to cohost, with their names directly after the bride's parents'.

All of these variations reflect a time when brides and grooms married quite young, straight out of their parents' homes. Now that so many couples get married later, they often want to issue the invitation themselves—particularly if they're paying for their own wedding. The dilemma is that they may also want to include their families somehow.

If this is the situation, consider the increasingly popular solution of stating the bride and groom's names first and adding "together with their families." This format is also useful in avoiding the sometimes delicate issue of stepparents. According to Julie Holcomb, owner of Julie Holcomb Printers, a letterpress company outside San Francisco, this style may depart from convention, but not from the essential wedding tradition: sharing your love with family and friends. "The wedding invitation might be the only good way to include everyone, the only gracious opportunity for a couple to acknowledge that these people are important to them," Holcomb says.

If a bride chooses to include names on her invitations, the most complicated question becomes whose. Divorces, deaths, and family estrangements all make the wording tricky. Instinct and good taste are the best guides if your family relationships are complicated. If, for example, the bride's father has passed away and her mother is the host, the mother's name is the only one that is necessary on the invitation. However, many people feel strongly about including a deceased parent. In this case, the wording should be phrased so that it is clear the deceased parent is not issuing the invitation: "The pleasure of your company is requested at the marriage of [bride's name], daughter of [the bride's mother's name] and the late [the bride's father's name]." Or, let's say the bride's parents are divorced, her father is remarried, and all of the above are hosts. Always start with the bride's mother's name, then her father's and stepmother's on a separate line, and have them invite guests "to the marriage of [bride's name]"—not the marriage of their daughter, since the bride is not the daughter of all three hosts. The wording should reflect each particular situation, however. If a stepmother raised the bride, and if the bride's birth mother has a less significant role in her life, the bride may include only her father and stepmother, using the words "their daughter."

By convention, ceremonies held in a church or synagogue "request the honour of your presence," reflecting the solemnity of the ritual, and those at a hotel or home use the warmer "pleasure of your company." But there's nothing inappropriate about wording the invitation to reflect individual personalities or to suit specific occasions. A wedding on the beach, for instance, might invite guests to "participate in the feast and festivity of the occasion."

Fortunately, none of the other decisions concerning invitations will involve so much tap dancing as the host line or involve as many possibilities as the request line. A couple will want to consider how they would like to be presented and whether just their names will suffice or whether they want to include titles; traditionally, the groom's name is preceded by "Mr." while the bride's name stands alone.

The decision for the time line will simply be whether "7:30" or "half after seven o'clock" best reflects the tone of your wedding. Formal events call for spelling out numbers, which might seem out of place for a more casual wedding. The same holds true for numbers in the date line and those in the location line, if, that is, the street address is included. Remember that all options are equally correct.

Also think about whether "Reception immediately following" should be on the invitation or whether it should be printed on separate cards to announce the reception, which is only necessary if a couple does not plan to invite everyone to the reception.

There is not as much flexibility with reply cards. Once upon a time guests replied on their own stationery. For those who long for the manners and grace of the past, R.S.V.P. can be printed in the lower left corner, or guests can be invited to kindly respond by a specified date. Be forewarned, though: If such

an approach is attempted today, there will likely be no head count to give to the caterer. Try to keep any prompting as simple as possible. An enclosed response card that reads "a favour of a reply is requested" by a specified date is a good choice because it still leaves room for guests to write a short message. More often, however, guests are simply asked to write their names on an "M line" and check whether they will or won't be attending.

Ideally, every component of the invitation should strike a compromise between practicality and charm. It is all a matter of what is emphasized—celebration or sanctity or a combination of the two. "I once had a customer who had been married before," says Holcomb. "She was practically in tears because she heard she'd have to use her married name on the invitation. I told her she could say whatever she wanted. The purpose of etiquette is to make things easier for people, not harder."

HOST LINE I. *The traditional format has the bride's parents hosting and inviting the guests.* 2. *If the groom's parents are sharing expenses, both sets of parents can act as hosts, with the bride's listed first.* 3. *Many couples want to mention the groom's parents, even if they are not hosting the wedding.* 4. *Divorced parents should be listed on separate lines with the mother's name first.* 5. *When either or both of the bride's parents has remarried, it is most proper that only the natural parents are listed, since they usually give the bride away; depending on your family's situation, however, stepparents can be included.* 6. *A good way not to leave anyone out is to invite the guests yourselves, and mention both families.* 7. *More couples are paying for their own weddings and playing hosts by themselves.*

REQUEST LINE I. *By strict convention, "the honour of your presence" is reserved for religious ceremonies. British spellings are still used for all types of formal weddings. 2. For weddings held at a hotel or a home, it's more appropriate to use warmer, less solemn wording. 3. Many families are opting to mix tradition (such as British spellings and formal constructions) with their own sentiments. 4. A reflection of the times: The couple issues a simple request, emphasizing the celebration.*

BRIDE AND GROOM LINE
1. *Traditionally, a bride takes no title before her name. Another option is to include titles for both the bride and groom; this is useful when one of you has an occupation that carries an official title, such as Dr. 2. One way to put yourselves on equal footing is to leave titles off altogether. This is also appropriate if both sets of parents are serving as hosts.*

DATE AND TIME LINES I. *Spelling out the day, date, and year lends sophistication, but you can also use a numeral for the year. Similarly, although the phrase "half after six o'clock" is classic, it may not be right for a less formal wedding. 2. When stating the time, only the hour is necessary; there's no need to note A.M. or P.M. Where the time of day may be unclear, use "in the morning" or "in the evening."*

LOCATION LINE I. *Make sure you have the proper name of your church. As with everything else, spell out "Saint" or any other abbreviations (except R.S.V.P.). 2. City landmarks and well-known hotels don't usually require addresses, unless you're inviting out-of-town guests who might need directions. 3. Any site that is not well known should include an address. Invitations are typically written without punctuation; line breaks take the place of commas, except to separate city and state, or to avoid confusion.*

Request Line

REQUEST THE HONOUR OF YOUR PRESENCE
AT THE MARRIAGE OF THEIR DAUGHTER
1

REQUEST THE PLEASURE OF YOUR COMPANY
AT THE MARRIAGE OF THEIR DAUGHTER
2

WOULD BE HONOURED TO HAVE YOU SHARE
IN THE JOY OF THE MARRIAGE OF THEIR CHILDREN
3

INVITE YOU TO CELEBRATE THEIR MARRIAGE
4

Bride and Groom Line

HILLARY BETH
TO
MR. MICHAEL JOHN FOSTER
1

HILLARY BETH EDWARDS
TO
MICHAEL JOHN FOSTER
2

Date and Time Lines

SATURDAY, THE TENTH OF APRIL
NINETEEN HUNDRED AND NINETY-NINE
AT HALF AFTER SIX O'CLOCK
1

SATURDAY, THE TENTH OF APRIL
NINETEEN HUNDRED AND NINETY-NINE
AT SIX O'CLOCK
2

Location Line

SAINT JOHN'S CHURCH
ATLANTA, GEORGIA
1

FOUR SEASONS HOTEL
ATLANTA, GEORGIA
2

OUR HOME
AT 4002 EAST BROOKHAVEN DRIVE
ATLANTA, GEORGIA
3

RECEPTION CARDS **1.** *When your reception and ceremony are at different locations, include the ceremony site at the bottom of the invitation.* **2.** *If the reception and ceremony share a site, there's no need to repeat location.* **3.** *If only some guests are invited to the reception, it's mandatory to enclose a separate card.* **4.** *When your reception doesn't immediately follow the ceremony, be sure to mention the time.* R.S.V.P. CARDS **1.** *For the most formal invitations, "R.S.V.P." appears on the invitation's lower left corner, indicating that guests should send a personal reply.* **2.** *Include an address on the invitation only if it differs from the one on the envelope.* **3.** *Separate cards are more common today; this one is conventional and convenient.* **4.** *This is a modern, time-efficient option.* **5.** *Postcards are the most casual approach.* **6.** *In the past, guests would reply on their own stationery.*

WEDDING PROGRAMS

The ceremony has been rehearsed, the bride and groom are in costume, they know their lines by heart. They even have a touch of stage fright. The wedding ceremony may be the most intensely emotional event of their lives—but it is also likely to be the most theatrical. And, as at any great performance, the members of the audience will appreciate having a program to follow.

A wedding program is never considered a necessity—which is what makes it so nice. It is a winsome little extra that shows attention to all the details. And because it is not required, it is not subject to strict rules of etiquette, which makes creating a program an easygoing, creative endeavor. But the program is no mere vanity: It serves the rather noble purpose of guiding guests through the ceremony you've planned so carefully, and it provides the couple with a way to communicate with everyone who has come to share the day.

The most basic program is straightforward and purposeful. The bride's and groom's names act as a title of sorts and are typically followed by the date and location of the wedding. The order of the service, often including titles of readings and songs, helps guests follow along. And listing the names of the celebrant, members of the bridal party, and others who have a role in the wedding, then giving a brief description of the person's relationship to the bride and groom enables everybody to put faces to the names they've heard before. Including the musicians, like an organist or a soloist, is optional, but it's a lovely way to thank them for their participation.

Incorporating other elements into the program can enhance the ceremony for the guests. Some couples include the words to readings, hymns, and vows that they've written themselves, so everybody can savor them—the recitations themselves are so fleeting. The program can also describe religious or cultural customs; when Joy Kaplan married Morey Wildes in Cedarhurst, New York, they knew that not all of their guests would be familiar with all of the rituals in the traditional Jewish ceremony. So they included explanations in the program. "We wanted people to feel involved, to feel comfortable," says Kaplan, who recalls that several friends told her later that the detailed program had allowed them to appreciate the ceremony even more. Also consider offering translations, if that would prove helpful to your friends and family.

To further personalize the program, some couples include a favorite poem or quotation that expresses their feelings about the day. It is also appropriate to write a brief thank-you to parents or other special people. To pay a tribute to deceased relatives or close friends, include a dedication to them in the program, or explain that a candle will be lit in their honor.

Once the information has been assembled, decide how to present it. Programs may be booklets, folded cards, or single sheets of paper or stiff stock, as small as postcards or as large as letterhead. They may be engraved or printed to match or complement your invitations. But having wedding programs professionally designed and assembled is not the only choice. Costs can be kept down by having a stationer print only the covers. And because the information required for the covers already exists—the names, the date, and the location of the ceremony—the covers can be made along with the invitations, which may reduce printing

BASIC PROGRAM *Etiquette doesn't dictate what a program should include, but this one can be considered the standard. On the cover are the couple's names and the date and location of the wedding. Inside are the names and roles of participants in the ceremony and the order of the service. Silver thread is strung around the off-white folded card and tied to a shimmering little tassel.* SINGLE SHEET *This is the most straightforward format. Clockwise from left: A tree tops this program; chartreuse on white looks summery; a calligraphed version can be printed many times; this program has the service on the front and the bridal party on back; this little square was designed on a home computer; vellum is joined to aqua paper with ribbon.* BOOKLET *The binding should complement the program's design. Clockwise from left: Pearl-beaded ribbon trails from creamy stock; a single staple is almost invisible; silver thread runs along the spine and is tied in the center; a note card, rubber-stamped with a monogram, gets matching ties; a white-on-cream booklet; a booklet bound with brown satin ribbon.*

costs. The inside pages can be created on a computer, then photocopied. Or, a stationer can make the pages, and they can be assembled at home.

Many couples choose to save even more money by making the complete programs themselves. You needn't be a designer to come up with something simple and lovely on a computer, especially since many desktop-publishing programs come with templates that you can customize and a wide selection of images to use. Recruit the help of a talented friend if working on a computer seems daunting. Copies can be printed out on a home printer, or they can be taken to a copy shop to be reproduced. When choosing paper, consider weight, texture, and color; thick stock in white or cream is always appropriate, but other options can be found at an art-supply store, a stationer, or even an office-supply store.

Good-quality note cards with a border or small image make perfect covers for computer-generated pages; some couples add their names, monograms, or any other information with a custom-made rubber stamp. There are stamps available with a single letter or image like a leaf or flower to embellish any hand-

made program. A single program can also be professionally calligraphed, then photocopied onto good paper. If binding pages together, search out the prettiest ribbon, even tassels and beads, at notions stores—and make sure the hole punch is small. Most important, proofread. Have one or two people who did not work on the program read over it carefully before hundreds are made.

There's no best time to complete the programs, but it's wise to set a deadline. Many a couple has been known to dash off to the copy shop the night before the wedding or to stay up until the wee hours tying tiny bows. It's best if the programs are ready at least two weeks in advance.

On the day of the wedding, have the ushers offer programs as they greet the guests, or assign the task to another friend or family member—this is an excellent way to include someone who is close to the bride and groom but not in the wedding party. Or, place a program on each seat or stack them in a tray or basket near the entrance. But don't forget to save a few for the wedding scrapbook. Years from now, this written record will stir as many memories as any photo.

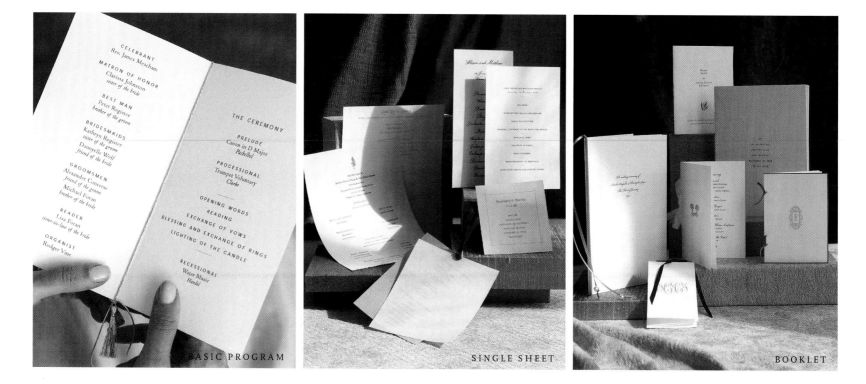

BASIC PROGRAM

SINGLE SHEET

BOOKLET

RECEPTION CARDS

Designing cards for a wedding reception can be an aesthetic tug-of-war. Should they be as formal as a wedding invitation or as personal as a thank-you note? The answer lies somewhere in the middle.

Wedding receptions traditionally call for three cards: the seating (or escort) card, which assigns a guest to his or her table; a place card, which indicates the chair in which he or she will sit; and a menu card, describing the meal.

History gives little indication of the origin of each card. Joy Lewis, owner of Mrs. John L. Strong Fine Stationery in New York City, says that the seating card was once called the gentleman's envelope. "A gentleman would discreetly open the envelope bearing his name to learn of his escort for the evening," she explains. "After slipping the envelope into his evening-suit pocket, he would introduce himself to this woman and ask to accompany her to dinner. It was his responsibility to entertain her throughout the party."

Place cards once followed a strict set of rules. In 1948, the *Vogue Book of Etiquette* decreed, "Like menu cards, place cards are made of heavy card, about two by two-and-three-quarters or three inches. They may be white or cream, but, if there are menu cards on the table, the place cards should be made of the same pasteboard. If the menu card has a beveled edge, silvered or gilded, the place card should also."

Today, without neglecting the importance of tradition, couples are freer to express their individuality through a range of original, beautiful ideas. Instead of the traditional monogram, symbolic motifs can be used to highlight the couple's cultural or ethnic heritage. Traditional calligraphy can be applied to unconventional cards; modern designs can be created with just a rubber stamp and a fountain pen. Computers have also lent a helpful hand to brides looking for less costly yet sophisticated results. With so many typefaces now available, it's easy to create something personal—a set of reception cards can be as unique as the couple getting married.

There remains, nonetheless, one basic rule: It's fine to mix and match, as long as the mixing matches. Maintaining unity in your choice of paper, colors, images, monograms, script, and typeface will tie the set together like a perfect knot.

SEATING CARDS are usually organized in alphabetical order on a table at the entrance. The cards may be folded so they stand up, or placed in an envelope for a more formal feeling. For large weddings, the card should give a person's full name; for smaller parties with less likelihood of confusion, a calligrapher may write first names only.

PLACE CARDS, though not required, help you influence the chemistry of each table. Possible flourishes include a beveled edge, a border, or an image. Wrap them around napkins, or set them behind or on a plate.

MENU CARDS may be engraved, printed, or calligraphed. A monogram or a motif is a powerful visual expression of unity.

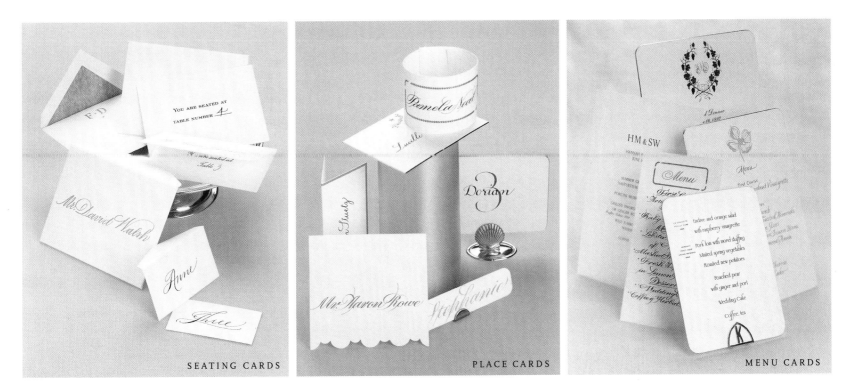

SEATING CARDS   PLACE CARDS   MENU CARDS

THANK-YOU CARDS

Nearly every aspect of planning a wedding tosses up one choice after another, so it may come as a relief to recognize that there is one custom no one has to debate: Every gift must be acknowledged with a personal, handwritten thank-you note. Preprinted or typed notes won't do. And even the most enthusiastic phone call, while it may be welcome, can't replace a written acknowledgment. If a bride receives one hundred gifts, she can plan to write that many notes.

Gifts will begin to arrive as soon as the engagement has been announced, so be prepared. A bride should think about what she wants her notes to say, both aesthetically and literally. The details deserve careful consideration: What kind of paper is appropriate? Whose initials or names go on the stationery? Who writes the notes? Who signs them? What, and how much, do you say? What is the acceptable time lapse between receiving a gift and sending a note expressing your gratitude?

Start with the foundation of a thank-you note—the paper. Selecting a style of writing paper has become simpler in recent years, according to Joy Lewis. "Handwritten correspondence has come to be used for ceremony and presentation only—thanking and inviting," she says. "Otherwise everyone uses the computer or the telephone." There are two common formats for thank-you notes: a stiff five-by-seven-inch card on which the correspondent can write on both sides, or an "informal," a small fold-over card typically about four by five inches. The informal may be engraved quite formally; its name comes from the placement of the fold at the top, in contrast to formal correspondence, such as wedding invitations, which fold at the side like a book.

Some couples order their writing papers at the same time as their wedding invitations, and, in the interest of establishing a style, carry through the same typeface and colors. Others treat thank-you notes as an entirely separate opportunity to exercise either formality or whimsy, and choose writing paper that's in deliberate contrast to the invitations. The most traditional colors are ecru and white, but lively color combinations for

thank-you notes can be chosen as long as the writing can be read clearly against the background.

If a bride is going to change her name, a couple should order one set of writing paper to use before the wedding and another to be used after. The prenuptial paper might carry the bride's maiden name or initials, both of their first names, or both sets of initials—but it's too soon to use a combined monogram. Engagement-phase envelopes should be printed or handwritten with the bride's return address. The paper for notes written after the couple is married traditionally bears either the wife's married monogram, her formal name (Mrs. John Smith), or the proper way in which she and her husband will be addressed (Mr. and Mrs. John Smith).

These traditional styles won't suit couples who prefer a more informal approach. For them, one option is to head the paper with the husband's and wife's first and last names. It doesn't matter whose name comes first, although Lewis says that traditionally a woman's name was placed second to reflect the quaint idea that a wife was protected when flanked by her husband's first and last names. A monogram can also be created that blends a couple's initials. A bride who plans to keep her maiden name can order paper that is headed by both hers and her husband's full names, stacked one above the other—again, there is no rule as to which comes first. Or names and monograms can be left out, and a favorite wedding photograph can be incorporated into a keepsake thank-you note.

The right paper and pen—blue or black ink—will make thank-you notes beautiful, but it's what is written that will make them meaningful. Before they are composed, however, make sure all of the facts are at hand. Establish a system to keep track of all the presents and who gave what and when. It does not have to be complicated: Make a computerized or handwritten list. This information can also be compiled on index cards and filed away. For those who tend to be more ceremonial, the gift cards can be annotated with the specifics, then stashed in a box or pasted in an album next to a snapshot of the gift.

The next step is to determine who will write the notes and who will sign them. Often the answer is that the bride will write some and the groom others, although this is a recent development: Brides used to write them all. That is partly because at one time gifts were considered to be the property of the bride. This custom is a vestige of a social order in which a woman might not have had much, if anything else, that belonged to her. When the economic status of women changed, wedding gifts became the property of both the bride and groom, and either or both can express their thanks.

To make it clear that whoever is writing is representing the bride and groom, say, for example, "John and I were delighted to receive…" then sign the letter, "Bonnie." Sometimes it's easier to split up the list according to the people the bride and groom know better, especially since there may be a few guests only one has met at the wedding. Thank-you notes can also be written by starting with, "We would like to thank you…" Only one person should do the actual writing, but as coauthors, the bride and groom should each sign in their own handwriting. The sign-off will indicate the degree of intimacy: The least intimate is "Sincerely"; after that comes some variation of "With affection," and finally, "Love."

The matter of to whom the note is addressed has also changed in recent years. A while back, thank-you notes were written from the bride to the wife of a couple. Now, it's more customary to write to both the husband and wife. Some couples prefer to do it the way their grandmothers did, though, and address the note to the wife; her husband's name, however, should also be included somewhere in the note.

There's no need to say too much after the salutation (which is always followed by a comma, not a colon, in handwritten letters); a four-sentence note can be plenty. But whatever is written, it should be personal and reflect the relationship with the giver and the nature of the gift. Points that should be included are a specific mention of the gift ("the Victorian dessert plates"), why they are meaningful ("because I enjoy setting a

CLASSIC

CONTEMPORARY

EMBELLISHED

STAMPED AND EMBOSSED

CLASSIC For the most formal thank-you cards, names or monograms are printed in black ink on white or ecru paper. The writing papers (top and bottom left) are engraved with the most traditional typestyles; the lined envelope (top) is a modern trend for informals. Under a feather emblem (center right), a bride and groom's first initials are engraved and centered above their last initial; this monogramming style was popular on eighteenth-century silverware. An ornate monogram (bottom right) is centered on a bordered informal. A bride and groom stack their names (center left), a good device for notes written during the engagement and for a bride who will keep her maiden name.

CONTEMPORARY As an alternative to formal thank-yous, paper can be trimmed with bold-colored borders, engraved with nontraditional typestyles, or embossed with whimsical emblems. An informal (top left) is embossed with a single initial. The fine quality of the lined envelope and bordered card (bottom left) compensates for it not being personalized. A couple's names are letterpressed in green ink (top right). A bee emblem (center right) separates the bride and groom's embossed initials. An informal (bottom right) is decorated with a pear.

EMBELLISHED To customize any paper, names and initials can be combined with simple details and personal touches. A wheat emblem (far right) is printed above a bride's initials on a fold-over note (right). A bride has enclosed petals from her bouquet (center). A simple leaf motif (left) is printed above the bride's and groom's names; this note was created on a computer.

STAMPED AND EMBOSSED An economical way to customize packaged paper is by having an embosser or rubber stamp made. The his-and-hers monogram embossed on blue deckle-edged paper (top left) and the rubber stamps for two couples (bottom) were made from custom calligraphy. A heart is embossed on the front of a rose-toned card (center); another heart on the envelope links the unmatched papers.

table with different china for each course"), and they will be used ("for our first annual holiday dessert party" and "we hope you'll be there!"). The words "thank you" usually go in the first sentence, although they can stand on their own at the end of the note.

How long is too long to wait before writing a thank-you note? Two months after you've returned from the wedding trip should be plenty of time to get the job done; three months is the maximum. For gifts arriving before the wedding, getting notes out as soon as they are received is usually easier than waiting until after the

event; since gifts do not come all at once, a couple of notes can be written a day to cover the recent arrivals. Occasionally, a bride and groom will receive hundreds of gifts and will not be able to write all the notes promptly, so they order printed acknowledgments that can be sent out stating that a personal note will follow.

When the backlog of notes piles up and begins to seem like an insurmountable task, it helps to remember that friends and relatives spent considerably more time selecting each gift than it takes to express the pleasure of their thoughtfulness.

{ SEATING }   { PROCESSION }   { CEREMONY }   { RECESSION }

Planning the Ceremony

She thought she'd thought of everything. They had the rings, the readings, and the programs; the ushers knew where to seat the guests, and her bridesmaids knew where to stand. They'd chosen the music for the ceremony—but hadn't told the musician exactly when to play it. So as the bridesmaids waited for their cue to start down the aisle, the opening notes to "Autumn" from Vivaldi's *The Four Seasons,* they were surprised to hear instead the unmistakable "Bridal Chorus" by Wagner—also known as "Here Comes the Bride." There was nothing to do but shove the first startled bridesmaid on her way.

Most likely, no one noticed. But a bride doesn't like surprises. The key to avoiding them is careful planning, starting early in the engagement with the basics: Where and when will you get married? Who will officiate? These decisions are personal ones, which depend on your religious beliefs as well as on the feeling you want for the entire wedding.

Consider the possibilities: When Janet Parker, an art director, was planning her marriage to Neal Hirschfeld, a screenwriter, they wanted "a simple wedding, a really nice party with a minimal ceremony," she says. They were married by a judge at a riverfront restaurant in New York City, where they also held the reception. For Mary Beth Griffith, an actress and dancer, and Peter Benson, an actor, "the ceremony was more important," she says. "When we picked the chapel at Smith College, we had no idea where we'd have the party."

A wedding ceremony can take place in a church, synagogue, hotel, or museum; at home, on the beach, on a mountaintop, or in a park; a minister, priest, rabbi, mayor, judge, justice of the peace, or county clerk can officiate. Don't make any plans until the elements of the ceremony have been discussed, especially religious requirements, with the prospective officiant. For example, the bride and groom may need to join a church's congregation or attend counseling before the wedding.

Jewish ceremonies can't be held on certain days of the year, including the Sabbath (Saturday weddings must take place after sundown) and holy days. An interfaith couple planning a religious ceremony may need to make special arrangements. And if a couple plans to diverge from tradition by writing their own vows, incorporating ethnic customs, or including children from previous marriages, they should confirm that the officiant is amenable. A couple should feel comfortable with the person performing your ceremony; if for any reason they do not, they should look for someone else. Make sure both the site and the officiant are available before booking either; have a backup date or two in mind.

Once there are answers to where, when, and who, there are many more questions for the officiant: Is another wedding taking place on the same day? Are there any fees? Does the house musician have to be used? Are there restrictions on music? How about photography? Can the site be decorated? Can guests throw birdseed or flower petals? Is there a place to dress? What time can the wedding party arrive? The officiant may also be familiar with state requirements concerning the marriage license; if not, call the local city hall. If a couple is not marrying in a house of worship, they can consult the contact at the site for answers to these questions.

The ceremony itself varies from religion to religion, and it is important to meet with the officiant to go over the way he usually performs it and discuss any modifications that must be made. For their wedding in Rockville, Maryland, Nanci Grossman, a mental-health therapist, and Gary Feldman, a podiatrist, "wanted a traditional Jewish ceremony," she says, "but we also wanted it to be gender equal." This meant changing the wording of "man and wife" to "husband and wife." Another common alteration is to change "love, honor, and obey" to "love, honor, and cherish."

Griffith and Benson wrote their own vows. "We wanted to put them into our own words," she says. Although this can be a lovely way to personalize the ceremony, there are a few things to keep in mind. Vows may include personal references, but they should sound timeless, never cute or silly. Imagine reading the vows twenty years from now; if they would sound dated or at all embarrassing, keep working on them. Don't make vows too long, and practice reading them aloud. A couple should have a copy with them for the ceremony, even if they've been memorized, and make sure the officiant has a copy. Don't feel pressured to write the wedding vows. As the judge who performed Parker's ceremony told her, "People have said these words for many, many years. You probably won't improve upon them."

There are often better ways to personalize a ceremony. A reading of poetry or prayer can allow the involvement of a special friend or relative. The bride may be escorted down the aisle by both parents—the custom in Jewish ceremonies—and the groom may also enter with his parents. Some couples light a unity candle to symbolize the joining of two families: At the start of the ceremony the bride's parents and the groom's parents each light a candle on either side of the altar;

at the end of the ceremony the bride and groom use the candles to light a single larger one in the center.

Parker and Hirschfeld added the Jewish custom in which the groom breaks a glass under his heel to their civil ceremony; it was a nod to his religion, and she liked this powerful ritual as the signal of the ceremony's close. Griffith, who holds a master's degree in liturgical dance, and Benson created a ceremony to reflect their interests and beliefs: She choreographed prayers into dance, and they incorporated Lutheran (his religion) customs into the Catholic (her religion) service, which was performed by three officiants; his sister Emily sang a Swedish song to celebrate his family's background.

As the plans for the ceremony are being made, remember that it will be set to music, which establishes the tone from the moment the first guest arrives until the bride and groom make their triumphant trip back up the aisle. The house organist, hired musicians, or members of the reception band can be asked to play. Ceremony music is generally classical, but modern songs may also be included. Discuss specifics with the musicians and officiant, choosing music for the following categories: prelude, processional, ceremony, recessional, and postlude. (For suggestions, see page 230.)

The prelude is the music played as guests arrive and are seated; it can be uplifting or solemn. After the mother of the bride takes her place, the processional begins, starting with a song that accompanies the bridal party down the aisle; after a brief pause a new song begins, and the bride makes her entrance to a suitably majestic piece. Music during the ceremony, often hymns or solos, is optional. The recessional is the celebratory music that begins as soon as the ceremony ends. The postlude maintains the joyous mood as the guests spill out and go to the receiving line.

Even if a couple has been to dozens of weddings, a rehearsal is crucial. It helps everyone feel at ease. Without it, questions will arise in the moments leading up to the ceremony, causing chaos. It should take place at the wedding site and is usually scheduled for the evening before the wedding, to be followed by

the rehearsal dinner. Anyone who has a role in the ceremony should attend; this includes the entire wedding party, officiant, readers, parents, and musicians; if someone can't be there, make sure he or she is briefed before the ceremony. At the rehearsal, walk through the entire ceremony twice. Establish pace and timing, and make sure the participants know their responsibilities. The illustrations and captions on the following pages provide guidelines for the traditional seating arrangements, procession, ceremony, and recession; your officiant should also be able to guide you. Some couples may choose to choreograph the ceremony in a new way. There's no rule that says the bride's guests must sit on one side and the groom's on the other.

Programs for the ceremony are optional, but they're helpful for the guests—"Oh! That's the groom's brother!"—and a keepsake for the scrapbook. They should include the wedding date and place; names of the bride, groom, officiant, wedding-party members, parents, and anyone else with a role in the ceremony; the titles of readings (and words if you wish); and music. They may also explain any rituals or traditions, remember deceased family or friends with a few words, and thank the bride and groom's parents.

When a bride wakes up on her wedding day, it's time to enjoy herself. She should relinquish her role as planner, and start being the bride. Some brides hire a bridal consultant to oversee things. Or they can ask the help of someone other than their mother, someone who's not as emotionally involved. An aunt, cousin, or family friend is a good choice; she can meet the catering coordinator, florist, and bandleader, answer their questions, and pay anyone who needs to be paid, so the bride and groom won't have to attend to such details.

But even the most organized bride can't anticipate everything. The flower girl could have a tantrum, or the officiant could get stuck in a traffic jam. Though they may seem like it at the time, these are not crises, not even close. Be flexible, focused, and relaxed. Remember, no matter what little surprises pop up, the end result will be the same: She will be married. ❧

THE FIRST ROWS *At a traditional, formal Christian wedding or a large civil ceremony, the bride's family and friends are seated on the left, the groom's on the right. Mark off the first few rows with flowers or ribbon as seating for immediate family and special guests (such as the flower girl's and ring bearer's parents, someone giving a reading, and close relatives). Divorced parents may sit together in the front row; if they are remarried or not on good terms, the father and his wife should sit in the third row. Ushers seat guests as they arrive, from front to back; the final guests to be seated are, in this order: grandparents, mother of the groom (with father walking behind), and mother of the bride. At a traditional, formal Jewish wedding, the bride's side is the right, the groom's, the left. The parents stand under the huppah during the ceremony; if parents are divorced, stepparents may sit in the aisle seats in the second and third rows or stand under the huppah if they are very close to the bride or groom.*

SEATING

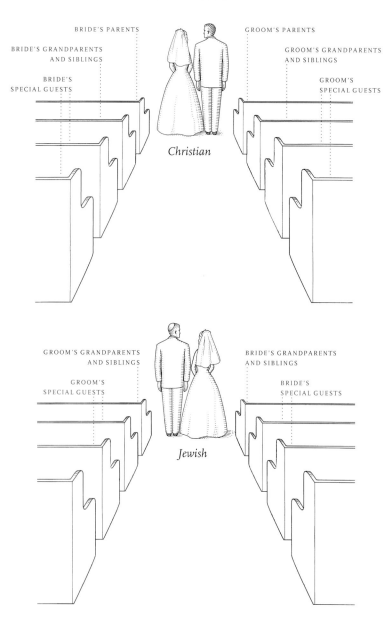

Christian

Jewish

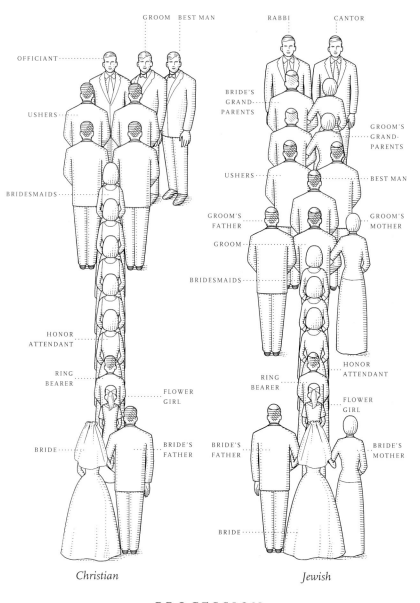

Christian

Jewish

PROCESSION

DOWN THE AISLE *Just before the procession begins in a Christian ceremony, the officiant takes his or her place, with the groom to the left, and the best man to his left, facing the guests. The ushers may stand at the front, or they may start the procession as shown here, walking in pairs. They are followed by the bridesmaids. The honor attendant enters next. As another option, the ushers and bridesmaids can enter together, in pairs, with the best man and honor attendant following. If a ring bearer and a flower girl participate, they are the last ones down the aisle before the bride, who is escorted by her father, on his left arm. Today a bride often asks her mother to walk on her other side. In a Jewish ceremony, grandparents, the groom's parents, and the bride's mother all join the procession. It is often led by the rabbi and the cantor, who sings the prayers during the service, but they may also enter from the side and await the others at the huppah. For any ceremony it is customary for the ushers and bridesmaids to be arranged in order of height, with the shortest attendants entering first.*

CEREMONY

THE FORMATIONS *In a Christian ceremony, as the ushers reach the altar, they usually form a diagonal line, with the first usher taking his place farthest from the groom. Bridesmaids do the same on the bride's side. The flower girl and ring bearer stand in front of the bridesmaids and ushers. When the bride reaches the altar, her honor attendant, the groom, and the best man turn toward the officiant. Alternatively, the bride and groom can face the guests, so the officiant has his back to the guests; or the honor attendant and best man can join the lines of bridesmaids and ushers, with the bride and groom standing on either side of the officiant, facing each other. As they reach the huppah in a Jewish ceremony, ushers and bridesmaids form diagonal lines from the front poles or simply gather around the huppah; the honor attendant and best man stand next to the bride and groom under the huppah, or outside it, with the bridesmaids and ushers. The bride's and groom's parents stand under the huppah as well. Small children can get fidgety during even the simplest ceremony, so it is perfectly acceptable for them to join their parents or take a seat on the altar once the ceremony has begun.*

Christian

Jewish

Christian

Jewish

RECESSION

JUST MARRIED *In a Christian ceremony, as the musicians start the celebratory recessional music, the bride and groom turn to each other, link arms, and walk briskly back up the aisle as husband and wife. They are followed by the rest of the wedding party, also in pairs, with the women on the men's right arms. The flower girl and the ring bearer (if they remained at the altar during the ceremony) come first (if there's only one or the other, he or she can walk alone), then the honor attendant and the best man, then the bridesmaids and ushers. Ushers can return to assist guests and direct them to the receiving line or reception site. In a Jewish ceremony, after the newlyweds come the bride's parents, then the groom's parents, the flower girl and the ring bearer, the honor attendant and the best man, and the bridesmaids and ushers; all are arm in arm, with the women on the men's left arms. Immediately following the ceremony, the bride and groom often take ten or fifteen minutes to themselves in yichud, the symbolic consummation of the marriage. During this time they can duck into a private room, where they may have something to eat (breaking the wedding-day fast) and reflect on their marriage. When they join their guests, they are announced as husband and wife and are greeted joyously.*

{ THE CEREMONY }
*Congratulations! You
are married, and the party is
about to begin.*

{ THE RECEIVING LINE }
*Couples today often forgo
this tradition, but it is the one
sure way to greet each guest.*

{ FORMAL PORTRAITS }
*Before joining the guests at
the reception, the wedding party has
their pictures taken.*

{ COCKTAIL HOUR }
*The first chance for everyone
to mix and mingle, to preview
the style of your party.*

Planning the Reception

Those few simple words—"I now pronounce you husband and wife"—are magical in more ways than one. As soon as you hear them, everything is beautiful. You are married. The months of planning are over, and for the rest of this glorious day a couple's only duties include mingling with friends and family, enjoying specially prepared food, dancing with each other, and feeling woozy with joy.

A wedding reception, after all, is simply a big party in honor of the bride and groom. Every one is as individual as the newlyweds, though most receptions follow a traditional timetable. Sticking to the schedule is important, but thankfully, not the bride and groom's responsibility. This job is better left to a professional—a bridal consultant, catering manager, or maître d'—who helps establish the schedule in the first place. (For a do-it-yourself wedding, assign a responsible friend or relative to the task.) For each wedding she works on, Elizabeth K. Allen, owner of

Elizabeth Allen Event Planning in New York City, maps out every detail of the day, including what time the flowers arrive, when the bridesmaids have their hair and makeup done, when the couple will have their portrait taken, when the best man will make his toast, and when the bride throws her bouquet.

If a couple isn't working with a bridal consultant, Allen suggests that they make a timetable themselves: At least a week before the wedding, sit down with the catering manager or maître d' and, if possible, the band leader, and go over the timing of everything. Type up the plan, and include any relevant contact names and numbers. Make sure each vendor has a copy, and give one to members of the wedding party; they will appreciate a written reminder of where they're supposed to be and when.

The schedule helps prevent confusion on the wedding day and helps the event run smoothly. "We've all been to those weddings where there are

huge gaps and lulls—and they are painful," says Allen. But it's also important, she says, that no one lives by the timetable. "You plan as much as you can," she says, "but there are human factors that have to be taken into consideration." So if it's 8:01 and the salad has yet to be served, don't panic. The maître d' may have asked the kitchen to hold off because the guests were still enjoying the cocktail hour or having such a good time on the dance floor. Trust the people who manage the event to communicate with each other, to read the energy in the room, and to keep things running smoothly.

So what, exactly, is the sequence of events? Following are guidelines for a dinner-dance reception preceded by a cocktail hour. The most formal and elaborate type of party, this usually lasts a total of five hours; a buffet, breakfast, lunch, tea, or cocktail reception is likely to be shorter and perhaps not as structured. But the elements remain the same;

{ DINNER }
*Guests collect their
table cards and find their places
in the dining room.*

{ THE FIRST DANCE }
*The bride and groom
glide across the dance floor to
their special song.*

{ THE TOASTS }
*The best man raises his
glass, and often the newlyweds
say a few words, too.*

{ CUTTING THE CAKE }
*With his hand over hers, the
newlyweds slice the cake together,
then share the first piece.*

regardless of the level of formality, most couples do include those familiar rituals—the first dance, the best man's toast, cutting the cake—that make weddings so wonderful.

As soon as the ceremony is over, the reception can take one of many directions: The wedding party and immediate family can assemble for photographs, if they had not been taken before. At many Jewish weddings, photographs are taken before the ceremony so that immediately after the bride and groom can duck into a private room, called a yichud, for a few minutes (ten or fifteen) in the symbolic consummation of marriage. "I even suggest this to my non-Jewish clients," says Mindy Weiss, of Mindy Weiss Party Consultants in Beverly Hills, California. "Breathe, smooch a little, have something to eat," she says.

The receiving line, if a couple chooses to honor the tradition of welcoming the guests in this way, can take place either directly following the ceremony or as the cocktail hour begins at the reception site, whichever is more convenient. But many couples are forgoing this practice. "Who wants to stand in a line for half an hour?" says Allen. "It's a lot of work for the bride and groom, and during the course of the evening, they will get to almost everyone." If there is a receiving line, the proper order is as follows: mother of the bride (first to greet the guests), mother of the groom, bride, groom, bride's honor attendant, and sometimes the best man and bridesmaids. Fathers often circulate with the guests, but they may join their wives in the receiving line. The attendants can be relieved of receiving-line duty. A couple should expect to spend between thirty minutes and an hour greeting everyone, depending on the number of guests, the number of people in the line, and the amount of visiting and chatting that takes place (which should be minimal; keep each interaction short and sweet).

At this point, either everyone is just making his way to the reception site or the cocktail hour is in full swing. Hors d'oeuvres are passed, and bars are open; the cocktail hour—anywhere from forty-five to ninety minutes—usually takes place in a separate area from the dining room, so that when those doors are thrown open, the beautifully set tables make a real impact. If a couple wants to be announced upon their entrance ("nine out of ten couples do," says Weiss), they'll wait outside the dining room while everyone else finds his or her seat. The band leader often does the announcing, but Allen has a charming suggestion: Since the bride's father (or parents) often welcomes the guests early in the evening, he can do so now, and introduce his daughter and new son-in-law at the same time.

As soon as the bride and groom make their grand entrance, they'll go straight to the dance floor for

{ TOSSING THE BOUQUET }
*When the bride parts with
her bouquet, the one who catches it
is said to be the next to marry.*

{ GOING AWAY }
*The newlyweds depart,
the guests wish them farewell, and
the party winds down.*

their first dance (some people prefer to wait until after the first course, or even until the end of the meal). After the first dance, the band will change songs to introduce the customary sequence of dances: The father of the bride cuts in and dances with his daughter while the groom dances with his mother; then the bride dances with the groom's father and the groom with the bride's mother; then the bride dances with the best man and the groom with the honor attendant; finally, all of the guests join you on the dance floor. "They've had the cocktails and hors d'oeuvres," says Weiss, "so we want them to get hungry again."

After this dance set, everyone is seated for the first course. The clergy member, a parent, or close family friend may say a blessing before the meal. At some receptions, guests dance between the courses. At others, the meal progresses straight from one course to another, followed by dancing (the time

allotted for the meal itself will vary). How structured these components are is largely up to the bride and groom, though the reception site itself may have an influence: If the dance floor is in another room, it makes sense to eat first, and dance later.

Toasts are another ritual that can take place one after the other, or one during each course. Just make sure that each speaker knows when his or her turn will be. The best man can make his toast during the first or second course, although some couples time the toast to take place just before the cake-cutting. According to Joseph Prezioso, director of banquet services at the St. Regis Hotel in New York City, "The best man is brought to the bride and groom, with the cake as a focal point. It's lovely." And it makes for great pictures.

If the father of the bride hasn't already welcomed the guests, he will usually also make a toast at some point during the meal. More and more, the bride

and groom are saying a few words as well. Other guests may want to make a toast, too, but plan (yes, wedding toasts are planned) accordingly, keep in mind that too many toasts can slow the evening down. The rehearsal dinner, which is a more intimate gathering, is generally a better time for all the kind words and funny stories from old friends.

The cake can be cut with all the guests still seated, or everyone can get up and dance, then gather around the cake closer to the end of the evening. To cut the cake, the groom places his hand over the bride's, and they cut one slice from the bottom layer. Feed each other from this single slice with your fingers, while the rest of the cake is whisked away to be cut into servings for the guests.

More dancing follows, with the band playing the fastest music yet. Thirty minutes before the reception is scheduled to end, the unmarried women assemble to vie for the bride's bouquet, as she tosses it over her shoulder. Some brides consider this and the garter toss, which would come next, too old-fashioned and don't participate in either ritual.

Near the end of the evening, if the party is heating up instead of cooling down, you can keep it going, but there will be some additional costs, including the band's extra sets (Allen recommends that overtime sets be in thirty-minute increments, not hourly ones), fees for the wait staff and bar, and perhaps a charge for the site, if it was booked on an hourly basis. All of these rates should be discussed beforehand and written into the contracts. But don't prolong the party if there are just a few guests out on the dance floor. "Most people like to end on a high note," says Prezioso, "to keep the memory of the excitement."

While the guests continue to dance, the bride and groom can slip out to change into their going-away clothes. Or they may want to prolong the magic of the day and stay clad in their wedding attire as they are given a joyous send-off by friends and family, and embark on their next adventure together.

TENT TYPES

{ PUSH-POLE TENT }
*The classic wedding tent,
this familiar style has a soft,
billowy silhouette.*

{ TENSION TENT }
*The tallest and most dramatic of
the three types, this tent has fewer interior
poles than the push-pole tent.*

{ FRAME TENT }
*This structure can fit in tight
spaces because it needs no clearance for
stabilizing ropes and stakes.*

Tents

Wedding tents are as American as can be. They're all about freedom: namely, the freedom to have a wedding where, when, and how a couple wants it. A wedding at home is appealing for many, but without the added room that tents provide, it might not be an option. Historic sites, public gardens, and parks are also popular places for weddings, often thanks to tents.

When people think about tents, the first thing that comes to mind is protection from the elements: the rain, cold, heat, and, sun. Indeed, if you could guarantee ideal conditions for your wedding day, the most compelling reason for having a tent would vanish since you wouldn't have to worry about where your guests would go if the weather took a turn for the worse. But practicality is just one of the reasons to have a tent.

Tents allow you to decorate as you choose, without having to work around a room's size, shape, features, and colors. "A tent is an empty canvas," says Preston Bailey, an event designer in New York City. "You

can transform it into an elaborately decorated space or do something more simple." And tents give you flexibility. As Christopher Robbins of Robbins-Wolfe Eventeurs in New York City says, "You're not limited by what a restaurant or hotel does. When you have a wedding under a tent, you can choose the caterer who will create just the menu you want. Wines and liquors can be much less expensive, too, since you're not paying hotel prices for them."

Most important, tents allow guests to enjoy the surroundings—beautiful gardens, stunning views, or sentimental settings like a backyard from the bride's childhood—which is why the majority of tent weddings could be more accurately described as garden weddings. Usually at such weddings, the ceremony is performed and cocktails are served outside the tent, which is used primarily as a place to dine and dance when the sun goes down; secondarily, it functions as emergency protection from unexpected rain. A

backup tent is also a good idea to consider; if the weather turns foul, the ceremony can be held in the dining tent, guests can move to the second tent for cocktails, and then go back to the dining tent once the tables and chairs have been set up.

If a couple is thinking about having a tent wedding, they should ask their caterer or event planner to refer them to tent-rental companies in their area. In initial phone calls, ask each company about its business practices. "Any tent company should carry liability insurance," says Jane Frost of Stamford Tent & Party Rental in Stamford, Connecticut, "and an installer should remain at the event to make adjustments, like putting up or taking down sidewalls [the tent flaps], especially if you're using multiple tents." To get an idea of the size of a company's operation, ask how many events it typically services in the busiest months: May, June, September, and October. The tents should be certified as flame-retardant, and the company should be willing to find out which permits and notices are required in your area. It's not a good idea to shrug off permits. "You run the risk of the building inspector shutting down your wedding," Frost says.

Any reputable company should arrange for a site inspection to give you an idea of what can be done and at what cost. "Most companies offer inspections at no charge and with no obligation," says Chris Starr of Starr Tents in Mount Vernon, New York. "We insist on inspecting the site before making a proposal." An experienced installer can spot situations that might raise the cost. Ground that looks flat enough for tables and chairs, for instance, might in fact be sloped; leveling it with flooring may be the only solution and could end up being expensive. "People often have an idea of where they want to put the tents," Frost says. "We discuss how the tents will fit into the setting and how people will move between them." Finally, ask the tent company to bring photographs of previous jobs, site plans they have drawn up, and references.

The tent company will want to know the number of people attending your wedding, whether you'll have buffet or sit-down service, and whether you'll have a band or a deejay. Formulas based on these factors determine the size of the tent—a seated dinner with danc-ing, for instance, would need about eighteen square feet per person. Some companies will let you set up contingency plans for more tents in case it rains. A kitchen tent is something else to consider; according to Robbins, it should be close enough to the dining tent that servers won't spend more time walking back and forth than they do serving. In the most elaborate setups, says Bailey, "people put up one tent for the ceremony, one for cocktails, and one for dinner and dancing. They want each space to have a distinct feel."

The kind of tent you choose is important in terms of cost and visual appeal. There are three major varieties: the push-pole tent, the tension tent, and the frame tent. The push-pole tent is the most common and familiar: The ceiling slopes gently downward from a row of tall center poles to a shorter set of poles called quarter poles, then out to the perimeter poles. From the outside, the tent's undulations have a soft, gentle look. This tent is usually the least expensive to rent.

The tension tent is newer, not as common, and slightly more costly to rent. "Because of the height of the center poles," says Frost, "the tension tent has a severe slope in the ceiling and a more open feeling in-side." A tension tent needs fewer interior poles than a push-pole tent, which simplifies the arrangement of tables and chairs. According to Frost, tension tents are the most stable of the three varieties in high winds.

The final variety, the frame tent, is ideal for tight spots; it needs no clearance around its sides, whereas the push-pole and tension tents need at least seven feet. Like the push-pole and tension tents, the frame tent can cover an area of almost any size. But only the frame tent can be as narrow as ten feet wide, so it's the best way to cover long, narrow areas connecting more than one tent or to form an entrance. Another advantage of the frame tent is that it has no interior poles. This tent is often more expensive than the other two, largely be-cause constructing it is more complicated. In contrast to the other types, which get their support from interi-or poles, the frame tent utilizes a complex structure of horizontal poles below the ceiling. (Decorators can conceal the framework with a canvas false ceiling.)

After determining the style of tent best suited to your wedding, the next decision concerns flooring. A floor prevents guests from walking on soft, uneven, or soggy ground. Because floors are an added expense, many people put in only a dance floor; others choose none at all. But if your wedding is in a month with high rainfall or if the tent will be erected on low ground, it's a worthwhile investment.

CEILINGS

{ PUSH-POLE CEILING }

*Tall center poles give height
to this ceiling and bring a sense
of space to the interior.*

{ FRAME CEILING }

*An elaborate framework
of poles supports the ceiling
of a frame tent.*

FLOORS

{ DANCE FLOOR }

*If you want grass under
your feet—and don't expect rain—
consider just a dance floor.*

{ FULL FLOOR }

*Almost any effect can be
created on a temporary tent floor,
including a ballroom pattern.*

The most desirable—and most expensive—choice is a plywood floor, which is laid over a custom-built subfloor that closely resembles the framing beneath the floor of a house. Plywood flooring requires a considerable amount of labor, but it will provide a sturdy raised floor over terrain of almost any type. Be sure entrance areas and steps are constructed for raised floors. Some people even build a variation of this floor over a pool if they have no other large area on their property for their party. The plywood can be painted in geometric or floral designs to carry out a decorative motif, or laid over with sod, or covered with artificial turf or carpeting.

For flat surfaces, especially paved ones (like tennis courts, driveways, or parking areas), a rigid plastic floor can be laid on top of the surface at roughly half the cost of plywood. A parquet-wood floor, assembled in sections, can be a dance floor. Artificial turf rolled right over the ground is the least expensive option, but it will not keep feet dry when it rains.

Sidewalls give further protection from wind, rain, and, if necessary, prying eyes. Sidewalls can be solid white for privacy, clear vinyl to let in light and the warmth of the sun, or cathedral-window walls, which are a more decorative option and also allow light in. The entire ceiling of the tent can be made of clear vinyl to bring the night sky a little closer, but it is suitable only for night weddings, since they don't offer protection from the sun and can become very hot during the day. "For winter or cold-weather events, doors are a nice option," Frost says. Heaters and air conditioners can also be used, which brings up the issue of facilities.

Both on the day of the site inspection and in the following months, the tent company should discuss any additional facilities needed to handle rest-room, electrical, and food-preparation requirements. A tent needs basic lighting and perhaps air conditioners or heaters; generators or natural gas will be necessary to power any of these. Most tent companies can provide whatever equipment is necessary. Caterers, however, usually prefer to handle the rentals of everything related to preparing and serving the food. They then pass the bill on to the couple. "Facilities might be coming from several vendors," Starr says, "so I sit down with everyone thirty to forty-five days before the event to make sure all of our schedules coordinate."

A tent company can also evaluate the adequacy of the bathrooms in a private home or any wedding site. Portable rest rooms are an option if plumbing is limited or nonexistent, or if the host doesn't want guests in the house. The most aesthetically pleasing and most expensive option is the mobile rest room with men's and women's rooms, each with tiled floors and walls, mirrors, washrooms, and private stalls. Also available are portable, free-standing rest rooms that, unlike the ones at construction sites, have flush toilets and sinks.

Once the tent requirements are determined, see how they fit into the wedding budget. Tent-rental prices vary by region, but in the Northeast, a basic fifty-by-seventy-five-foot tent that accommodates up to two hundred people could run from $6,000 to $10,000, which includes lighting, flooring, and the cost of delivery, setup, and removal. (Eliminate the extras, and the cost may be as little as $3,000.) Add a twenty-square-foot kitchen tent, and the cost increases by another few hundred dollars. And don't count on squeezing in a few extra guests beyond a tent's capacity. A dozen extra people could force a substantial leap in tent size and significantly increase costs, so take the guest count seriously.

How does the cost of a tent wedding fare against other options? According to Robbins, "If you compare it with a typical catering hall, a tent will be more expensive because you're renting everything. If you compare it with the best hotel in the area, the cost is about the same." And for a wedding that will bear a personal imprint, that could be a very good deal indeed.

WALLS

{ CATHEDRAL WINDOWS }

*To bring views inside,
clear vinyl windows are built
into some sidewalls.*

{ CLEAR SIDEWALLS }

*Vinyl sidewalls keep
warmth in and rain out without
obscuring the scenery.*

ENTRANCES

{ COVERED ENTRY }

*A small frame tent
appended to a larger tent creates
a formal entryway.*

{ STEPS }

*For a tent with raised
flooring over uneven terrain,
steps are a must for access.*

GRANDPARENT · BEST MAN · BRIDE · GROOM · HONOR ATTENDANT · GRANDPARENT

OFFICIANT · BRIDE'S MOTHER · GROOM'S FATHER · OFFICIANT'S SPOUSE · BRIDE'S FATHER · GROOM'S MOTHER

FAMILY TABLE

Seating

The last thing a bride and groom want to do on their wedding day is dictate to their guests how to have a good time. But telling them where to sit during the reception is more a favor than a command. "Not knowing where to sit makes people uncomfortable, and it is disrespectful of hosts to put them in that position," says John Loring, design director of Tiffany & Co. Historically, the seating plan at a wedding was designed to encourage comfortable conversation and to honor special guests. This still holds true today.

Naturally, the bride and groom will be the center of attention, and the people selected to sit with them will consider it a privilege. So the perfect place to begin is with the bride and groom. In most situations, the options will be: to sit at a traditional bride's table with the wedding party, to sit at a small table by themselves, or to sit with parents and selected relatives and friends.

Whatever the arrangement, one principle always applies: The bride and groom sit next to each other.

Since the newlyweds will circulate for much of the party, they'll want to be seated with people who will not be offended by their absences from the table; so even though the couple might think it would be a nice gesture to ask a widowed great-aunt to dine with them, it's best if they resist this urge. Instead, start with the following protocol, or a variation thereof.

At a traditional bride's table, the bride and groom are seated with their attendants, alternating men and women (see above). With larger wedding parties, sitting together is often not possible. "Because our wedding party couldn't fit at one table, we decided to seat just our bridesmaids and their dates with us," says Jennifer Butler, a lawyer who was married at the Boathouse Cafe in New York City's Central Park. "While most of the bridesmaids were childhood pals, the groomsmen didn't know each other well. Instead, we sat them at different tables with their dates and friends." For smaller wedding parties, the spouses or dates can be

seated at the bride's table. If there's no room, seat them together at a table in close proximity. At a second wedding, children of the bride and groom may be seated at the bride's table, or nearby with a relative.

In recent years, some couples have chosen to sit at a centrally located table for two. This romantic arrangement will guarantee that the newlyweds have some time alone. But it can also be off-putting to guests who may fear they'll interrupt an intimate moment.

Many couples find a table with their parents is a good way to ensure a few moments with family during a day that will be pulling everyone in different directions. Grandparents and siblings may also be seated at this table; some couples also include the best man and honor attendant as well as the officiant and the officiant's spouse.

Once it has been decided where the bride and groom will sit, the next focus should be on families' and parents' friends, advises Susan Holland, an event designer and caterer in New York City. "Friends will fall easily

USHER · BRIDESMAID · BEST MAN · BRIDE · GROOM · HONOR ATTENDANT · USHER · BRIDESMAID

BRIDE'S TABLE

BRIDE'S MOTHER · OFFICIANT · GROOM'S MOTHER · BRIDE'S FATHER

GROOM'S FATHER · OFFICIANT'S SPOUSE

PARENTS' TABLE

into tables, so they can be left for last." Since it is likely the bride and groom will not know every guest on their parents' lists, they should let their parents decide the placement of their friends and relatives.

Regardless of who is paying for the wedding, the bride's parents are considered the hosts. For this reason, being seated at the parents' table is thought of as a position of honor. There can be one parents' table, consisting of both sets of parents, or two tables, or more, depending on each family's situation. If the groom's parents are divorced, for instance, and not on good terms, it might be best to seat them separately. Just be sure to give both tables equal importance; one parent can sit with the bride's parents, the other parent with the officiant. The parents' table can be slightly larger than other guest tables and should be close to the bride's table.

When creating guest tables, there are a few guidelines that serve well. "Seat people with similar experiences and interests together," says Holland. Some

couples may even go all out and arrange the seating order of each table. Unlike a dinner party, where couples are often placed at different tables, there is a romantic nostalgia at weddings that makes most couples want to sit together. And although it's tempting to seat single guests all together at one table, this can be awkward. Instead, intersperse single guests among couples with, perhaps, one other single person seated at his or her side. Finally, it's best to seat children with their parents, but teenagers typically prefer a table all their own.

To communicate guests' table assignments, set out alphabetized table-number cards so guests can locate them easily, at least an hour before the reception. You could also have a waiter circulate during cocktails, handing guests their cards. A seating chart on display is also a lovely way to inform guests of their tables. One tip that's useful is to split the room in half, with even tables on one side, and odd numbers on the other. This way, wait staff can direct guests swiftly to their seats.

Typically, the bride's table is numbered "one" or left unnumbered. An extralush centerpiece or a display of the bridesmaids' bouquets will also help to distinguish it.

Practice some sensitivity with table placement: Family and close friends should not be clustered around the newlyweds, leaving other guests feeling excluded. Take into account any special needs of your guests, such as elderly people who may have difficulty seeing and hearing; seating them in well-lit areas, away from the noise of the band, will give them a better vantage point.

To visualize the seating arrangements, it's helpful to map out the floor plan on paper, with circles representing the tables and adhesive notes with each guest's name attached in the appropriate spot. You may want to group friends and relatives together. But unlike at the ceremony, where the couple's guests sit on opposite sides, the reception is a time for joining both families and their friends, and it is a meaningful gesture for the table arrangements to reflect this philosophy.

{ FOR THE CEREMONY }   { FOR THE RECEPTION }

Music

Choosing the music for a wedding can seem a daunting task. A couple is, after all, choosing the soundtrack for the most important day of their lives. The prospect can become less overwhelming if the music is thought of in terms of audio "snapshots": What favorite music should be played when guests arrive for the ceremony? What music will best capture the bride's many emotions as she walks down the aisle toward life with her future spouse? What music is most natural in the setting chosen for the reception, be it a ballroom, garden, country club, or mountaintop? Once a couple has a strong sense of the moods they want to create, selecting specific pieces becomes manageable.

The music must, of course, be considered in the context of the musical accompaniments chosen— the two go hand in hand. If, for example, the majestic sound of trumpets heralding the wedding ceremony is appealing, there is no need to research and consider all of the possible selections for the classical guitar. Fortunately, many beautiful melodies will transcend specific instrumentation, and a selection that is as timeless as "Embraceable You"or Vivaldi's "The Four Seasons" can be as beautifully represented by a harpist as by a jazz trio or big band.

If deciding what style of music best suits a wedding proves difficult, there is no need to panic. Weddings offer abundant opportunities to use many genres. Consider a musical menu such as this: several lovely selections by Bach, Albinoni, and Geminiani played by a string quartet, filling the church and arriving guests with a combination of welcome and reflection; a solemn but exquisite contemporary tune, such as Mark O'Connor's "Appalachia Waltz," as an unexpected, unique "here comes *this* bride" processional; a blend of classic and off-the-beaten-path standards played by a fine piano-bass jazz duo as the backdrop for cocktails and dinner; and for dancing, the classic songs of thirties tango star Carlos Gardel performed by an authentic tango quintet. Confusing? No, wonderful. Your wedding will last just one day, but if selected with thought, taste, and individual style, the music at this single celebration will linger for a lifetime.

The charts that follow break down the ceremony and reception into their most basic parts: the prelude, processional, interlude, and recessional for the ceremony and the cocktail hour, and first dance, dinner, and dancing for the reception. There are suggestions for songs from several musical genres that work very well in each. In total, there are more than 200 repertoire and song suggestions that combine many of the most popular wedding-music selections with more imaginative options that can help make every wedding unique. The categorization is not absolute, and suggestions in one category can often work perfectly well in another.

MUSIC FOR THE CEREMONY

{ TRADITIONAL }		{ TRADITIONAL ALTERNATIVES }		{ CONTEMPORARY }	
{ PRELUDE }					
Albinoni *Oboe Concerto in D Minor (Adagio)*	Handel *Water Music (Air)*	Bach *Lute Suite BWV 1006a in E Major (Gavotte en Rondeau)*	Francisque *Courante (from Three Lute Dances)*	Jim Brickman *Angel Eyes*	
Bach *Air on the G String*	Haydn Serenade *(from String Quartet Op. 3, No. 5)*	Bach *Sei Lob und Preis mit Ehren*	Handel *Concerto Grosso in D Major, Op. 3, No. 6 (Vivace)*	Jim Brickman *The Gift*	
Bach *Bist du bei mir*	Mozart *Ave Verum Corpus*	Bach *Violin Concerto No. 2 in E Major (Allegro assai)*	Marcello *Oboe Concerto in D*	Carolan's *Welcome Irish traditional*	
Bach *Jesu, Joy of Man's Desiring*	Schubert *Serenade*	Chopin *Nocturne in E Flat, Op. 9, No. 2*	Minor *(Adagio)*	Dan Fogelberg *Longer*	
Bach *Sinfonia (from Cantata No. 156)*		Debussy *Prelude to the Afternoon of a Faun*	Mozart *Sonata in E Flat (Adagio)*	Barbra Streisand *Evergreen (from "A Star Is Born")*	
Handel *Largo (from "Xerxes")*			Satie *Gymnopédie No. 1*		
{ PROCESSIONAL }					
Charpentier *Prelude to Te Deum*	Mozart *Wedding March (from "The Marriage of Figaro")*	Bach *Sinfonia (from Cantata No. 156)*	Mendelssohn *Sonatas for Organ, Op. 65, No. 3 (con moto maestoso)*	Gabriel's *Oboe (from "The Mission")*	Andy Statman *Flatbush Waltz*
Clarke *Trumpet Voluntary (Prince of Denmark's March)*	Pachelbel *Canon in D*	Couperin *Hymn Fanfare from The Triumphant*	Monteverdi *Toccata (from "L'Orefo")*	Jeremy Lubbock *The Vow*	Yo-Yo Ma, Edgar Meyer, Mark O'Connor *Appalachia Waltz*
Concerto in D Major (Largo)	Purcell *Trumpet Tune and Air*	Gabrieli *Canzon V*	Mussorgsky *Promenade (from Pictures at an Exhibition)*	*Procession (from "The Sweet Hereafter")*	
Handel *Water Music (Coro)*	Stanley *Trumpet Voluntary*	Handel *Royal Fireworks Music (Overture)*	Tchaikovsky *Coronation March for Czar Alexander III*		
Marcello *Psalm XIX*	Vivaldi *Guitar*	Haydn *St. Anthony's Chorale*	Vivaldi *The Four Seasons (Winter, Largo)*		
	Wagner *Bridal Chorus (from "Lohengrin")*				
{ INTERLUDE }					
Bach *Arioso*	CHRISTIAN	Bach *Erbame dich (from "St. Matthew's Passion")*	Massenet *Meditation (from "Thaïs")*	*All I Ask Of You (from "Phantom of the Opera")*	Paul Stookey *The Wedding Song*
Bach *Sheep May Safely Graze*	*All Things Bright and Beautiful*	Debussy *Clair de lune*	Offenbach *Barcarolle (from "Tales of Hoffman")*	Will Ackerman *Unconditional*	James Taylor *The Water Is Wide*
Bach-Gounod *Ave Maria*	*Joyful, Joyful, We Adore Thee*	Debussy *Rêverie*	Rachmaninoff *Vocalise*	*Amazing Grace traditional*	Tuck and Patti *Takes My Breath Away*
Fauré *Sanctus*	*Love Divine, All Love Excelling*	Delibes *Flower Duet (from "Lakme")*		Leonard Bernstein *A Simple Song*	
Franck *Panis Angelicus*	*O Perfect Love*	Elgar *Salut D'Amour*		Andrea Bocelli, Celine Dion *The Prayer*	
Gluck *Minuet, Melody (from "Orfeo ed Euriduce")*	*Simple Gifts*	Fauré *Pavane*		John Denver *Annie's Song*	
Handel *Let the Bright Seraphim*		Handel *Minuet (from "Berenice")*		Simon and Garfunkel *Benedictus*	
Handel *Where'er You Walk (from "Semele")*	JEWISH				
Schubert *Ave Maria*	*Dodi Li*				
Vaughan *Williams The Call*	*Erev Ba*				
	Jerusalem of Gold				
	Shalom Alechem				
	Yedid Nefefsh				
{ RECESSIONAL }					
Beethoven *Ode to Joy (from "Ninth Symphony")*	Mouret *Rondeau (theme from "Masterpiece Theatre")*	Bach *Badinerie (from Orchestral Suite No. 2)*	Grieg *Triumphal March*	The Beatles *The Long and Winding Road*	
Handel *The Arrival of the Queen of Sheba*	Purcell *Rondeau (from "Abdelezar")*	Bach *Brandenburg Concerto No. 1 (Allegro)*	Mozart *Exsultate, Jubilate*	Cole Porter *From This Moment On*	
Handel *La Rejouissancé (from "Royal Fireworks Music")*	Purcell *Trumpet Tune in C*	Bach *Brandenburg Concerto No. 4 (Allegro)*	Telemann *Air de Trompette*	George Winston *Joy*	
Handel *Water Music (Hornpipe)*	Walton *Coronation March*	*Camprá: Rigaudon*	Tartini *Sonata in G Major*	Suzanne Ciani *Anthem*	
Mendelssohn *Wedding March (from "Midsummer Night's Dream")*	Widor *Toccata*	*Concerto grosso in D Minor, Op. 2, No. 3 (Presto)*	Vivaldi *The Four Seasons (Spring, Allegro)*	Vince Guaraldi *Linus & Lucy ("Peanuts theme")*	
		Geminiani			

	{ STANDARDS }		{ CONTEMPORARY }		{ CLASSICAL/OTHER }	
	"Standards" are the classics of the American popular songbook. Written by such composers as George Gershwin, Irving Berlin, and Cole Porter, these songs are associated equally with some of their most enduring interpreters, from Frank Sinatra to Ella Fitzgerald to Nat "King" Cole.		*These selections cover a range of music, from popular and alternative love songs to country tunes to reggae and the spices of world music. Some are inseparable from their original recordings, making them great for deejay weddings. If you are planning live music, use these as a departure for discussion with your musicians.*			
{ COCKTAILS }	Berlin *I'm Putting All My Eggs in One Basket* Gershwin *'S Wonderful* Gordon *There Will Never Be Another You* Mercer *Too Marvelous for Words* Porter *Let's Do It (Let's Fall in Love)*	Porter *You'd Be So Nice to Come Home To* Van Heusen *I Thought About You* Warren, LaTouche, Fetter, Duke *Taking a Chance on Love*	Bela Point *Spanish Point* Billy Joel *Just the Way You Are* Bryan Adams *I Do It for You (Everything I Do)* Buena Vista Social Club *Chan Chan* Caetano Veloso *Os Passistas*	Cassandra Wilson *Solomon Sang* Cyndi Lauper *Time After Time* Filipa Pais, Antonia Chainho *Fado da Adica* K.D. Lang *The Air That I Breathe* Los Lobos *This Time*	Albeniz *Sevilla* Beethoven *Minuet (from Septet, Op. 20)* Boccherini *Minuet in A Major* Fauré *Sicilienne (from "Pelléas et Mélisande")* Gluck *Dance of the Blessed Spirits (from "Orfeo ed Euriduce")*	Haydn *London Trio No. 1 in C Major* Haydn *Serenade (from String Quartet in F Major, Op. 3, No. 5)* Mozart *Eine Kleine Nachtmusik* Verdi *Brindisi (from "La Traviata")*
{ FIRST DANCE }	Berlin *Let's Face the Music and Dance* Comdon, Stern, Greene, Styne *Just in Time* Fields, McHugh *I Can't Give You Anything but Love* Gershwin *Embraceable You* Gershwin *Love Is Here to Stay*	Kahn, Jones *It Had to Be You* Kern, Fields *The Way You Look Tonight* Mancini *Two for the Road* Porter *Night and Day* *Some Day My Prince Will Come (from "Snow White")*	Bob Marley *Is This Love?* Emmylou Harris, Linda Ronstadt, Dolly Parton *Feels Like Home* Etta James *At Last!* Jim Brickman, Martina McBride *Valentine* Marc Cohn *True Companion*	Mary Chapin Carpenter *Grow Old With Me* Neville Brothers *Utterly Beloved* Sam Cooke *You Send Me* Shania Twain *From This Moment On* *When I Fall in Love (from "Sleepless in Seattle")*	Gounod *Waltz and Chorus (from "Faust")* J. Strauss *Vienna Blood Waltz* *Luke and Leia (love theme from "Return of the Jedi")* *Milonga Triste (from "The Tango Lesson")*	Walton *Touch Her Soft Lips and Part (from "Henry V," forties version)*
{ FATHER/BRIDE } { MOTHER/GROOM }	Burke, Gerlach *Daddy's Little Girl* Gershwin *Someone to Watch over Me*	Louis Armstrong *What a Wonderful World* Natalie Cole, Nat "King" Cole *Unforgettable* Trenet *I Wish You Love*	Bob Carlisle *Butterfly Kisses* Celine Dion *Because You Loved Me*	Cesaria Evora *Flor Na Paul* Sarah McLachlan *I Will Remember You* Natalie Merchant *Kind and Generous*		
{ DINNER }	Berlin *The Best Thing for You* Berlin *Cheek to Cheek* Berlin *It Only Happens When I Dance With You* Gershwin *I Was Doing All Right* Hupfeld *As Time Goes By*	Loesser *(from "Guys and Dolls") If I Were a Bell* Mercer, Arlen *This Time the Dream's on Me* Rodgers, Hart *Isn't It Romantic* Rodgers, Hart *My Romance* Schwartz, Dietz *Dancing in the Dark* Youmans, Caeser *Tea for Two*	Alison Krauss *Stay* Bill Frisell *One of These Days* Cesaria Evora *Petit Pays* Charlie Haden, Pat Metheny *Waltz for Ruth* Eric Clapton *Wonderful Tonight*	Joe Cocker *You Are So Beautiful* Patricia Barber *Light My Fire* Richard Marx *Now and Forever* Stevie Wonder *All in Love Is Fair* *With One Look (from "Sunset Boulevard")*	Bach *Lute Suite in G Minor, BWV 995 (Gavotte)* Chopin *Nocturne in E Flat Major, Op. 9* Chopin *Polonaise in A Flat Major* Debussy *Rêverie* Haydn *Divertimento No. 2 for Flute, Violin & Cello in G Major*	Haydn *London Trio No. 3 in G Major* Kreisler *Liebeslied* Liszt *Consolation No. 3* Mozart *Divertimenti for String Quartet* Tchaikovsky *Romeo and Juliet (theme)*
{ DANCING }	Brian Setzer Orchestra *This Cat's on a Hot Tin Roof* Cherry Poppin' Daddies *Zoot Suit Riot* Chick Webb *Stomping at the Savoy* Count Basie *Jumpin' at the Woodside*	Count Basie *One O'Clock Jump* Duke Ellington *Take the "A" Train* Glenn Miller *In the Mood* Glenn Miller *Moonlight Serenade* Glenn Miller *String of Pearls* Louis Prima *Jump, Jive an' Wail*	Dido *Here With Me* The Cranberries *Dreams* Heatwave *Always and Forever* The Honeydrippers *Sea of Love* Ibrahim Ferrer *Marieta* LeAnn Rimes *How Do I Live*	Mary Chapin Carpenter *Passionate Kisses* Percy Sledge *When a Man Loves a Woman* Savage Garden *Truly Madly Deeply* *Unchained Melody (from "Ghost")* Ziggy Marley and the Melody Makers *Beautiful Day*		

{ BUTTERCREAM }   { FONDANT }

Wedding Cake 101

Like the best marriages, wedding cakes are built on firm foundations. The former rely on trust and love, while the latter depend on sturdy separators and dowels. Knowing how much work goes into creating either one just might spoil the romance.

But once you understand the architecture of a wedding cake, the prospect of making one yourself will become much less intimidating. Basic baking skills and supplies, patience, and time are all you need to create a beautiful, classic wedding cake. An industrious bride can do much of the work in advance of the wedding and recruit helpers for assembling and decorating it on her wedding day. Or even a keen amateur baker can offer to make a cake as the most personal and special of wedding gifts.

Still, making a wedding cake is not for the faint of heart. Though no one skill is difficult to master, each step must be executed precisely: The cake layers must be perfectly straight, the wooden dowels must be perfectly even, and the icing has to be perfectly smooth. Be sure to practice well before the day of the wedding, and don't be too ambitious with your first cake. Once you've mastered basic cake construction, you can experiment with more elaborate shapes, colors, decorations, and designs.

The wedding cakes above and on the following pages, made by Martha Stewart and contributing editor Wendy Kromer, are elegant enough for any party but still simple enough to make. Both are constructed from various tiers of yellow cake with apricot-jam filling (see the Recipes section); one is finished with Swiss-meringue buttercream, and the other is covered with rolled fondant. Buttercream is a versatile icing but not the best choice for an outdoor wedding in the summer, since the buttercream—made from pure butter—can melt in the heat. Fondant, which is available from baking-supply stores, is easy to work with and produces a porcelain finish; it holds up well and even helps preserve a cake. Both of these wedding cakes are decorated with fresh flowers, an inexpensive and romantic adornment.

The cake layers and buttercream can be frozen for several weeks, and the jam filling will keep well in the refrigerator. Store-bought fondant is ready when you are. The day before the wedding, completely prepare the tiers, first placing them on foam-board bases, then refrigerate the finished tiers overnight.

To transport the tiers, put each one in its own box (with double-sided tape between the foam-board base and box), and place on the flattest surface in your car, out of direct sunlight. At the reception site, assemble and decorate the cake. Real flowers should be added as close to serving time as possible so they look fresh.

After all your hard work, not much time will pass between the instant the cake has been completed and the ritualistic first cut. Take a moment to appreciate your creation—everyone else will, too.

BUTTERCREAM CAKE

1. Each cake layer needs a sturdy base. Trace the cake pans onto a piece of foam-board three-sixteenths-of-an-inch thick (available at art-supply stores). Cut out the rounds. Bake the cakes in parchment-lined cake pans, and let them cool slightly. Remove the cakes from the pans, and do not peel off the parchment. Once completely cool, place each cake right-side up on a foam-board round, wrap in plastic, and refrigerate for at least six hours; this makes the layers firm and easy to handle. The cakes can also be frozen at this point.

2. If a cake layer doesn't bake level—they often don't—even it out with a serrated knife. Use a turntable to help make the cake even all around.

3. Place a small dollop of the buttercream in the center of one cake tier. Put another foam-board round on top of the tier, then invert the cake onto the foam-board. Remove the original foam-board base and parchment. The bottom of the cake is now the top, and the dollop of buttercream prevents the cake layer from sliding off the foam-board; the cake will remain on this foam-board round from now on.

4. Split the cake. Place the cake on a turntable. Hold a serrated knife against the edge of the cake, then rotate the turntable, working the knife through the cake.

5. Brush the cut surface of the bottom half of the cake layer with a sugar syrup, flavored with liqueur or orange zest if desired. This syrup will moisten the cake and add a subtle flavor.

6. Pipe the buttercream around the perimeter of the bottom half of the cake. Use a pastry bag fitted with a standard-size coupler. This "dam" of buttercream will keep the jam filling in place.

7. Within the buttercream perimeter, fill the bottom layer with jam filling one-eighth-of-an-inch thick; don't use so much that the top layer slips and slides.

8. Replace the top layer, cut side down, and brush with sugar syrup. Let set for two to three minutes.

9. Ice the top of the cake layer with buttercream using an offset spatula to give the tier a "crumb coat." This thin layer of icing will seal the cake. Start from the center and work out, making sure to push the buttercream over the sides of the tier.

10. Smooth the icing. The crumb coat will be covered by more icing later, so it doesn't have to be perfectly smooth at this point. Chill the tier in the refrigerator to set the icing, about thirty minutes to one hour, until the buttercream doesn't stick to you when you touch it. Repeat steps one through ten with the remaining cake layers.

11. Give the tiers a final coating of buttercream. Use an offset spatula to smooth the tops of the cake tiers, and a tool called a bench scraper for the sides. Before you ice each tier, wipe off the spatula, dip it in hot water, then wipe it off again; using this warm, clean spatula will make a clean, finished edge.

12. The icing should be smooth and uniform. But

perfection is nearly impossible; if you see an air bubble or another small flaw, make that side the back of the cake. Refrigerate the cake tiers.

13. Prepare the cake board at least eight hours before assembling the cake. The board should be at least four inches wider than the cake and strong enough to support its weight, which for this four-tiered cake can easily exceed fifty pounds. Boards are available at baking-supply stores; this one, made of flake board, was cut for us at a hardware store. Spread a thin layer of royal icing over the cake board; it's not necessary to ice the center, but the icing must be brought to the edge of the board. Let the royal icing dry completely, for at least eight hours or overnight.

14. Insert a quarter-inch dowel vertically into the bottom tier of the cake; mark it three-eighths-of-an-inch above the top of the tier. Remove it, and cut eight dowel pieces to this length. These will be the supports for the next tier. Use five cut dowels to form a circle an inch-and-a-half in from the edge of the tier that will be placed on top (hold an empty cake pan over the finished tier to determine placement); use the other three dowels to form a triangle inside the circle. Repeat the process on each cake tier—except the top one—using fewer dowels in different configurations as the tiers get smaller. Do not place the dowels directly in the center of the tiers. At this point, the cakes can be refrigerated overnight.

15. Assemble the cake on its serving table. Dab some royal icing onto the center of the cake board to keep the cake from moving, and place the bottom tier on it. Add the next tier, resting it on the dowels; the three-eighths-of-an-inch space between the tiers will hide the bases of the flowers that you'll use for decorations. Once all of the tiers are stacked, cut a dowel a quarter-inch shorter than the height of the cake. Using a knife or a clean pencil sharpener, whittle one end to a point, and with a mallet, gently drive the dowel through the center of all the cakes and foam-board bases. Do not hammer too close to the cake, and push the end in with your fingers.

16. Use a pastry bag fitted with a large leaf tip to pipe buttercream leaves along the top edges of the tiers.

17. Trim the flower stems close to the base. Use unsprayed flowers (you may want to use edible ones like violets and nasturtiums). The hydrangeas, violas, and scabiosa used on this cake are from Martha's East Hampton, New York, garden. Decorate the base of each tier with the flowers. The monogram, which sits on the top tier, is made from twenty-four-gauge wire with small sprigs of thyme wired to it.

18. Starting at the back of the cake, use a hot-glue gun to attach ribbon around the perimeter of the cake board. With this final touch, the wedding cake is now ready to be admired by the guests before being sliced by the bride and groom. (See the finished cake on page 158.)

FONDANT CAKE

This fondant-covered cake decorated with hydrangeas is made of three graduated square tiers. The construction is the same as described for the buttercream cake. Before you begin working with the fondant, prepare all of the cakes by baking, filling, and crumb-coating each with a thin layer of buttercream icing. The tiers should be stored in the refrigerator at this point. This square cake calls for a square cake board; if you can't find one, have one cut out of flake board at a hardware store.

Fondant must be at room temperature before you can use it. Once you've covered the cake with the fondant, do not refrigerate it; the fondant can become dewy. Finished tiers or the completed cake can stand at cool room temperature overnight.

1. Start by kneading fondant as you would bread dough. Your work surface should be smooth; dust the area very lightly with cornstarch to keep the fondant from sticking, then knead fondant until it feels soft and pliable.

2. On the same work surface, roll out the fondant; the ideal thickness is between one-quarter and one-eighth of an inch. If you notice any air bubbles as you roll the fondant, prick them with a clean straight pin. Roll out enough fondant to cover the entire top and sides of the tier you are working on; excess fondant can be reused for the remaining tiers as long as it has not come into contact with buttercream.

3. Lift the fondant with both hands, and lower it onto the prepared cake tier, working quickly so that the fondant doesn't dry out.

4. Dust your hands with cornstarch if necessary, and smooth out the top and sides of the cake tier, pushing out any air bubbles. The fondant will adhere to the buttercream crumb coat.

5. Run a pizza wheel or a knife along the edge of the cake, cutting away any excess fondant. Complete the process on the remaining tiers, then assemble cake as described in step 15 of the buttercream cake.

CAKES

WEDDING CAKE 101

See pages 233 to 236 for photographs and instructions on how to assemble a wedding cake. This is a good, moist yellow cake that will keep for several days in the refrigerator and also freezes well. Bake it one day, and split, fill, and frost it the next. Brush it with sugar syrup to enhance the flavor; you can also substitute almond extract for vanilla.

To make a 14-inch tier, make a triple batch, pour it into a prepared 14-by-3-inch pan, and let it sit while you make another triple batch. Pour that right on top, and bake for about 1 hour and 45 minutes, or until a wooden skewer comes out clean. Rotate pan halfway through baking. Lay a piece of foil on top if it starts to get too brown. For remaining tiers, continue making triple batches and filling pans in this manner until each one is three-quarters full. Baking times will vary for each, so watch carefully, and test for doneness. Use the filling of your choice; the easiest one is based on preserves. Heat your favorite flavor until warm, and strain through a sieve. Spread while warm.

MOIST YELLOW CAKE
makes one 8-inch cake

8 tablespoons (1 stick) unsalted butter, softened, plus more to coat parchment

1⅓ cups cake flour, sifted, plus more to coat parchment

1 cup sugar

1 teaspoon pure vanilla extract

2 large eggs

1 teaspoon baking powder

Pinch salt

1½ cup milk

1. Heat oven to 325°. Butter 8-inch cake pan, line with round of parchment, and butter and flour parchment. Cream butter and sugar in bowl of electric mixer fitted with paddle attachment until light in color and fluffy, about 5 minutes. Add vanilla extract. Add eggs one at a time.

2. Sift together flour, baking powder, and salt three times. Add to egg mixture in three additions, alternating with milk, starting and ending with flour.

3. Pour batter into pan; bake until top is golden and tester inserted into center comes out clean, 45 to 50 minutes. Cool in pan for 10 minutes. Turn out onto a wire rack; remove paper; cool completely.

SWISS-MERINGUE BUTTERCREAM
makes 3 cups

If buttercream becomes too soft, stir over ice water to stiffen. If it has been refrigerated, bring to room temperature; rewhip.

1¼ cups sugar

5 large egg whites

Pinch cream of tartar

2 cups (4 sticks) unsalted butter, cut into small pieces

1 teaspoon pure vanilla extract

1. In small saucepan over medium heat, bring sugar and ⅓ cup water to a boil. Boil until syrup reaches soft-ball stage (238° on a candy thermometer).

2. Meanwhile, beat egg whites on low until foamy. Add cream of tartar; beat on medium high until stiff but not dry.

3. With mixer running, pour syrup into egg whites in a steady stream; beat on high until stream is no longer visible, about 3 minutes. Beat in butter, piece by piece. Add vanilla; beat 3 to 5 minutes, until frosting is smooth and spreadable. If it looks curdled during beating process, continue beating to smooth it out.

SUGAR SYRUP
makes 2 cups

1½ cups sugar

3 tablespoons liqueur, such as Grand Marnier, Kirsch, or Frangelico

Combine sugar and 1 cup of water in a small saucepan. Set over high heat; boil until the sugar dissolves. Remove from heat; stir in the liqueur. Let cool; brush the layers with syrup.

ROYAL ICING FOR CAKE BOARD
makes enough for one 20-inch round cake board

3 large egg whites

1 pound confectioners' sugar, sifted

Combine ingredients in bowl of electric mixer with paddle attachment; beat until smooth. Icing should be thin enough that a ribbon of icing, dropped on surface of batter, smooths out within 8 seconds. If too thick, whisk in water 1 teaspoon at a time. Using offset spatula, coat board with icing. Let dry. Trim edge with ribbon.

CROQUEMBOUCHE
serves 15/pictured on page 169

Make the caramel and assemble as close to serving time as possible.

For pâte-à-choux puffs:

1½ sticks unsalted butter

¼ teaspoon salt

1 teaspoon sugar

1½ cups sifted all-purpose flour

6 large eggs

1 egg beaten with 1 teaspoon water, for egg glaze

For mocha crème pâtissière:

6 large egg yolks

½ cup sugar

½ cup sifted all-purpose flour

2 cups milk

3 tablespoons unsalted butter

2 ounces semisweet chocolate

2 teaspoons instant espresso powder mixed with 2 teaspoons hot water

For caramel:

2 cups sugar

2 tablespoons corn syrup

To make puffs:

1. Heat oven to 425°. Melt butter in 1½ cups water with salt and sugar. Remove from heat; add flour. Return to heat; beat vigorously 2 to 3 minutes. (A film should form on bottom of pan.) Cool slightly; add eggs, one at a time, beating vigorously.

2. Using a pastry bag with a coupler and ½-inch-wide plain tip, pipe mounds 1 inch high and ⅓ inch in diameter on parchment-lined baking sheet. Brush with egg glaze; smooth tops. Bake 20 to 25 minutes, until puffed and golden. Cool on racks. (The puffs can be frozen until ready to assemble.)

To make crème pâtissière:

1. Beat egg yolks, gradually adding sugar, until mixture is thick and pale yellow. Beat in flour. Scald milk and add in dribbles, reserving ½ cup. Place mixture in pot over high heat; stir vigorously until it boils and thickens. If too thick to pipe, add reserved milk. Remove from heat.

2. Beat in butter, one tablespoon at a time. Melt chocolate; add to mixture with espresso. Let cool completely. Just before assembling, fill pastry tube fitted with ¼-inch-wide tip with crème. Insert tip into puffs; pipe in crème to fill.

To make caramel:

1. Combine ⅔ cup water, sugar, and corn syrup in medium saucepan; bring to a boil. Do not stir. Cover; boil until sugar has dissolved. Uncover; boil 5 minutes, or until syrup is amber. Remove from heat.

2. Dip bottom of each puff into caramel; arrange in a pyramid. Cut tip from a balloon whisk, dip into caramel, and whirl strands of caramel around croquembouche to form a spun-sugar web.

CHOCOLATE CHESTNUT CAKE
serves 100 generously/pictured on page 172

For cake layers:

1 cup whole hazelnuts (4¼ ounces)

8 tablespoons (1 stick) unsalted butter, cut into small pieces, plus more for pans

1 cup all-purpose flour, plus more for pans

4 ounces best-quality semisweet chocolate, chopped

1½ cups sugar

2 tablespoons heavy cream

2 tablespoons pure vanilla extract

¼ cup unsweetened cocoa powder

1½ teaspoons baking soda

½ teaspoon baking powder

½ teaspoon salt

9 ounces vacuum-packed chestnuts, ground

2 large eggs

For ganache:

3 pounds best-quality semisweet or bittersweet chocolate

2 cups heavy cream

8 tablespoons (1 stick) unsalted butter, cut in pieces

⅔ cup sour cream

For sugared fruit and laurel leaves:

40 Small pieces of fruit, such as Seckel pears, lady apples, and grapes

10-14 marrons glacés (candied chestnuts)

50 Fresh, unsprayed laurel leaves and sprigs
Fresh or powdered egg whites
Superfine sugar

To make cake layers:

1. You will need two 4-inch square layers, two 6-inch square layers, two 9-inch square layers, and three 16-inch round layers. A half-batch of batter makes one 4-inch and one 6-inch layer; 1½ batches makes two 9-inch layers; 1 batch makes one 16-inch layer.

2. Heat oven to 350°. Toast hazelnuts for 8 minutes; rub in a towel to remove skin. When cool, process in food processor until finely ground, about 30 seconds.

3. Heat oven to 325°. Brush baking pans with butter. Line bottom of pans with parchment, brush with butter again, and dust with flour, shaking out excess.

4. Combine chocolate, butter, and 1 cup hot water in a double boiler; melt over low heat, about 5 minutes. Transfer chocolate mixture to an electric mixer.

5. Stir sugar into chocolate mixture. Let cool to room temperature, about 10 minutes. Add cream and vanilla; stir with a rubber spatula.

6. Sift together flour, cocoa powder, baking soda, baking powder, and salt. Add ground chestnuts, hazelnuts, and dry ingredients to melted-chocolate mixture. Beat on low for 30 seconds. Add eggs one at a time, mixing 30 seconds, scraping sides of bowl after each addition.

7. Pour batter into prepared pans (filling 4-inch and 6-inch pans ½ inch full, 9-inch pans ¾ inch full, and 16-inch pans with all the batter). Bake 4-inch, 6-inch, and 16-inch layers for about 35 minutes, 9-inch layers about 45 minutes; cakes are done when toothpick inserted in center comes out clean.

8. Let cool completely on a rack. Invert

onto appropriate-size cardboard round or squares, remove parchment, and immediately reinvert onto another round so cakes are right-side up. Wrap with plastic wrap; store at room temperature.

To make ganache:

1. You will need 3 batches for the filling and 1 for the glaze (the batch for the glaze should be made just before using). Chop chocolate into small pieces; melt with cream in double boiler over medium heat. Transfer to stainless-steel bowl. Add butter; stir until butter is melted.

2. Fold in sour cream until completely incorporated. If not using within 2 hours, cover with plastic wrap, pressing it directly on surface, and refrigerate.

To make sugared fruit:

Beat 4 egg whites (or more as needed; use powdered whites if concerned about consuming raw eggs) with a fork. Brush apples and pears with whites; roll in sugar; shake off excess. Let dry on parchment-covered sheet pans. Store at room temperature in a nonhumid environment for 24 hours. Sugar grapes, chestnuts, and laurel leaves (paint leaves only halfway; leave stem end plain) just before using.

To assemble cake:

1. Make 3 batches of ganache; place over a large bowl of ice and water to cool, whisking continuously; do not let it solidify. Transfer to an electric mixer with whisk. Whip until soft peaks form.

2. Spread ¼ cup ganache on one 4-inch cake layer (on cardboard); place other 4-inch layer (without cardboard) on top. Repeat with other sizes, using 1 cup ganache between 6-inch layers; 2 cups between 9-inch layers; 5 cups between 16-inch layers. Use icing spatula to apply thin coating of ganache to each tier. Refrigerate tiers until firm, at least 1 hour.

3. Make one batch of ganache for glaze; it should be warm to the touch (125° on an instant-read thermometer).

4. Place 16-inch tier on the wire rack over baking sheet with edges (so excess ganache can be reused). Ladle 16 to 18 ounces ganache on top of tier; spread with offset spatula, pushing ganache over edges. Pour more ganache over bare spots. Set tier aside. Repeat for remain-

ing tiers, using 4 to 6 ounces for 4-inch tier, 8 to 10 ounces for 6-inch tier, and 10 to 12 ounces for 9-inch tier.

5. Place a masonite board on cake turn-table. Smear board with 2 tablespoons ganache; place 16-inch tier on top. Insert ¼-inch-diameter wooden dowel into cake; mark where dowel is flush with glaze; cut 5 pieces to that length. Insert 4 dowels in a square pattern, and 1 in center.

6. Place 9-inch tier, on cardboard, on top, centered over cake. Repeat dowel procedure with 9-inch tier; place 6-inch tier on top. Repeat procedure; place 4-inch tier on top.

7. Decorate as desired with sugared fruit and leaves.

APPLESAUCE CAKE
serves 60/pictured on page 173

You will need to prepare three batches of batter to make three twelve-inch layers and three six-inch layers; each batch makes one large and one small layer. You will also need four half-inch-diameter, eight-inch-long wooden dowels to assemble.

For cake layers (one batch):

1 cup (2 sticks) unsalted butter, room temperature, plus more for pans

2 cups superfine sugar, plus more for pans

2¾ cups all-purpose flour

¾ teaspoon baking soda

1½ teaspoons baking powder

1½ teaspoons ground cinnamon

½ teaspoon ground nutmeg
Pinch ground cloves

¼ teaspoon salt

2 large eggs, room temperature

2½ cups chunky applesauce

1 cup chopped pecans

1 teaspoon pure vanilla extract

2 tablespoons Calvados (a French apple-flavored brandy) or brandy

1 Granny Smith apple, peeled, cored, and very thinly sliced

For assembling cake:
Cream-Cheese Filling (recipe follows)
Confectioners' sugar

2-4 cups granulated sugar

½ cup corn syrup

30 crab and lady apples, washed and dried
Unsprayed, nontoxic apple-tree branches

To make cake layers:

1. Heat oven to 325°. Butter one 12-by-2-inch round cake pan and one 6-by-2-inch round cake pan. Line bottoms with parchment; butter. Dust with superfine sugar. Tap out excess sugar; set pans aside.

2. In large bowl, sift together flour, baking soda, baking powder, cinnamon, nutmeg, cloves, and salt. Set aside.

3. In bowl of electric mixer fitted with paddle attachment, cream butter and superfine sugar on medium until fluffy, about 5 minutes. Add eggs, one at a time, beating 2 minutes after each. Add applesauce; beat to combine.

4. Fold in flour mixture and pecans. Fold in vanilla, Calvados, and apple slices. Fill 6-inch pan with 1⅓ cups batter and 12-inch pan with remaining batter.

5. Bake cakes until they spring back when you touch centers, about 1 hour for smaller cake and 1 hour 15 minutes for larger cake. Transfer to wire rack; let cool completely, about 1½ hours. Turn out cakes; wrap in plastic until ready to use.

To assemble cake:

1. Place one 12-inch layer on serving platter. Spread 1¼ cups cream-cheese filling over cake. Place second large layer on top; spread with another 1¼ cups filling. Top with remaining large cake layer, top side up.

2. Cut 5-inch round out of cardboard; place round in center of top cake layer. Around cardboard, mark four equidistant points with a toothpick. Remove cardboard; mark four more points ¾ inch in from first marks. Stick dowel into each new point, making sure dowels are straight. Sift confectioners' sugar over top.

3. Place one 6-inch cake layer over cardboard round, pressing gently so cardboard is not visible. Spread cake with ½ cup filling. Top with a second small layer; spread with ½ cup filling. Top with remaining small layer, top side up. Sift confectioners' sugar over top. Place this tier on top of dowels, centering it perfectly.

4. Line two baking sheets with parchment. Combine 2 cups granulated sugar, ⅓ cup corn syrup, and ⅓ cup water in

a medium bowl; mix until consistency of wet sand. Transfer to medium saucepan. Place over high heat; cover. When sugar begins to turn brown, 6 to 8 minutes, uncover, stir with a wooden spoon, and reduce heat to medium low. Cook, stirring, until sugar becomes clear and golden caramel, 4 to 6 minutes more. Remove from heat.

5. Using slotted spoon, dip apples into caramel, coating completely. Allow excess caramel to drip off; transfer apples to lined baking sheets; allow caramel to harden. If caramel becomes too dark and stiff, make second batch with another 2 cups sugar, ⅓ cup corn syrup, and ⅓ cup water.

6. Decorate cake with apple-tree branches and dipped apples. Serve.

CREAM-CHEESE FILLING
makes 3½ cups

1 pound cream cheese, room temperature
6 tablespoons unsalted butter, room temperature
2 cups confectioners' sugar

1. In bowl of electric mixer fitted with paddle attachment, beat cream cheese on medium-low until smooth, about 1 minute. Add butter; beat until smooth, 2 minutes.

2. On low speed, add sugar; mix until combined. Transfer filling to airtight container; chill until firm, 4 hours or overnight. Store, refrigerated, up to 3 days.

FORTUNE-COOKIE FAVORS
makes 50/pictured on page 185

5 tablespoons unsalted butter
4 large egg whites
1 cup superfine sugar
¾ cup plus 1 tablespoon all-purpose flour
3 tablespoons Dutch cocoa
Pinch salt
3 tablespoons heavy cream
½ teaspoon pure almond extract
½ teaspoon pure vanilla extract
50 paper fortunes

1. Heat oven to 400°. In small saucepan over low heat, melt butter; set aside.

2. In bowl of electric mixer, combine egg whites and sugar; beat on medium until frothy, 30 seconds. Add flour, cocoa, and salt; beat until combined. Add melted butter, cream, and almond and vanilla extracts; beat until combined, 30 seconds.

3. Drop a heaping teaspoon of batter onto a Silpat baking mat fitted in a baking pan, or use a nonstick baking sheet. Repeat with remaining batter, spacing dollops 5 inches apart. Using back of a spoon, spread each one into a 4-inch circle. Place pan in oven; bake cookies until edges darken slightly, about 5 minutes.

4. Transfer pan to heat-resistant surface. Working quickly, slide offset spatula under cookie; flip over. Roll cookie into loose tube; insert paper fortune into middle so edges extend from cookie. Using the index finger, make indentation in center of tube; pinch each end together with other hand. Repeat rolling-and-folding process with remaining cookies. Store in airtight container up to a week.

DRINKS

WHITE-WINE SANGRIA
serves 25/pictured on page 142

1 cup sugar
Grated zest of six kumquats
2 lemons, cut into ⅛-inch-thick rounds
2 limes, cut into ⅛-inch-thick rounds
4 mandarin oranges, cut into ⅛-inch-thick rounds
2 star fruit, cut into ⅛-inch-thick slices
2 cups green grapes, halved
3 liters pinot grigio
1 750-ml bottle sparkling grape juice
¼ cup brandy

1. Place sugar, zest, and 1 cup water in saucepan; bring to boil. Once sugar has dissolved, reduce heat; simmer 30 minutes. Remove from heat, strain, and let cool.

2. Combine the syrup and the remaining ingredients in large container. Cover; refrigerate 2 hours or overnight. Serve over ice.

CANTALOUPE PUNCH
serves 44/pictured on page 143

Juice extractors work best; you can also purée fruit in a blender and strain it.

20 cups freshly squeezed cantaloupe juice (about 8 medium cantaloupes)
2 cups freshly squeezed lemon juice (about 12 lemons)
4 cups freshly squeezed lime juice (about 36 limes)
4 cups light rum
Lemon Simple Syrup (recipe follows)
16 cups ice cubes

Combine ingredients except ice in 2-gallon container. When ready to serve, add ice.

LEMON SIMPLE SYRUP
makes 4 cups

3 cups sugar
Zest of 8 lemons, thinly sliced

In saucepan over medium heat, combine sugar with 3 cups water. Cook, stirring, until sugar dissolves, 5 to 6 minutes. Add zest; reduce heat. Simmer 10 minutes. Remove from heat; let cool. Strain; transfer to airtight container. Store, refrigerated, up to 1 week.

STRAWBERRY-CHAMPAGNE PUNCH
serves 44/pictured on page 143

10 cups freshly squeezed orange juice (about 30 oranges)
4 cups freshly squeezed strawberry juice (about 3 pounds strawberries)
1 cup freshly squeezed lemon juice (about 6 lemons)
1 cup Campari
16 cups Asti Spumante
16 cups ice cubes
16 strawberries, for garnish

In 2-gallon container, combine juices; chill. Before serving, add Campari, Asti Spumante, and ice cubes; garnish with strawberries.

PINEAPPLE-APRICOT PUNCH
serves 44/pictured on page 143

2 cups freshly squeezed cranberry juice (40 ounces fresh or frozen cranberries)
12 cups freshly squeezed pineapple juice, strained (about 21 pounds of pineapple)

2 cups freshly squeezed lime juice (about 18 limes)
1 cup freshly squeezed lemon juice (about 6 lemons)
15 cups apricot nectar
12 cups ice cubes
Cranberry Cubes (recipe follows)

Combine all ingredients except ice and cranberry cubes in 2-gallon container. Just before serving, add ice and cranberry cubes.

CRANBERRY CUBES
makes 140 cubes

4 cups freshly squeezed cranberry juice (85 ounces fresh or frozen cranberries)

Pour juice into ten ice-cube trays or decorative molds. Freeze. Soak a cloth in hot water, wring; apply to backs of molds. Tap backs, or use a paring knife, releasing ice. Store frozen in an airtight container until ready to use.

HONEYDEW PUNCH
serves 44/pictured on page 143

20 cups freshly squeezed honeydew juice (4 large honeydew melons)
6 cups freshly squeezed lime juice (about 54 limes), plus 3 limes cut into ¼-inch-thick rounds
Mint Simple Syrup (recipe follows)
16 cups ice cubes
12 sprigs fresh mint

In a 2-gallon container, combine juices and simple syrup. Just before serving, add ice, and garnish with mint and lime.

MINT SIMPLE SYRUP
makes 6 cups

4 cups sugar
8 ounces fresh mint leaves

1. In medium saucepan set over medium heat, combine sugar and 4 cups water. Cook, stirring occasionally, until sugar has dissolved, about 9 minutes. Stir in mint leaves; remove pan from heat. Let cool.

2. Strain through fine sieve, pressing mint with a wooden spoon to extract liquid. Discard mint; transfer to an airtight container. Store, refrigerated, up to 3 days.

MINT VODKA GIMLET
makes 2/pictured on page 145

2½ tablespoons Mint Simple Syrup
(recipe above)
4 ounces vodka
½ cup freshly squeezed lime juice
½ bunch mint, top sprigs picked, for garnish
2 wedges lime, for garnish

Fill cocktail shaker halfway with ice. Add mint syrup, vodka, and lime juice. Shake. Fill two glasses with mint sprigs and ice cubes. Pour gimlet over ice. Garnish with another mint sprig and lime. Serve.

ORANGE-BLOSSOM NECTAR
makes 1 cocktail/pictured on page 145

½ cup sanding sugar
2 tablespoons grated orange zest
1 wedge lemon
1 ounce (2 tablespoons) bourbon
¼ cup freshly squeezed orange juice
¼ cup papaya or mango nectar
½ ounce (1 tablespoon) Cointreau
or Triple Sec
Orange blossoms, for garnish

1. In small bowl, combine sugar and orange zest. Run lemon wedge around rim of martini glass. Invert glass, and dip into sugar mixture, coating rim. Set aside, and repeat with remaining glasses.
2. Fill a cocktail shaker halfway with ice. Pour in bourbon, orange juice, and nectar. Shake until chilled; strain into glass. Top off with Cointreau; garnish with orange blossoms. Serve immediately.

CARIBBEAN LOVE PUNCH
makes 25 to 30 servings/pictured on page 145

1 ripe pineapple, peeled and cored
1 cup freshly squeezed lemon juice
¼ cup Simple Syrup (recipe follows)
1 teaspoon ground nutmeg
1 teaspoon ground cinnamon
1 teaspoon ground allspice
1 750-ml bottle dark rum
1 750-ml bottle spiced rum
1 quart pineapple juice
1½ quarts freshly squeezed orange juice
1½ cups ginger ale

1. Thinly slice half of pineapple; set aside. Cut remaining half into chunks.
2. In a blender or food processor, com-bine pineapple chunks, lemon juice, sim-ple syrup, and spices. Blend on high until well mixed. Pour into large punch bowl.
3. Add rums, juices, and ginger ale; stir well. Add ice, garnish with reserved pineapple slices; serve.

THE RASMOPOLITAN
makes 1 cocktail/pictured on page 145

1 ounce (2 tablespoons) citrus-flavored vodka
1 ounce (2 tablespoons) raspberry-flavored vodka
½ ounce (1 tablespoon) Chambord
1 tablespoon freshly squeezed lime juice
1 tablespoon Simple Syrup (recipe follows)
2 tablespoons cranberry juice
Raspberries, for garnish

Fill cocktail shaker halfway with ice. Add vodkas, Chambord, lime juice, sim-ple syrup, and cranberry juice. Shake or stir until well chilled. Strain into martini glass. Garnish with raspberries; serve.

SIMPLE SYRUP
makes 1⅓ cups

1 cup sugar

In a small saucepan over medium-high heat, combine sugar and 1 cup water. Bring mixture to a boil; cook, stirring oc-casionally, until sugar has completely dis-solved, about 2 minutes. Remove from heat; set over an ice bath until chilled. Store in a covered plastic container.

CRANBERRY MARTINI
makes two 4-ounce drinks/pictured on page 145

Red sanding sugar
1 lime wedge
10 whole cranberries
8 ounces vodka
1 ounce cranberry juice
1 teaspoon vermouth

1. Place sanding sugar into a saucer big enough to encompass rim of a martini glass. Rub rim of each glass with lime wedge. Dip glass into sugar; rotate until rim is evenly coated. Place glasses in freezer for at least 10 minutes to chill.
2. Skewer 2 toothpicks with 5 cranber-ries each; set aside.
3. In a cocktail shaker filled with ice, mix vodka, cranberry juice, and ver-mouth. Strain into chilled glasses; garnish with cranberry skewers. Serve immediately.

BICYCLE BUILT FOR TWO
makes 8 to 10 servings/pictured on page 145

¼ cup sanding sugar
Powdered food coloring
1 wedge lemon
10 ounces (1¼ cups) brandy
10 ounces (1¼ cups) ruby port
6 ounces (¾ cup) Cointreau
½ cup plus 2 tablespoons freshly squeezed orange juice
½ cup plus 2 tablespoons freshly squeezed lemon juice
1½ cups ginger ale

1. In small bowl, combine sanding sugar and food coloring to achieve desired shade. Run lemon wedge around rim of a tall glass. Dip glass into sugar, coating rim. Set aside; repeat with remaining glasses.
2. Combine remaining ingredients in a large pitcher, and stir well. Fill glasses with ice, add cocktail, and serve.

PIMM'S CUP
serves 8 to 10/pictured on page 144

½ pint (6 ounces) strawberries, hulled and cut into quarters
1 lemon, sliced into ⅛-inch rounds
1 lime, sliced into ⅛-inch rounds
1 blood orange, sliced into 1-inch wedges
3 cups Pimm's Cup
48 ounces 7-Up or ginger ale
2 cucumbers, cut into ¼-inch lengths

1. In large pitcher, combine fruit and Pimm's. Refrigerate for 3 to 4 hours.
2. Fill glass halfway with ice. Add about ⅓ cup Pimm's mixture. Fill glass with 7-Up; stir. Garnish with cucumber; serve.

AFTERNOON DELIGHT
makes 1 cocktail/pictured on page 144

1½ ounces (3 tablespoons) tequila
½ cup tomato or vegetable juice
¼ cup freshly squeezed orange juice
3 tablespoons freshly squeezed lime juice
½ teaspoon ground cumin
Large dash Tabasco sauce
Large dash soy sauce
Cherry tomatoes, small fresh chiles, and cucumber slices, for garnish

Fill a cocktail shaker halfway with ice. Pour in tequila, vegetable, lime, and orange juices. Add cumin, Tabasco sauce, and soy sauce. Stir very well; strain into a glass. Garnish with choice of vegetable; serve immediately.

HORS D'OEUVRES

VIOLET NOSEGAYS
makes 65/pictured on page 139

Edible violets give these flower-shaped cookies their special look. Be sure the flow-ers are free from any sort of sprays or pesti-cides (see the Guide for sources).

1 cup (2 sticks) unsalted butter
½ cup granulated sugar, plus more for sprinkling
1 tablespoon pure vanilla extract
2¼ cups all-purpose flour
½ cup hazelnuts
2 cups cream cheese, softened
½ cup confectioners' sugar
Edible violets, for garnish

1. Heat oven to 325°. In large bowl of electric mixer, cream butter and sugar on medium-high until smooth. Add vanilla and flour; mix on low until combined.
2. On a lightly floured surface, roll out dough to ⅛ inch. Using a 2-inch round scallop cutter, cut out nosegays.
3. With a No. 5 plain pastry tip, cut out a circle of small rounds around edges. Gather remaining dough into a ball, and roll out again. Reuse dough only once, discarding any dough after second roll.
4. Place cookies on ungreased baking sheet; bake until light brown, about 20 minutes. Let cool on wire racks, then lightly sprinkle with granulated sugar.
5. Heat oven to 350°. Spread hazelnuts on a baking sheet; toast for 10 to 15 min-utes, until they give off an aroma and skins begin to blister. Shake pan occasionally. Let cool; rub nuts in a towel to remove most of the skins, then finely chop.
6. Combine nuts with cream cheese and confectioners' sugar. Spoon mixture into pastry bag fitted with a coupler and a small star tip; pipe onto cookies. Gar-nish each nosegay with an edible violet.

BLUEBERRY PINWHEELS

makes 30/pictured on page 139

You can garnish these cookies with any small, firm berry.

1 cup (2 sticks) unsalted butter
½ cup sugar, plus more for sprinkling
1 tablespoon pure vanilla extract
1 large egg
2½ cups all-purpose flour
1 large egg yolk mixed with 1 tablespoon water, for glaze
1 cup good-quality apricot preserves
Fresh blueberries, for garnish

1. Heat oven to 325°. In bowl of electric mixer, cream butter and sugar on medium-high until smooth. Add vanilla and egg; mix on low until smooth. Mix in flour.
2. Roll out dough on a lightly floured surface to ⅛ inch; cut out 3-inch rounds. Cut 5 evenly spaced lines from edge toward center, leaving ½ inch at center intact. Fold left corner of each wedge toward center; press down, creating a pinwheel.
3. Brush pinwheels with egg glaze, and sprinkle with sugar. Bake until light brown, about 20 minutes.
4. Let cool on wire racks. Dab preserves into center; garnish with a blueberry.

PRALINE CALLA LILIES WITH LEMON CREAM

makes 30/pictured on page 139

You can make the cones beforehand, but assemble right before serving.

4 tablespoons unsalted butter
¼ cup light-brown sugar
¼ cup light corn syrup
1 teaspoon pure vanilla extract
½ teaspoon almond extract
¼ cup sliced almonds, coarsely chopped
3 tablespoons all-purpose flour
2 cups mascarpone (Italian cream cheese)
Zest of 1 lemon, finely chopped
2 tablespoons confectioners' sugar

1. In small saucepan over medium-high heat, combine butter, brown sugar, and corn syrup; bring to a boil. Remove from heat; stir to dissolve sugar. Add extracts and almonds. Stir in flour; let batter cool.
2. Heat oven to 350°. Oil baking sheet.

Using 2 spoons, drop ½ teaspoon of batter at a time onto sheet to make 4 cookies, leaving 3 inches in between. Bake for 10 minutes, or until golden brown.
3. Let cool for 1 minute; remove from sheet with spatula, being careful not to tear cookies. Quickly roll each cookie to form a cone. Cool completely on wire racks. Repeat until batter is used up, placing cookies at least 3 inches apart. You will only need to oil baking sheets once.
4. Just before serving, combine mascarpone, lemon zest, and confectioners' sugar. Spoon into a pastry bag fitted with a coupler and star tip; pipe mixture into center of each cookie.

MERINGUE MUSHROOMS

makes 25/pictured on page 139

The stems and caps can be made ahead of time; store in an airtight container.

Meringue:
½ cup sugar
2 large egg whites
Pinch cream of tartar
Pinch salt
Cocoa powder, for dusting

Ganache:
1 cup heavy cream
8 ounces bittersweet chocolate, chopped

1. In a heavy saucepan over low heat, bring sugar and ¼ cup of water to a boil. Cover and boil on medium-high heat for 5 minutes. Remove cover, and wash down any sugar crystals clinging to pan with a brush dipped in cold water. Continue to boil until syrup reaches hard-ball stage, 240° on a candy thermometer.
2. While syrup is cooking, beat egg whites in bowl of electric mixer on low until foamy. Add cream of tartar and salt; beat on medium-high until egg whites hold stiff peaks. With mixer on medium, add hot syrup slowly; beat for 10 minutes, or until meringue is stiff and cool.
3. Heat oven to lowest possible temperature (about 175°). Spoon meringue into a pastry bag fitted with a coupler and a No. 1A round metal tip. To make mushroom tops, pipe 25 quarter-size rounds onto baking sheet lined with

parchment paper. Smooth tops by dipping your finger in cold water and lightly smoothing any peaks. To make stems, use a No. 12 tip; create even cylinders of meringue by pulling bag straight up and away from pan while piping. Smooth tops. Dust tops and stems with cocoa powder. Bake for 2 to 2½ hours, or until meringues are dry.

To make ganache:
1. Heat cream in a heavy pot to just below boiling. Remove from heat; stir in chocolate until smooth. Let cool.
2. Spoon ganache into a pastry bag fitted with a coupler and star tip. To assemble mushrooms, pipe a small ganache star onto bottom of each cap; attach stem.

ASPARAGUS WITH BASIL-TARRAGON DIPPING SAUCE

serves 25/pictured on page 139

4 pounds asparagus
2 large bunches basil, leaves picked and washed
2 bunches tarragon, leaves picked
1 tablespoon olive oil
4 ounces crème fraîche
1½ teaspoons sherry-wine vinegar
Salt
½ cup heavy cream

1. Bring large pot of salted water to a boil. Trim asparagus to desired length, peeling tough outer skin. Place asparagus in boiling water for 30 seconds. Drain and immediately plunge into an ice bath to stop cooking process. Drain and dry.
2. Bring a saucepan of salted water to a boil. Add basil leaves; boil for 30 seconds. Remove with a slotted spoon, and immediately plunge into an ice bath. Repeat with tarragon leaves. Drain leaves from ice bath, and squeeze out water.
3. Put herbs and oil in a food processor; purée until smooth. Strain through cheesecloth into a measuring cup, squeezing cloth to get out all the liquid. Discard solids. Measure 5 tablespoons liquid, and fold into crème fraîche. Fold in vinegar; add salt to taste.
4. In bowl of electric mixer, whip cream on medium-high until stiff peaks form. Fold in crème fraîche. Serve immediately.

MINI CARPACCIO TEARDROPS

makes 35/pictured on page 139

We used very rare, instead of raw, beef to make this variation on an Italian classic.

½ eye of round (about 3 pounds)
Salt and pepper to taste
1 teaspoon olive oil
¼ pound sun dried tomatoes
loaf store-bought herb or peasant bread, sliced ½ inch thick
1 cup Basil Aïoli (recipe follows)
35 basil leaves, washed and dried

1. Season beef with salt and pepper; let rest one hour. Heat oven to 375°. Heat oil in large ovenproof sauté pan over high heat. Brown beef on all sides. Place in oven; roast until instant-read thermometer reaches 115°, 15 to 20 minutes. Let cool; chill overnight. Slice as thin as possible.
2. Bring pan of water to a boil. Drop in 18 sun dried tomatoes; boil for 30 seconds. Drain and cut in half.
3. Cut bread into 35 teardrop shapes; spread with aïoli. Place tomato on round end of bread; place basil at 90-degree angle. Arrange beef slice on top; serve.

BASIL AÏOLI

makes about 3 cups

1 bunch basil leaves
3 large egg yolks
½ tablespoon freshly squeezed lemon juice
1 clove garlic
½ teaspoon salt
1 cup olive oil

1. Blanch basil in pot of boiling water for 30 seconds. Drain and plunge into ice bath to stop cooking. Drain and dry.
2. Combine all ingredients except oil in a blender; purée until smooth. Pour in oil; mix until combined. Store in refrigerator.
Note: Raw eggs should not be used in food prepared for pregnant women, young children, or anyone whose health is compromised.

SAVORY BLINTZES

makes 25 to 30/pictured on page 139

Each crêpe filling recipe makes enough for one batch of crêpes. Double the crêpes recipe if you want to serve both fillings.

Crêpes:

8 tablespoons (1 stick) unsalted butter
1 cup all-purpose flour
1 teaspoon salt
4 large eggs
2 cups plus 2 tablespoons milk

For grilled pear, cambozola, and walnut filling:

4 Bosc pears, unpeeled
Olive oil
½ cup walnut halves
¼ wheel (about 1 pound) cambozola, an
   Italian soft blue cheese, cut into
   1-by-1½-inch slices
3 tablespoons unsalted butter

For wild mushroom and apple filling:

1 tablespoon olive oil
2 shallots, peeled and finely chopped
½ pound white mushrooms, stems
   removed, coarsely chopped
½ pound shiitake mushrooms, stems
   removed, coarsely chopped
2 Granny Smith apples, peeled, cored,
   and diced
3 tablespoons all-purpose flour
1 cup heavy cream
2 tablespoons fresh thyme, chopped
2 tablespoons freshly squeezed lemon juice
1 tablespoon finely chopped lemon zest
   Salt and freshly ground pepper
3 tablespoons unsalted butter

To make crêpes:

1. Melt butter. Combine flour and salt in a medium bowl. Add eggs; whisk until smooth. Whisk in butter and milk.

2. Lightly oil 8-inch nonstick crêpe pan; heat over medium-low heat. Add 2 tablespoons batter; swirl to evenly coat bottom of pan. When crêpe surface looks dry, remove from pan; place uncooked side down on parchment to cool. Repeat with remaining batter. Stack cooled crêpes with parchment paper between each until ready to use.

To make pear filling:

1. Heat grill or cast-iron grill pan to medium-high. Slice pears lengthwise; brush with oil. Grill for 3 to 4 minutes per side, until hot. Let cool; core and coarsely chop.

2. Heat oven to 350°. Spread walnuts on baking sheet; toast, stirring occasionally, until just golden brown, about 5

minutes. Remove from heat; let cool slightly; coarsely chop.

3. Place a crêpe, uncooked side down, on a flat surface; place slice of cambozola at center. Top with teaspoon each of pear and walnuts. Fold 3 sides into center, then roll toward unfolded side.

4. Melt butter in medium pan over low heat. Place as many blintzes as will fit in pan; sauté until golden on both sides, 2 to 3 minutes per side. Serve immediately.

To make wild-mushroom filling:

1. Heat oil in large saucepan over medium-low heat. Add shallots; sauté until tender, 3 to 4 minutes. Add mushrooms. Cook 2 minutes, and add apples; cook another 3 minutes. Stir in flour; cook an additional 2 to 3 minutes. Add cream and thyme; cook 5 more minutes, or until thick. Remove from heat; stir in lemon zest and juice. Salt and pepper to taste.

2. Fill crêpes with 1 teaspoon filling; roll and sauté in butter as described in step 4 of pear filling.

CREAM SCONES
makes 35 to 40/pictured on page 139

½ cup yellow cornmeal
3 cups all-purpose flour
1 tablespoon baking powder
½ cup sugar
¾ cup currants or golden raisins
6 tablespoons (¾ stick) unsalted butter,
   softened
3 large eggs, beaten
¾ cup heavy cream
1 large egg yolk mixed with 1 tablespoon
   sugar and 1 tablespoon water, for glaze
6 ounces (1 bottle) Devonshire cream
   (available at specialty-food shops)
1 cup fruit preserves of your choice

1. Heat oven to 325°. Combine cornmeal, flour, baking powder, sugar, and currants in bowl of electric mixer. Cut in butter until mixture is coarse. Beat in eggs and cream until combined; do not overmix.

2. On lightly floured surface, roll out dough to ½ inch. Cut dough into leaf shapes with sharp knife, or use 2-inch scalloped or heart-shaped cutter. Place on the ungreased baking sheet. Brush tops with

egg-yolk glaze; bake until golden, about 25 minutes. Cool on wire racks; serve with Devonshire cream and fruit preserves.

BEET-PINK QUAILS' EGGS
makes 24/pictured on page 149

Quails' eggs have a tough membrane between shell and egg. To peel, lightly tap on work surface; roll along surface with palm of hand to feel shell cracking.

2 large beets, scrubbed
12 fresh quails' eggs
1 eight-ounce container cream cheese, softened
⅛ teaspoon salt
⅛ teaspoon finely ground pepper
1 small seedless cucumber, trimmed
10 sprigs fresh chervil

1. Heat oven to 450° with rack in center. Trim beet stems to 1 inch. Place whole beets in large piece of foil; fold up to make packet. Cook until tip of knife inserts easily into beets; timing will vary greatly with size of beets, 35 to 75 minutes. When cool enough to handle, peel. Reserve one beet. Grate remaining beet on small holes of a box grater, to yield 1 cup. Fill large glass measuring cup, or other non-reactive bowl, with 4 cups water. Add 1 cup grated beet; stir well; let steep, stirring occasionally. Reserve unused portion of beet.

2. Put eggs in medium saucepan; cover with several inches cool water. Place, covered, over high heat, stirring occasionally, until just before water comes to a boil. Uncover, reduce to a simmer; cook 1½ minutes, stirring eggs gently. Transfer to large bowl filled with ice water; let cool completely, about 5 minutes. Pat each egg dry, and peel; transfer to reserved beet liquid. Let eggs steep for 30 minutes at room temperature.

3. Grate remaining portion of unused beet with a ginger grater (or very small holes of a grater) over bowl to yield 6 to 8 tablespoons. Press grated beets into a fine strainer with back of a spoon to yield 2 tablespoons plus 1 teaspoon juice. Place cream cheese, salt, and pepper in a bowl. Add juice; combine. May be made a day ahead and stored, covered, in refrigerator.

4. Use a half-inch melon baller to cut out twelve small rounds from remaining cooked beet. Reserve. Run five-hole zester along cucumber to make very thin stripes. Cut out 12 small rounds from cucumber with melon baller. Reserve.

5. To assemble, fill small piping bag fitted with small leaf tip (Wilton #349) with chilled beet-pink cream cheese. Reserve. Remove eggs from liquid. Pat dry. Cut each in half lengthwise with sharp knife. Smooth yolks with knife blade if needed. Pipe out leaf of cream cheese onto each half egg. Garnish a beet or cucumber round and sprig of chervil. Serve slightly chilled or at room temperature.

SHOWER TEA SANDWICHES
makes about 3 dozen/pictured on page 148

The cream-cheese spreads are used as the base for each of the sandwiches.

3 one-pound loaves white sandwich bread,
   preferably unsliced
   Flavored Cream Cheeses (recipe follows)
   Tea-Poached Chicken (recipe follows)
1 large seedless cucumber (14 ounces),
   very thinly sliced
½ pound sliced smoked salmon
2½ ounces fresh salmon roe
1 ounce caviar, optional
3 to 4 ounces baby leaf lettuce, such as
   mâche, mizuna, shiso leaves, and sprouts
1 bunch fresh dill
1 bunch fresh chives
2-3 tablespoons black sesame seeds
2-3 tablespoons white sesame seeds

Trim crusts. Slice bread into ½-inch-thick pieces. Spread each slice with cream-cheese spread. Arrange ingredients in decorative patterns. Sandwiches look best with chicken, cucumbers, and salmon arranged along edges of bread, overlapping slightly. Trim edges in straight lines, cutting through bread and ingredients to leave clean edges on all sides. Make salmon sandwiches first, reserving trimmings for salmon cream cheese. Tuck small green leaves in between layers. Keep sandwiches covered with damp cloth until serving. Refrigerate if not serving right away. Sandwiches are best eaten within 2 to 3 hours.

FLAVORED CREAM CHEESES
makes 1 cup

16 ounces cream cheese
1 tablespoon wasabi paste, or to taste
2½ tablespoons freshly squeezed
  lemon juice (1 lemon)
  Salt to taste
2 ounces trimmings from sliced smoked
  salmon in Shower Tea Sandwiches
1 tablespoon salmon roe, optional

1. Place 4 ounces cream cheese in
a food processor. Add wasabi, 2 teaspoons lemon juice, and salt to taste.
Process until smooth. Transfer to a
small bowl.
2. Place another 4 ounces cream cheese
in clean food processor. Add salmon
scraps, salmon roe, and 2 teaspoons
lemon juice; process until smooth.
Transfer to small bowl; set aside.
3. Process remaining 8 ounces cream
cheese with remaining 3½ teaspoons
lemon juice in a clean food processor.

TEA-POACHED CHICKEN
makes enough for 18 tea sandwiches

*Poaching the chicken in tea adds flavor
and creates a striking dark border when the
chicken is sliced.*

4 tea bags strong tea (½ ounce loose tea)
  such as Russian caravan, Darjeeling, or
  Chinese Oolong
1 star anise
1 cinnamon stick
4 half chicken breasts, boned

1. Bring 8 cups of water to a boil in
a medium saucepan. Add tea, star anise,
and cinnamon stick. Cover saucepan; let
steep for 10 minutes. Squeeze and discard
tea bags. Return tea to a simmer.
2. Add chicken; poach until cooked
through, 20 to 30 minutes. Strain; let
stand to cool. Slice chicken into long,
thin pieces. Set aside; cover with damp
kitchen towel if not using right away.

SPICY CHEESE TWISTS
makes 24/pictured on page 147

2½ cups bleached bread flour
1¼ teaspoon salt, plus more for sprinkling
8 tablespoons (1 stick) cold, unsalted butter, cut into small pieces

4 ounces cream cheese, cut into pieces
2 large eggs
2 teaspoons each whole cumin,
  fennel, and caraway seeds
½ cup freshly grated Parmesan
1 tablespoon freshly ground pepper
1 tablespoon heavy cream

1. Pulse flour and salt in food processor. Add butter and cream cheese;
pulse until resembles fine cornmeal.
With machine running, add 1 egg,
and gradually add 1 to 3 tablespoons
ice water; process until dough begins
to come together. Transfer to board;
knead into ball with your hands.
2. Transfer dough to lightly floured
surface. Gently flatten with floured
hand into two 6½-by-4-inch rectangles. Wrap in plastic. Chill at least 1
hour, or until firm.
3. Place cumin, fennel, and caraway
seeds in small dry skillet. Toast over
medium heat, shaking pan to keep
from burning, 2 to 3 minutes. Transfer
to spice grinder; grind slightly. Let
cool 1 minute; combine with Parmesan and pepper.
4. In small bowl, whisk together
remaining egg and cream. Heat oven
to 375° with rack in center. Line two
baking sheets with parchment. Sprinkle the work surface with half of the
Parmesan-spice mixture. Roll out half
chilled dough over mixture, flouring
surface of dough as needed until dough
is ⅛ inch thick and about 11 by 16
inches. Trim to measure 10 by 15
inches. Cut into ¾-by-15-inch strips.
5. Brush the egg wash over the
dough. Sprinkle with salt. Transfer
the strips to baking sheets, laying them
widthwise across sheets; dough will
hang over sides. Twist each strip until
it is short enough to fit inside the pan;
pinch edges onto the rim to secure.
Freeze 4 minutes, or refrigerate for
10. Bake 12 to 15 minutes, until gold-
en brown. Transfer the sheet to a rack
to cool. Let twists cool on a baking
sheet. Repeat with remaining dough.
The spicy cheese twists may be made
a day ahead and stored tightly covered
in a large plastic container.

CREAMY-CRISPY
STONE-GROUND GRITS CUBES
makes 42/pictured on page 149

4 cups whole milk
1½ teaspoons salt
¼ teaspoon freshly ground pepper
1½ teaspoons paprika
1½ cups stone-ground grits, plus
½ cup for rolling
2 tablespoons unsalted butter
½ cup grated Gruyère cheese
3 cups solid vegetable shortening
  Roasted-Pepper Filling (recipe follows)
4 sprigs each fresh dill, tarragon,
  and parsley, for garnish
  Butter-flavored cooking spray

1. Fill bottom of double boiler with
1 inch water. Set aside. In top of double
boiler, place milk, salt, pepper, and paprika. Place top of double boiler directly
on heat; bring just to a boil. Whisking
constantly, slowly add grits. Whisking,
cook grits over low heat for 10 minutes.
2. Meanwhile, bring water in bottom
of double boiler to a boil. Place just-
cooked grits that are in top of double
boiler over, but not touching, boiling
water in bottom. Cover; cook 20 minutes more, stirring often, over low heat.
Stir in butter until melted. Cool about
2 minutes. Stir in cheese.
3. Line 9-by-13-inch pan with plastic; spray with cooking spray. Transfer
mixture to pan; smooth into 1-inch-
thick block (will take up about half of
pan). Let cool at room temperature
about 1 hour. Cover with plastic; refrigerate overnight or until cold.
4. Turn cool mixture out onto clean
piece of plastic. Trim edges to straighten.
Using a ruler and a knife, cut mixture
evenly into 1-inch cubes. Wipe knife
occasionally with damp paper towel to
clean. Roll cubes in stone-ground grits.
5. Meanwhile, melt shortening in a
heavy 8- or 9-inch skillet until a candy
thermometer registers 330°. Fry cubes,
3 to 4 at a time to ensure oil temperature remains high enough for proper
frying, until golden, 1 to 2 minutes.
Drain on paper towel. When cool
enough to touch, use small (size 22)
melon baller to hollow out top of each

cube; discard top. Fill each cube with
rounded half teaspoon of roasted-
pepper filling. May be reheated in a
300° oven for 10 to 12 minutes just
before serving. Garnish each with dill,
tarragon, and parsley.

ROASTED-PEPPER FILLING
makes ⅓ cups; enough for 42 cubes

3 red or yellow bell peppers
2 garlic cloves, peeled and minced
1 small tomato, skinned, seeded, and
  cut into ¼-inch pieces
¼ teaspoon red-pepper flakes
½ ounce tasso ham, cut into ⅛-inch strips,
  about ¼-inch long
  Salt and freshly ground black
  pepper to taste
  Olive-oil cooking spray

1. Roast peppers over gas flame or
in oven until just blackened. Transfer
to bowl; cover with plastic; let sweat
about 15 minutes. Peel, stem, and seed
peppers. Cut into ¼- to ⅛-inch-thick
slices. Reserve.
2. Lightly spray saucepan with cooking spray. Add garlic; cook over low
heat until soft, 4 to 6 minutes. Add
remaining ingredients plus reserved
peppers. Cook over medium-low heat,
stirring, until tomato has reduced and
there is not much liquid in pan, 10
to 14 minutes.

ASPARAGUS TARTS
makes 3 tarts, 30 pieces/pictured on page 149

*Preserved lemons are available in specialty
stores in jars. To make a quick version,
blanch zest of one lemon, strain with cool
water, and let sit thirty minutes covered with
white vinegar and one tablespoon salt.*

1 pound thin asparagus
  Asparagus Tart Shells (recipe follows)
  Goat-Cheese Filling (recipe follows)
  Preserved lemon zest (1 lemon)

1. Trim asparagus to 5 to 6 inches,
removing woody ends. Blanch in pot
of boiling salted water until cooked
through, 1 to 3 minutes. Transfer immediately to bowl of ice water to stop
cooking. When cool, drain. Pat dry.
2. To assemble, use small offset spa-

tula to spread cheese over bottom of each tart. Arrange asparagus lengthwise to cover bottom of each tart. Tuck pieces of zest between edges of asparagus. Cut tarts widthwise into ten 1¼-inch-thick pieces.

ASPARAGUS TART SHELLS
makes 3 shells

1¼ cups all-purpose flour
½ teaspoon salt
¼ teaspoon freshly ground pepper
½ tablespoon finely chopped lemon zest
8 tablespoons (1 stick) cold, unsalted butter, cut into small pieces
1 large egg
1 tablespoon heavy cream

1. Combine flour, salt, pepper, and zest in food processor. Add butter; process until resembles coarse meal, 8 to 10 seconds.
2. Add ⅛ to ¼ cup ice water in a slow, steady stream through feed tube of a food processor with the machine running until the dough holds together, about 30 seconds. Knead on lightly floured board to combine if needed. Press into 6-inch disk; wrap tightly with the plastic; refrigerate one hour or until chilled. May be frozen, double-wrapped in plastic, up to 2 months.
3. On lightly floured surface, roll dough into 14-by-8-inch piece, ¼ inch thick. From one side of dough, cut six strips lengthwise for sides, each ¼ inch wide by 14 inches long. Set aside. Roll out remaining dough widthwise another 2 inches so piece measures 14 by 10 inches and is ⅛ inch thick. Cut three 2-by-14-inch rectangles of dough for bottoms. Set aside.
4. In small bowl, whisk egg and cream. Lightly score long edges of three rectangles. Lightly brush scored edges with egg wash. Lay two strips lengthwise over scored edges of each rectangle. Brush strips with egg wash. Prick each tart, except side strips, with tines of a fork to prevent crust from rising while it cooks. Transfer tarts to baking sheet. Refrigerate 30 minutes.
5. Heat oven to 375° with rack in center. Bake 8 minutes, rotating pan

for even cooking; prick bottom dough if rising too much. Cook 5 to 7 minutes, until golden. Let cool on rack, 20 to 30 minutes. Shells may be made one day ahead and kept in airtight plastic container at room temperature.

GOAT-CHEESE FILLING
makes ¾ cup; enough for 3 tarts

2¾ ounces soft goat cheese, room temperature
⅛ teaspoon freshly ground pepper
1 tablespoon fresh chives, cut into ⅛-inch pieces
1½ teaspoons freshly grated lemon zest
¼ cup heavy cream

1. Mix goat cheese, pepper, chives, and zest with fork in bowl until combined.
2. Whip cream to soft peaks; fold into goat-cheese mixture. Cover with plastic; refrigerate until needed.

CRISPY CAESAR CUPS
makes 24/pictured on page 149

To make a bed for these hors d'oeuvres, grate five to seven ounces of Parmesan into long, thin strips.

For the bread cups:
4 tablespoons unsalted butter, melted
⅛ teaspoon cayenne
1 clove garlic, peeled and mashed to a paste
½ teaspoon salt
¼ teaspoon freshly ground pepper
24 slices thin white sandwich bread

For the filling:
10 inner romaine lettuce leaves
Caesar Dressing (recipe follows)
Frico Topping (recipe follows)
Mini Croutons (recipe follows)

1. Heat oven to 375° with rack in upper third. Using a fork, combine butter, cayenne, garlic paste, salt, and pepper in a bowl. Reserve at room temperature.
2. Cut crusts off bread. On dry surface, flatten one slice of bread with rolling pin to ¹⁄₁₆ inch. Cut circle with a 2½-inch-round cookie cutter. Brush butter mixture onto one side of bread. Press bread round, buttered-side up, into hole of a 24-mini-muffin tin (each cavity measuring 2 inches

in diameter and ¾ inches deep), letting bread scallop inside edges. Repeat until all bread slices are used.
3. Bake until bread is toasty and golden, 6 to 8 minutes. Transfer to a baking rack to cool. The cups may be made a day ahead and kept in an airtight container at room temperature.
4. Before serving, stack lettuce, and cut across into ⅛-inch-thick strips. Transfer to a medium bowl. Toss with Caesar dressing. Fill each bread cup with lettuce; top with frico topping and croutons.

CAESAR DRESSING
makes ⅔ cup, enough for 24 Caesar cups

½ teaspoon grated lemon zest plus
1 tablespoon freshly squeezed lemon juice (1 lemon)
1 large egg yolk
1 small garlic clove, peeled and mashed to a paste
¼ teaspoon freshly ground pepper
¼ teaspoon salt
5 tablespoons extra-virgin olive oil
5 flat anchovy fillets, rinsed, patted dry, and minced
¼ cup freshly grated Parmesan

Whisk lemon zest, juice, yolk, garlic, pepper, and salt in a bowl. Slowly whisk in oil. Add anchovies and Parmesan. Adjust seasoning. Place in refrigerator to chill. May be made a day ahead. Note: Raw eggs should not be used in food for pregnant women, babies, young children, or anyone whose health is compromised.

FRICO TOPPING
makes enough for 24 Caesar cups

2 ounces Asiago cheese
½ teaspoon all-purpose flour
Olive-oil cooking spray

1. Grate cheese lengthwise into long strips on large holes of a box grater to make about ½ cup. Transfer to bowl. Toss with flour.
2. Spray a nonstick 7½-inch skillet with cooking spray; warm over medium-high heat. Sprinkle 1 teaspoon cheese in pan to make a 2-inch circle; cheese pieces should touch slightly but

have some space between them to make lacy pattern. Cook over medium-low heat until barely golden, about 1 minute; turn with offset spatula; cook about 30 seconds until golden. Transfer to paper towel to cool. Respray pan each time; continue until all cheese is used. When cool, break pieces into smaller shards, about 1 by ½-inch. May be made a day ahead and kept in an airtight container at room temperature.

MINI CROUTONS
makes about 72

1 slice thin white sandwich bread, crust removed
Pinch paprika
Pinch salt

Cut bread into ¼-inch cubes. Warm nonstick skillet over medium heat. Add bread cubes; sprinkle with paprika and salt. Keep moving cubes until golden on all sides, 2 to 3 minutes. Let cool; reserve. May be made a day in advance and kept in airtight container at room temperature.

PEPPERED TIGER PRAWNS WITH YELLOW-PEPPER AÏOLI
serves 12 to 15; pictured on page 150

1 four-ounce potato
1 yellow bell pepper
20 black tiger prawns, peeled, tails left on, and deveined
20 fresh basil leaves
20 thin slices pancetta
1¾ cups extra-virgin olive oil
1 tablespoon cracked peppercorns
40 asparagus stalks, trimmed
¼ cup balsamic vinegar
2 teaspoons chopped garlic
Salt and freshly ground pepper
2 large egg yolks
Juice of 2 lemons

1. Boil potato in salted water; drain. Let cool, then peel and roughly chop.
2. Heat grill. Roast pepper on grill or gas burner, blackening skin on all sides. Place in stainless-steel bowl; cover with plastic wrap. When cool enough to handle, peel, seed, and core. Chop roughly; set aside.

3. Wrap each shrimp in a basil leaf and a slice of pancetta; place in a baking pan.

4. Mix ¾ cup olive oil and peppercorns in small bowl; pour over shrimp. Marinate until ready to grill.

5. Grill the shrimp until opaque through to the center, about 3 minutes per side; set aside.

6. In a large pot of salted boiling water, cook the asparagus until just tender but still crisp and bright green. Plunge into ice water to cool. Drain and set aside.

7. Meanwhile, in small bowl, mix together ¼ cup olive oil, vinegar, 1 teaspoon garlic, and salt and pepper to taste. Toss asparagus with vinaigrette; grill until lightly charred.

8. To make aïoli, combine egg yolks, potato, remaining teaspoon garlic, lemon juice, and roasted pepper in food processor; purée. Add ¾ cup olive oil in a slow, steady stream until well blended; do not overblend. Season to taste.

9. Arrange asparagus on platter; place shrimp on top. Serve aïoli on the side. Note: Raw eggs should not be used in food for pregnant women, babies or young children, the elderly, or anyone whose health is compromised.

GRILLED VEGETABLE ANTIPASTO

serves 12 to 15/pictured on page 150

Experiment with whatever vegetables are fresh and in season.

1½ cups extra-virgin olive oil
¼ cup red-wine vinegar
½ cup chopped fresh basil
2 eggplants, sliced
4 fennel bulbs, sliced
2 red bell peppers, sliced
2 yellow bell peppers, sliced
4 zucchini, sliced
2 red onions, sliced
2 oranges, sliced
3 tablespoons tarragon vinegar
¼ cup chopped shallots
Zest from 2 oranges, chopped
Salt and freshly ground pepper
1 tablespoon chopped flat-leaf parsley

1. Heat grill. Combine 1 cup olive oil, red-wine vinegar, and basil; toss all sliced vegetables in the mixture. Grill until brown and tender.

2. Arrange grilled vegetables on platter; garnish with orange slices.

3. Combine tarragon vinegar, shallots, orange zest, remaining ½ cup olive oil, and salt and pepper to taste; spoon over vegetables and garnish with parsley.

SALMON FLATBREAD NAPOLEONS

makes 40 circular and 40 square napoleons/pictured on page 150

After cutting rounds and squares from dough to make flatbreads, cut any left-over dough with tiny aspic cutters, and use to top each napoleon.

For the flatbread:
Cornmeal for sprinkling
¾ teaspoon dry yeast
Pinch sugar
2 tablespoons plus 1 teaspoon olive oil
1¾ cups plus 2 tablespoons all-purpose flour, plus more for dusting
½ teaspoon each whole fennel and dill seeds
¾ teaspoon table salt
Coarse salt, for sprinkling

Filling ingredients:
7 ounce salmon filet
Coarse salt and freshly ground pepper
Herbed Green Hummus (recipe follows)
½ cup black-olive tapenade
4 to 5 black olives, pitted and thinly sliced
1 to 2 scallions, trimmed and very thinly sliced widthwise
2 ounces salmon roe
2 to 3 ounces cucumber, sliced paper-thin and cut into triangles
1 to 2 teaspoons Dijon mustard
2 teaspoons mustard seeds
2 tablespoons chopped chives
4 to 5 small radishes, cut into thin rounds
1 bunch flat-leaf parsley
¼ cup golden caviar

1. Heat oven to 375° with one rack in center and one right underneath. Sprinkle cornmeal over two rimmed baking sheets; set aside. Combine yeast, sugar, and ⅛ cup warm water (about 110°) in electric mixer; let stand until foamy, 3 minutes. Add ½ cup warm water, 1 tablespoon oil, flour, fennel and dill seeds, and table salt. Using dough hook, mix on low,

scraping sides, until dough is smooth and elastic, 6 to 10 minutes. Transfer to lightly floured surface; knead, forming dough into a ball.

2. Cut dough into two equal pieces; shape into flattened circles; cover loosely with plastic. Remove one; dust with flour. Roll into 20-by-20-inch piece, 1⁄16-inch thick.

3. Lightly brush dough with 2 teaspoons oil; sprinkle with coarse salt. Use a 1¼-inch-round cookie cutter to cut out 120 rounds. Transfer to prepared baking sheets, salt-side up. (If using smallest aspic cutters to cut out scraps for garnish, do so now; place on a separate baking sheet sprinkled with cornmeal. Bake separately 6 minutes at 200°.) Bake until edges and bottoms are crisp and slightly golden, 5 to 8 minutes, rotating pans halfway through baking time. Immediately transfer flatbreads off sheets to rack to cool. Roll out second half of dough to same measure. Use ruler to mark 1¼-inch squares; cut with a sharp knife, yielding 120. Brush squares with remaining 2 teaspoons of oil, sprinkle with salt, and bake as above. May be made 2 days ahead and stored in airtight container at room temperature.

4. Rub salmon with salt and pepper. Heat medium nonstick skillet over medium-high heat until hot but not smoking, 3 to 4 minutes. Cook salmon until cooked through but moist in center, 4 to 6 minutes each side. Let cool; flake into small pieces, about ¾ inches. Reserve.

5. To assemble, layer and combine ingredients with flaked salmon in any order, using all or just some. Each napoleon needs three round or three square flatbreads. Top each with salmon roe, caviar, scallions, mustard seed, or olives.

SMOKED-SALMON PETITS FOURS

makes about 60/pictured on page 150

15 slices white bread
8 ounces cream cheese, room temperature
½ teaspoon lemon zest
Freshly ground pepper
12 ounces Scottish smoked salmon, sliced as thinly as possible
1 lemon
3 tablespoons capers
Chives and edible blossoms

1. Heat oven to 300°. Trim crusts of bread; quarter each slice. Arrange on baking sheets; bake until lightly toasted, about 5 minutes per side.

2. Cream together cream cheese, zest, and pinch of pepper; spread over toasts. Arrange salmon over cream cheese. Squeeze lemon over salmon. Garnish with capers, chives, and edible blossoms. Sprinkle with pepper.

HEART-SHAPED QUESADILLAS

makes 48/pictured on page 150

The salsa and tortillas can be prepared several days ahead; assemble the quesadillas just before serving.

1 ripe mango, peeled and finely diced
½ cup finely diced jicama
½ cup finely diced red onion
½ jalapeño, seeded and finely diced
Juice of 1 lime
2 tablespoons olive oil
½ teaspoon coarse salt
¼ cup chopped fresh cilantro
16 six-inch flour tortillas
1½ cups (about 7 ounces) grated Monterey Jack cheese
6 ounces soft goat cheese, crumbled

1. In a medium bowl, combine the mango, jicama, red onion, and jalapeño. Add the lime juice, olive oil, salt, and cilantro; toss to combine throughly. Set the mango salsa aside.

2. Using a 2¼-inch heart-shaped cookie cutter, cut six hearts from each tortilla. Cover with a damp paper towel, or store in a resealable plastic bag until you are ready to prepare the quesadillas.

3. Heat a medium nonstick skillet over medium-high heat. Place six heart-shaped tortillas in skillet. Sprinkle each with 1 teaspoon Monterey Jack cheese and ½ teaspoon goat cheese. When cheese begins to melt, place a second heart on top of each tortilla. Flip quesadillas; cook until cheese is completely melted and quesadillas are golden brown, about 3 minutes. Repeat with other tortillas. Transfer to a serving tray; top each with 1 teaspoon mango salsa. Serve hot.

ACID-FREE PAPER: *NY Central Art Supply, Talas*

BAKING SUPPLIES: *Bridge Kitchenware, Broadway Panhandler, Lamalle Kitchenware, Martha By Mail, New York Cake & Baking*

BEADED ORNAMENTS: *Martha By Mail*

BONE FOLDERS: *NY Central Art Supply, Talas*

BOOKBINDING CLOTH: *NY Central Art Supply*

BOUQUET HOLDERS: *D. Blumchen & Co.*

BUBBLE BOTTLES: *Dillon Importing Co.*

BUTTONS: *M&J Buttons*

CAKE BOXES: *C&S Confections, Modpac Catalog*

CAKES: *Wendy Kromer, Gail Watson, Sylvia Weinstock Cakes*

CAKE STANDS: *Martha By Mail*

CALLIGRAPHERS: *Gail Brill Design, Judith Ness Calligraphy & Design, Lisa Maria Niccolini, Diana Sharkey Design, Soolip Paperie & Press, Tail of the Yak*

CANDLES: *Biedermann & Sons, Candlestick, The Candle Shop, Danica Design, Felissimo, Pier 1 Imports, Tallows End Gift Shop*

CANNING JARS: *Glashaus, Home Chef*

CATERERS: *Paula LeDuc Fine Catering*

CAVIAR: *Martha By Mail, Petrossian, Urbani Truffles USA*

CELLOPHANE BAGS: *Martha By Mail, New York Cake & Baking*

CHAMPAGNE GUMDROPS: *The Sweet Life*

CHOCOLATES: *Distributor Concepts, Lucky Star Sweets*

CORSAGE PINS: *B&J Floral Supply, Bill's Flower Market, Dorothy Biddle Service, Hersh Sixth Avenue Buttons*

CRAFT WIRE: *Metalliferous*

CRYSTALLIZED FLOWERS: *Meadowsweets*

DOILIES: *Artifacts, Ehlers Co., Martha By Mail, Royal Lace*

DRAGÉE ALMONDS: *Crossings, Economy Candy, Nassau Candy Co.*

DRIED WHEAT: *Dry Nature Design*

EDIBLE FLOWERS: *The Herb Lady, Indian Rock Produce*

EMBOSSERS: *Martha By Mail, Stampworx 2000*

EMBROIDERY: *Penn & Fletcher*

ENGRAVING: *K&Z Engraving*

FABRIC: *ABC Carpet & Home, B&J Fabrics, Britex Fabrics, Rosen & Chadick, Silk Trading Co.*

FABRIC FLOWERS: *Bell'Occhio, Cinderella Trimmings, Dulken & Derrick, Lins International, M&J Trimmings, Ruben et Fleur, Sein Import Co.*

FAUX HORSEHAIR: *Concord Merchandise Corporation*

FAVOR CONTAINERS: *Cannon's, Consolidated Plastics, Country Kitchen, Glerup-Revere, Linnea's, Martha By Mail, Spectrum Ascona*

FISHBOWLS: *Martha By Mail*

FLORAL FOAM: *B&J Floral Supply*

FLORAL PINS: *B&J Floral Supply, Bill's Flower Market, Dorothy Biddle Service*

FLORAL TAPE: *B&J Floral Supply, Dorothy Biddle Service, Kervar Inc.*

FLORAL WIRE: *B&J Floral Supply, Bill's Flower Market*

FLOWERS: *Fischer & Page*

FLOWER TUBES: *B&J Floral Supply*

FOAM-BOARD: *Pearl Paint, Sam Flax*

FONDANT: *New York Cake & Baking Distributor*

GLASS CLOCHE: *Smith & Hawken*

GLASSINE: *Kate's Paperie, NY Central Art Supply, Paper Source*

GLASSINE ENVELOPES: *APEC, Papivore/Marie Papier*

GUM PASTE: *New York Cake & Baking Distributor*

HOLE PUNCHES: *Martha By Mail, Pearl Paint, Sax Arts & Crafts*

HORS D'OEUVRES KIT: *Martha By Mail*

ICING TIPS: *New York Cake & Baking Distributor*

INVITATIONS: *Crane & Co. Inc., Dempsey & Carroll, Kate's Paperie, Mrs. John L. Strong Fine Stationery, SoHo Letterpress, Tail of the Yak, Tiffany & Co.*

LABELS: *Heirloom Woven Labels, Martha By Mail, University Products/Lineco, Madison Signatures*

LANTERNS: *Ad Hoc Softwares, Leekan Designs, Martha By Mail, Pearl River Mart Department Store*

MARZIPAN: *New York Cake & Baking Distributor*

MATCHBOOKS: *Atlas Match, LLC*

MENU CARDS: *Ross-Cook Engraving*

METAL PAILS: *Creative Kids Stuff*

METALLIC TRIMMINGS: *Tinsel Trading*

MONOGRAMMING: *Penn & Fletcher*

MUSHROOM BASKETS: *Archetique Enterprises*

ONIONSKIN PAPER: *NY Central Art Supply*

ORGANZA: *B&J Fabrics*

PAINT: *Martha Stewart Everyday Colors, Pearl Paint, Sherwin Williams*

PAPER: *Bell'occhio, JAM Paper & Envelope, Kate's Paperie, NY Central Art Supply, Pantry Press, Paper Access, Sam Flax, Soolip Paperie & Press, Dieu Donne Papermill*

PAPER BAGS (FOR CANDLES): *Bemiss-Jason Corporation*

PAPER BOXES: *Cannon's, C&S Confections, Chocolate Universe, Country Kitchen, Glerup-Revere, Kari-Out, Linnea's*

PAPER EDGERS: *Fiskars*

PÂTE DE FRUITS: *Crossings*

PEPPERBERRIES: *Dry Nature Design, OKS Flowers*

PENS: *Kate's Paperie, Mont Blanc, Papivore/Marie Papier, Tiffany & Co.*

PHOTO ALBUMS: *Kate's Paperie, Martha By Mail, Papivore/Marie Papier*

PICTURE FRAMES: *Banana Republic, Calvin Klein, Century Framing, John Esty, NY Central Art Supply, Tiffany & Co.*

PINKING SHEARS: *Hersh Sixth Avenue Buttons Inc., Judson Cutlery Co.*

PLACE-CARD HOLDERS: *AdHoc Softwares, Cardel, Martha By Mail, Papivore/Marie Papier, Tail of the Yak*

PLACE CARDS: *Julie Holcomb Printers, Ross-Cook Engraving, Madison Signatures*

POMEGRANATES: *OKS Flowers*

PORTFOLIO BOXES: *Talas*

POTS: *Archetique Enterprises, Bill's Flower Market, The Grass Roots Garden, Planter Resource, Potluck Studios, Smith & Hawken, Takashimaya, Tinsel Trading*

PRESSED FLOWERS: *Nature's Pressed*

PRINTERS: *Deanco Press, Julie Holcomb Printers, Papivore/Marie Papier, SoHo Letterpress, Soolip Paperie & Press, Tail of the Yak*

RENTALS: *Broadway Famous Party Rental, Party Rental Ltd.*

RIBBONS: *Bell'occhio, Britex Fabrics, Hyman Hendler & Sons, M&J Trimmings, Martha By Mail, Masterstroke, Midori Ribbon, Offray, Paper Source, So Good, Tail of the Yak, Tinsel Trading, YLI*

ROSEBUD RIBBON: *Artistic Ribbon, Inc.*

ROTARY CUTTERS: *Fiskars*

RUBBER STAMPS: *Empire Stamp & Seal, Kate's Paperie, Stampworx 2000, Tail of the Yak*

SANDING SUGARS: *New York Cake & Baking Distributor, Martha By Mail*

SCRAPBOOKS: *Kate's Paperie*

SEAM BINDING: *Masterstroke*

SHADOW BOXES: *Skyframe*

SILK FLOWERS: *Cinderella Trimmings, Dulken & Derrick, Tinsel Trading, Bell'occhio, Lins International*

SILK STEMS: *Tinsel Trading*

SILPAT BAKING MAT: *Bridge Kitchenware, Broadway Panhandler, Martha By Mail, New York Cake & Baking Distributor*

SILVER JULEP CUPS: *Wm. Court, Global Table, Kitchen Kaboodle, William Wayne & Co.*

SOAP-MAKING KIT: *Martha By Mail*

SPARKLERS: *Rubinstein's & Son*

STATIONERY: *Crane & Co., Dempsey & Carroll, db Firenze, Pineider Stationery, Mrs. John L. Strong Fine Stationery, Paper Access, Papivore/Marie Papier, Stampendous, Tiffany & Co.*

STEM WIRE: *Cinderella Trimmings*

STEPHANOTIS HOLDERS: *B&J Floral Supply*

SUGARED ALMONDS: *Crossings, Economy Candy, Nassau Candy*

TEA LIGHTS: *Biedermann & Sons*

TABLE CARDS: *Julie Holcomb Printers, Ross-Cook Engraving*

TEA: *The Metropolitan Tea Company, Takashimaya*

TENTS: *Durkin Awnings & Tent Rentals*

TISSUE PAPER: *Kate's Paperie*

TOPIARIES: *Atlock Farm*

TULLE: *B&J Fabrics, Falk Industries Inc.*

TWINE: *The Caning Shop, Tinsel Trading*

VASES: *Ad Hoc Softwares, L. Becker Flowers, Planter Resource*

VELLUM: *Kate's Paperie, NY Central Art Supply*

VOTIVE HOLDERS: *Biedermann & Sons, Illuminations, Martha By Mail*

WAXED TISSUE PAPER: *B&J Floral Supply*

WAXED TWINE: *Caning Shop*

WREATH FORMS: *B&J Floral Supply, Oregon Wire*

ABC CARPET & HOME
888 Broadway, New York, NY 10003;
212-473-3000.
Fabric

AD HOC
410 West Broadway, New York, NY
10012; 212-925-2652.
Glass lanterns, vases, place-card holders

AERO LTD
132 Spring Street, New York, NY 10012;
212-966-1500.
Place-card holders

APEC
800-221-9403.
Glassine envelopes

ARCHETIQUE ENTERPRISES
123 West 28th Street, New York, NY
10001; 212-563-8003.
Mushroom baskets, pots

ARTIFACTS INC.
903-729-4178.
Heart-shaped paper doilies

ARTISTIC RIBBON INC.
22 West 21st Street, New York, NY
10010; 212-255-4224.
Ribbon rosebuds

ATLAS MATCH, LLC.
800-628-2426.
Matchbooks

ATLOCK FARM
545 Weston Canal Road, Somerset, NJ
08873; 732-356-3373.
Topiaries

B&J FABRICS
263 West 40th Street, New York, NY
10018; 212-354-8150.
Fabrics, organza, tulle

B&J FLORAL SUPPLY
103 West 28th Street, New York, NY
10001; 212-564-6086.
*Floral foam, pins, tape, tubes, wire,
stephanotis holders, waxed tissue paper,
wreath forms, ribbons*

BANANA REPUBLIC
888-277-8953.
Silver picture frames

L. BECKER FLOWERS
217 East 83rd Street, New York,
NY 10028.
*Antique vases, antique terra-cotta pots,
hand-blown vases*

BELL'OCCHIO
8 Brady Street, San Francisco, CA 94103;
415-864-4048 or www.bellocchio.com.
Antique ribbons, paper, silk flowers

BEMISS-JASON CORPORATION
800-544-0093.
Paper bags for candles

DOROTHY BIDDLE SERVICE
348 Greeley Lake Road, Greeley, PA
18425; 570-226-3239 or
www.dorothybiddle.com.
Corsage pins, floral tape

BIEDERMANN & SONS
P.O. Box 8407, Northfield, IL 60093;
800-446-8150
Floating candles, tea lights, votive holders

BILL'S FLOWER MARKET
816 Sixth Avenue, New York, NY 10001;
212-889-8154.
Corsage pins, floral wire, pots

D. BLÜMCHEN & CO.
162 East Ridgewood Avenue, P.O.
Box 1210M, Ridgewood, NJ 07451;
201-652-5595.
Bouquet holders

BRIDGE KITCHENWARE
214 East 52nd Street, New York, NY
10022; 212-688-4220.
Baking supplies, Silpat baking mats

GAIL BRILL DESIGN
333 Valley Road, Cos Cob, CT 06807;
203-869-4667. By appointment only.
Hand calligraphy and invitation design

BRITEX FABRICS
146 Geary Street, San Francisco, CA
94108; 415-392-2910 or
www.britexfabrics.com.
Fabrics, ribbons, lace

**BROADWAY FAMOUS
PARTY RENTAL**
212-269-2666.
Party rentals

BROADWAY PANHANDLER
477 Broome Street, New York, NY
10013; 212-966-3434.
Baking supplies, Silpat baking mats

C&S CONFECTIONS
55 East 52nd Street, New York, NY
10055; 212-759-1388.
Cake-slice boxes, paper sacks, paper boxes

CALVIN KLEIN
800-294-7978.
Picture frames

CANDLESHTICK
181 Seventh Avenue, New York, NY
10011; 212-924-5444.
Candles

THE CANDLE SHOP
118 Christopher Street, New York, NY
10014; 888-823-4823.
Columns, floating candles, pillars

THE CANING SHOP
800-544-3373 or www.caning.com.
Waxed linen twine

CANON'S
2638 Kirkwood Highway, Newark, DE
19711; 302-738-3321.
Paper favor boxes

CENTURY FRAMING
105 Christopher Street, New York, NY
10014; 212-989-1058.
Picture frames, easels

CHOCOLATE UNIVERSE
2131 Carey Way, Pittsburgh, PA 15203;
412-481-4004.
Paper favor boxes

CINDERELLA TRIMMINGS
48 West 37th Street, New York, NY
10018; 212-564-2929.
Fabric flowers, floral decorations, stem wire

**CONCORD MERCHANDISE
CORPORATION**
1026 Sixth Avenue, New York, NY
10018; 212-840-2720.
Faux horsehair

CONSOLIDATED PLASTICS
800-362-1000.
Metal favor containers

COUNTRY KITCHEN
3225 Wells Street, Fort Wayne,
IN 46808; 219-482-4835.
Paper favor boxes

CRANE & CO.
800-572-0024.
Custom invitations, stationery

CROSSINGS
800-209-6141.
Dragée almonds, patés de fruit

CREATIVE KIDS STUFF
800-353-0710.
Tin pails

DANICA DESIGN
Route 90, Rockport, ME 04856;
207-236-3060.
Candles

DB FIRENZE
53 East 58th Street, New York, NY
10022; 212-688-8777.
Stationery

DEANCO PRESS
767 Fifth Avenue, New York, NY 10153;
212-371-2025.
Offset printing

DEMPSEY & CARROLL
800-444-4019.
Custom invitations, stationery

DIEU DONNÉ PAPERMILL
433 Broome Street, New York, NY
10013; 212-226-0573.
Handmade Paper

DILLON IMPORTING CO.
800-654-3696.
Bubbles

DISTRIBUTOR CONCEPTS
888-447-0611.
Chocolate cards

DRY NATURE DESIGN
129 West 28th Street, New York, NY
10001; 212-695-8911.
Dried wheat, pink pepperberries

DULKEN & DERRICK
12 West 21st Street, New York, NY 10010;
212-929-3614.
Fabric floral designs, silk flowers

DURKIN AWNINGS & TENT RENTALS
800-498-3028.
Tents

ECONOMY CANDY
800-352-4544 or
www.economycandy.com
Sugared almonds

EHLERS CO.
800-434-5377.
Paper doilies

EMPIRE STAMP & SEAL CO.
800-660-9782.
Rubber stamps

JOHN ESTY
636 Hudson Street, New York, NY
10014; 212-691-3753.
Custom framing

FALK INDUSTRIES
P.O. Box 483, Canal Street Station,
New York, NY 10013; 212-966-2800.
Tulle

FELISSIMO
800-565-6785 or www.felissimo.com
Pillar candles

FISCHER & PAGE
134 West 28th Street, New York,
NY 10001; 212-645-4106.
Flowers

FISKARS
7811 West Stewart Avenue, Wausau, WI
54401; 715-842-2091 or www.fiskars.com.
Paper edgers, rotary cutters

GLASHAUS
450 Congress Parkway, Crystal Lake,
IL 60014; 815-356-8440.
Canning jars

GLERUP-REVERE
P.O. Box 31419, Seattle, WA 98103;
206-545-1850.
Favor boxes

GLOBAL TABLE
107-109 Sullivan Street, New York, NY
10012; 212-431-5839.
Julep cups

GRANDMA'S CUPBOARD
1297 Krumroy Road, Akron, OH 44306;
330-784-1712.
Paper favor boxes

THE GRASS ROOTS GARDEN
131 Spring Street, New York, NY 10012;
212-226-2662.
Terra-cotta pots

HEIRLOOM WOVEN LABELS
P.O. Box 428, Moorestown, NJ 08057;
865-722-1618.
Custom labels

THE HERB LADY
52792 42nd Avenue, Lawrence, MI 49064;
616-674-3879.
Candied and edible flowers

HERSH SIXTH AVENUE BUTTONS INC.
800-391-6615.
Corsage pins, pinking shears

JULIE HOLCOMB PRINTERS
510-654-6416.
Letterpress printing, place cards, table cards

HOME CHEF
415-927-3290.
Canning jars

HYMAN HENDLER & SONS
67 West 38th Street, New York, NY
10018; 212-840-8393.
Ribbons

ILLUMINATIONS
800-226-3537 or www.illuminations.com.
Votive holders

INDIAN ROCK PRODUCE
888-302-6182.
Edible flowers

JAM PAPER & ENVELOPES
800-473-6666 or 201-467-6666.
Envelopes, paper, seals

JUDSON CUTLERY INC.
631-981-4083.
Pinking shears

K&Z ENGRAVING
45 West 47th Street, New York, NY
10036; 212-719-1137.
Engraving

KATE'S PAPERIE
800-809-9880.
Paper, rubber stamps, scrapbooks, photo albums, vellum, wooden boxes, glassine, tissue paper, fountain pens

KERVAR
119 West 28th Street, New York, NY
10021; 212-564-2525.
Floral tape

KITCHEN KABOODLE
800-366-0161.
Silver julep cups

WENDY KROMER
212-929-4108. By appointment only
Specialty cakes and cookies

LAMALLE KITCHENWARE
36 West 25th Street, New York, NY
10010; 212-242-0750.
Baking supplies

PAULA LEDUC FINE CATERING
1350 Park Avenue, Emeryville, CA 94608;
510-547-7825.
Catering

LEEKAN DESIGNS
93 Mercer Street, New York, NY 10012;
212-226-7226.
Paper lanterns

LINS INTERNATIONAL
562-407-0616 or
www.linsinternational.com.
Silk flowers

LUCKY STAR SWEETS
212-595-0968.
Monogrammed chocolates

M&J BUTTONS
1008 Sixth Avenue, New York, NY
10018; 212-391-6200.
Buttons

M&J TRIMMINGS
1008 Sixth Avenue, New York, NY
10018; 212-391-9072.
Ribbons, flower appliqués

MADISON SIGNATURES
800-783-9590.
Labels, menu cards, place cards

MANHATTAN FRUITIER
105 East 29th Street, New York, NY
10016; 212-686-0404 or
www.manhattanfruitier.com.
fresh and dried fruit baskets

MARTHA BY MAIL
800-950-7130 or www.marthabymail.com.
Baking supplies, beaded ornament kit, cake stands, caviar, doilies, favor tins, fishbowls,

hole-punch kit, hors d'oeuvres kit, labels, memories book, paper lanterns, place-card holders, sanding sugars, Silpat baking mats, silvery string, soap-making kit, votive holders

MARTHA STEWART EVERYDAY COLORS
available through Kmart, 800-866-0086 or
Sears stores, 800-972-4687 or www.sears.com
Paint

MASTERSTROKE CANADA
416-751-4193 or
www.masterstrokecanada.com.
Ribbons, seam binding

MEADOWSWEETS
888-827-6477.
Crystallized flowers

METALLIFEROUS
34 West 46th Street, New York, NY
10036; 212-944-0909.
Craft wire, round-nose pliers

THE METROPOLITAN TEA CO.
416-588-0089.
Specialty teas

MIDORI RIBBON
708 6th Avenue North Seattle, WA 98109;
206-282-3595.
Organdy ribbon

MOD-PAC CATALOG
800-666-3722.
Cake boxes

MONT BLANC
800-995-4810.
Pens

MRS. JOHN L. STRONG FINE STATIONERY
699 Madison Avenue, New York, NY
10021; 212-838-3775.
Custom stationery, invitations

NASSAU CANDY CO.
516-433-7100.
Sugared almonds

NATURE'S PRESSED
P.O. Box 212, Orem, UT 84059;
801-225-1169.
Pressed flowers

JUDITH NESS CALLIGRAPHY & DESIGN
212-348-5863.
Calligraphy

NY CENTRAL ART SUPPLY
800-950-6111.
*Acid-free tissue, bone folders, bookbinding
cloth, glassine, onionskin, paper, picture
frames, vellum*

NEW YORK CAKE & BAKING
DISTRIBUTOR
800-942-2539.
*Baking supplies, cellophane bags, fondant,
gum paste, marzipan, sanding sugars*

LISA MARIE NICCOLINI
914-738-3049.
Calligraphy

OFFRAY
www.offray.com.
Ribbons

OKS FLOWERS
123 West 28th Street, New York, NY
10001; 212-268-7231.
Red pepperberries, dried pomegranates

OREGON WIRE
800-458-8344.
Wreath forms

PAPER ACCESS
23 West 18th Street, New York, NY
10011; 212-463-7035.
Paper, stationery

PAPER DIRECT
800-272-7377 or www.paperdirect.com.
Notecards, paper

PAPER SOURCE
800-248-8035.
Glassine, paper, ribbon

PARTY RENTAL LTD.
888-774-4776.
Party rentals

PEARL PAINT
308 Canal Street, New York, NY 10013;
212-431-7932.
Acrylic stains, foam-board, hole punches

PAPIVORE/MARIE PAPIER
117 Perry Street, New York, NY 10014;
212-627-6055.
*Glassine envelopes, notecards, pens, photo
albums, place-card holders, printing*

PEARL RIVER MART
277 Canal Street, New York, NY;
212-431-4770.
Chinese red lanterns

PENN & FLETCHER
242 West 30th Street, New York, NY
10001; 212-239-6868.
Custom embroidery and monogramming

PERFUMES ISABELL
800-472-2355.
Votive dinner lights

PETROSSIAN
182 West 58th Street, New York, NY
10019; 212-245-2217.
Caviar

PIER 1 IMPORTS
800-447-4371.
Candles

PLANTER RESOURCE
106 West 28th Street, New York, NY
10001; 212-206-7687.
Pots, vases

POTLUCK STUDIOS
23 Main Street, Accord, NY 12404;
914-626-2300.
Pots

ROSEN & CHADICK
246 West 40th Street, New York, NY
10018; 212-869-0142.
Velvets

ROSS-COOK ENGRAVING
CO., INC.
135 West 29th Street, New York, NY
10001; 212-563-2876.
Invitations, menu cards, place cards, table cards

ROYAL LACE
800-669-7692.
Paper doilies

RUBAN ET FLEUR
8655 S. Sepulveda Boulevard, Los Angeles,
CA 90045; 310-641-3466.
Velvet leaves

RUBINSTEIN'S & SON
24 East 17th Street, New York, NY
10003; 212-924-7817.
Sparklers

SAM FLAX
425 Park Avenue, New York, NY 10022;
212-620-3060.
Foam-board, paper

SAX ARTS & CRAFTS CATALOG
800-558-6696.
Hole punches

SEIN IMPORT CO.
150 West 28th Street, New York, NY
10001; 212-645-2468.
Fabric flowers

DIANA SHARKEY DESIGN
212-757-0445.
Calligraphy

SHERWIN WILLIAMS
800-457-9566.
Spray and enamel paints

THE SILK TRADING CO.
360 South LaBrea Avenue, Los Angeles,
CA 90036; 323-954-9280.
Silk fabric

SKYFRAME
96 Spring Street, New York, NY 10012;
212-925-7856.
Shadow boxes

SMITH & HAWKEN
800-776-3336.
Glass cloches, terra-cotta pots

SO GOOD
28 West 38th Street, New York, NY
10018; 212-398-0236.
Ribbons

SOHO LETTERPRESS
71 Greene Street, New York, NY 10012;
212-334-4356.
Invitations, printing

SOOLIP PAPERIE & PRESS
8646 Melrose Avenue, West Hollywood,
CA 90069; 310-360-0545.
Calligraphy, letterpress printing, paper

SPECTRUM ASCONA
800-356-1473.
Clear favor boxes

STAMPENDOUS
800-869-0475.
Cards, hole punches, paper

STAMPWORX 2000
800-998-7826.
Embossers, rubber stamps

THE SWEET LIFE
63 Hester Street, New York, NY 10002;
212-598-0092.
Champagne gumdrops

TAIL OF THE YAK
2632 Ashby Avenue, Berkeley, CA 94705;
510-841-9891.
*Calligraphy, card holders, invitations,
printing, ribbons, rubber stamps*

TAKASHIMAYA
800-753-2038.
Flower pots, teas

TALAS
568 Broadway, New York, NY 10012;
212-219-0770.
Acid-free paper, portfolio boxes

TALLOWS END GIFT SHOP
888-661-5903.
Candles

TIFFANY & CO.
800-526-0649.
*Custom invitations, stationery, picture
frames, pens*

TINSEL TRADING CO.
47 West 38th Street, New York, NY
10018; 212-730-1030.
*Metallic ribbons and thread, silk stems,
silk thread, twine, floral decorations*

UNIVERSITY PRODUCTS
800-628-1912.
Labels

URBANI TRUFFLES USA
800-281-2330.
Caviar and truffles

GAIL WATSON
212-967-9167 or
www.gailwatsoncake.com.
Custom wedding cakes

SYLVIA WEINSTOCK CAKES
273 Church Street, New York, NY
10013; 212-925-6698.
Custom wedding cakes

WILLIAM-WAYNE & CO.
800-318-3435
Silver julep cups

WM. COURT
5030 Champion Boulevard, Suite G-8,
Boca Raton, FL 33496; 561-997-8609.
Silver julep cups

YLI
800-296-8139.
Ribbons

Photo Credits THE PEOPLE WHO CAPTURED THE MOMENTS TO REMEMBER

WILLIAM ABRANOWICZ
pages 18, 21 (top right), 24 (right), 27-29 (left), 30, 31, 33 (right), 34, 35, 103 (bottom right), 114, 115, 116 (bottom left), 118, 119, 121, 124, 125, 133 (middle center, middle right, bottom right), 135 (right), 192, 195 (top right), 196, 197

ANTHONY AMOS
pages 45, 140, 142, 143, 148, 158 (right), 233-236

SANG AN
pages 202, 203 (left), 204 (top and bottom left, bottom right)

CHRISTOPHER BAKER
pages 120 (bottom left), 136, 155 (middle right), 163, 174 (right)

DAVID BARTOLOMI
page 21 (top left)

HARRY BATES
illustrations pages 220, 221, 228, 229

FERNANDO BENGOECHEA
pages 33 (left), 51 (middle right), 222 (far left)

KAIJA BERZINS-BRAUS
page 223 (center right), 224 (right)

ANITA CALERO
page 155 (top center), 172

PHILIPPE CHANG
page 230 (left)

SUSIE CUSHNER
pages 80 (top), 86 (bottom center), 133 (bottom center), 144 (middle), 186, 187 (left)

BEATRIZ DA COSTA
pages 181 (top right), 184 (top and bottom center), 187 (top and bottom center, top and bottom right), 188, 208 (center left), 214

CARLTON DAVIS
pages 195 (bottom left), 200 (top left)

TERRY DEROY GRUBER
pages 218 (far right), 223 (center left)

JOHN DOLAN
pages 8 (bottom right), 39 (top left), 46 (left), 47, 51 (top left), 84

BOBBY FISHER
page 218 (far left)

DANA GALLAGHER
pages 21 (bottom left), 38, 39 (bottom left), 42, 51 (middle left), 67 (top right), 70, 72, 74 (top and bottom right), 75, 76, 79, 107 (right), 108 (bottom left), 120 (top left), 130 (top right), 132 (middle), 144 (top), 145 (top center, middle left and center, bottom), 151, 170, 173, 203 (right), 210-213, 217

GENTL & HYERS
pages 22, 23, 29 (right), 37, 44 (top left and middle right), 51 (bottom center), 71, 103 (bottom left), 104, 106, 109, 116 (bottom right), 126, 133 (top center, middle left), 134, 135 (left), 147, 149, 150 (top left, bottom right), 155 (top right, middle center, bottom left and right), 156, 157, 159, 166, 175 (left), 176, 177, 181 (top and bottom left), 195 (top left and bottom right), 223 (far right)

THAYER ALLYSON GOWDY
page 230 (right)

LISA HUBBARD
pages i, 14, 80 (middle left and bottom left, center, right), 81-83, 96, 183, 190, 198, 199, 200 (center top and bottom right), 201, 206

THIBAULT JEANSEN
pages 120 (bottom right), 139 (bottom right), 223 (far left)

CHRIS JOHNSON
pages 63, 108 (top right)

JOHN KERNICK
page 46 (top and bottom center, top and bottom right)

KEN KOCHEY
pages 36, 39 (top right), 40, 53, 103 (top left), 127, 139 (top left), 171, 218 (center left)

STEPHEN LEWIS
pages 29 (top and bottom center), 41 (right), 44 (top right, middle left and bottom left), 86 (top and bottom right), 88, 91, 93, 94, 95, 116 (top right), 131, 133 (top right), 184 (left), 185 (top and bottom left), 222 (far right)

GEOFF LUNG
pages 155 (middle left), 158 (left), 168

AMY NEUNSINGER
pages 24 (left), 26, 41 (left), 43, 44 (bottom right), 86 (top center), 103 (top right), 105, 107 (left), 108 (top left), 116 (top left), 120 (top right), 123 (right), 132 (top), 133 (bottom left), 139 (bottom left), 145 (top left), 150 (top right, bottom left), 160, 181 (bottom right), 184 (right), 185 (top and bottom center, right), 204 (top right), 225 (center), 227 (center right)

VICTORIA PEARSON
pages 2, 48, 51 (top center, middle center, bottom left, bottom right), 52, 54-61, 65, 67 (bottom right), 68, 69, 73, 74 (top and bottom left), 77, 78, 80 (middle right), 85, 87, 92, 133 (left), 141, 144, (bottom), 152, 155 (top left), 161, 164, 165, 167, 178, 182, 189

MARIA ROBLEDO
pages 51 (top right), 62, 64, 66, 67 (top and bottom left), 117, 130 (bottom left)

MALLORY SAMSON
page 21 (bottom right)

VICTOR SCHRAGER
pages 4, 110, 111, 112, 128, 129, 174 (left), 175 (right), 208 (far left, center right), 215

MATTHEW SEPTIMUS
pages 224 (left), 226 (far left, center left, far right), 227 (far left, center left)

JERRY SIMPSON
page 8 (top right)

DANIELLA STALLINGER
pages 32, 39 (bottom right), 226 (center right)

SARA VALENTINI
page 139 (top right)

JASON WALZ
pages 218 (center right), 222 (center left), 225 (left and right), 227 (far right)

SIMON WATSON
pages 6, 25, 100, 108 (bottom right), 113, 122, 123 (left), 130 (top left), 145 (middle right), 146, 155 (bottom center), 162, 169, 205, 222 (center right)

ANNA WILLIAMS
pages 86 (left), 130 (bottom right), 132 (bottom), 145 (top right), 208 (far right)